D1250608

WALTER & ME

STANDING IN THE SHADOW OF SWEETNESS

EDDIE PAYTON

with PAUL BROWN and CRAIG WILEY

TRIUMPH
BOOKS

Library of Congress Cataloging-in-Publication Data

Payton, Eddie.
  Walter & me : standing in the shadow of sweetness / Eddie Payton with Paul T. Brown and Craig Wiley.
    p. cm.
  ISBN 978-1-60078-763-8 (hardback)
  1. Payton, Walter, 1954–1999—Anecdotes. 2. Payton, Eddie. 3. Football players—United States—Biography. 4. Brothers—United States—Biography. I. Brown, Paul T. II. Wiley, Craig. III. Title.
  GV939.P39P4 2012
  796.3320922—dc23
  [B]
                                    2012026473

This book is available in quantity at special discounts for your group or organization. For further information, contact:

    Triumph Books LLC
    814 North Franklin Street
    Chicago, Illinois 60610
    (312) 337-0747
    www.triumphbooks.com

Printed in U.S.A.
ISBN: 978-1-60078-763-8
Design by Patricia Frey
Photos courtesy of the author unless otherwise indicated

Contents

Author's Note

This book is based primarily upon the author's recollections. Whenever possible, the author's version of events has been confirmed with sources such as books, magazine articles, and personal interviews. Conversations have been recreated as precisely as possible according to the memories of the individuals involved.

All proceeds earned by Eddie Payton from the sale of this book will go to the Payton Family Foundation. The money raised by the foundation supports the Walter "Sweetness" Payton Memorial Scholarship. Scholarships are awarded each year to economically disadvantaged students from around the country. For more information, visit paytonfamilyfoundation.com.

Foreword

I don't have to read an unauthorized biography of Walter Payton to know what kind of man he was. I coached him. I knew him myself. He was my friend. And when it comes to someone writing a book about my friend, I have to ask, how well did the writer really know him? Did he grow up with him? Was he on the field with him? Did he live with him? Was he a parent? Was he a coach? Was he a brother? In the case of Jeff Pearlman, the answer to those questions is clearly "no." Pearlman wrote a book about Walter, but it was written only from a distance. It was all secondhand. He put together a few things he'd heard—some of them from people who have very little credibility—to paint a picture that just doesn't look much like the Walter I knew.

One thing we all know is that Walter Payton was a great football player. That is unquestionable. Even Pearlman can talk about Walter's skills on the field and be taken seriously, because we have the evidence on film. We measure greatness by what we see a person do, and as a football player, Walter did it all. He was a majestic runner, he was a vicious blocker, he controlled the ball with magic, and he caught the ball with grace. He even passed the ball a little before I got to Chicago.

What's more, though, is that Walter was the consummate teammate, a born and respected leader. Everyone looked up to him, even the players who physically towered over him. He was the key guy on our 1985 Super Bowl team, yet he put the team above himself. He was a true cornerstone in every sense of the word. A lot of NFL players do great things, but few are truly great the way Walter was, and none are greater. If I had to pick one player from any era to start a football team with, it'd be him.

Have there been other guys who ran with the ball better than Walter? Maybe. I'll let you argue about that. But you can't argue about the fact that nobody ran *harder* than Walter. Nobody left more on the field. Nobody had a bigger heart or a greater will to win. But that's not all. Walter was so much more than a football player. I've known a lot of superb athletes in my life and have met a lot of the current players in the NFL. Never have I met a guy who was or is as giving, sharing, or understanding as Walter was. He took time to be with regular people. He visited kids who needed a hero. He paid attention to and truly respected the fans who watched him play every Sunday. He was a part of them, and they were a part of him. Walter did the little things that some of the egomaniacs in the game today won't do...and he did them because he wanted to, because that's what defined him. He didn't just spend time with the common man; he was one of them. He just happened to be uncommonly gifted.

Was Walter a perfect person? Are you? Listen, we're all human beings. We're all in this thing together, trying to find our way, and, yes, we all mess up every now and then. I think to err is human, and to forgive is divine. I don't know every single detail about Walter's personal life, and I can't say for certain that he never did anything wrong. When it comes to his marriage, I know that he and Connie did separate, but that's about all I know. But the Walter Payton I knew was good for everything that mattered to me: people, football, and, in particular, the Chicago Bears. He'll always hold a high place in my book, and you couldn't pay me enough to ever crack the cover of Pearlman's book. I know he tried to say you can't just look at the excerpts, but I saw all I needed to see in those excerpts. It's pathetic to write something like that about an individual who isn't here to defend himself. If the person has passed and can't respond, then just let the speculation rest with him. Period.

Obviously, if you're going to look for negative things and pick through someone's life, you'll probably find something that isn't all that great. If you look at anyone closely enough, a blemish or two will appear. That's just part of having skin, which is something we all have. It may seem like some of us have armor instead of skin, but I assure you, those guys are still human. So what if we found a chink in Walter's armor? We're talking about a guy who had so many great qualities that, when you add them up, his shortcomings all but disappear. He had characteristics that anyone would want in a son or a friend or a neighbor or a father. A man should be judged on the whole, and the whole of Walter Payton was pretty damn good. So, let's not listen too much to the guys who didn't know Walter. They only have fragments to share and cannot possibly give us the whole. Instead, let's listen to someone who really knew the man.

I only knew Eddie Payton through Walter, but I saw firsthand what he could do on that football field. I wish I'd had Eddie returning kicks for me, I can tell you that. He was the brother of the greatest player of all time, but he was a pretty damn good player himself. He taught Walter well when they were at Jackson State, and, like Walter, Eddie was a quality person off the field. I know Walter was very proud of Eddie and thought a lot of his big brother. I know this because I coached Walter and saw him every day. It was obvious that his brother was a big part of his life. They had a bond that just couldn't be broken. It was a bond that only siblings can share. Having grown up with Walter, Eddie knew him better than most. He's certainly more than a writer just trying to fit some fragments together. So, let's stop listening to those who didn't wholly know my friend. Instead, let's hear from someone who was there from the beginning and all the way through to the end. Let's hear from Eddie Payton.

—Mike Ditka

Preface

My first exposure to a Payton came on a sweltering summer's night in 1971. The occasion was the Mississippi High School All-Star Game played in Veterans Memorial Stadium in Jackson, Mississippi. My father and I had annually attended this event, during which we'd scour the program between periods of watching the play on the field. We were always looking for the next Archie Manning, who we'd seen play in the same affair four years prior, when both rosters were filled with only white players. It didn't take long for a running back from the South squad to stand out, and it wasn't because he was one of only a handful of black kids on the field. White, black, or purple, this kid was special. I remember asking Dad where he had signed to play college ball, and to our great surprise, he was listed in the program as "unsigned."

"I hope Mississippi State is recruiting him," I remarked to my dad. "We need a lot of help."

"I might write Coach Shira a letter and tell him about this kid," Dad said (he was a notorious letter-writer to the MSU athletic department back in the day).

"What's his name, Dad?"

"Walter Payton," Dad said, glancing at the program. "Says here he's 5'10", 185 pounds…but he looks bigger than that."

Well, he sure ran bigger. Walter Payton ripped through, over, and around the North team. Walter was the clear star of the game. I followed the college recruiting process for the rest of the summer, wondering if (or hoping that) the college at which I was a junior (Mississippi State) would get lucky (or smart) and sign this Walter Payton phenomenon.

As it'd turn out, not a single Southeastern Conference school, including Mississippi State, would recruit Walter. Just before the start of the school year, Walter signed with Jackson State College (which became Jackson State University in 1974). I remember wondering if Jackson State even knew what it was getting. Little did I know, its staff was way ahead of the game. You see, they already had a guy named Payton on the team. His first name was Eddie. He was ripsnortin' up and down the field. I'll leave it to you to turn the pages to learn how special these two Paytons would become together at Jackson State and on their own at the next level.

Becoming a fan of the Payton brothers was easy. They were both from Mississippi, and they were both great football players. Unfortunately, I didn't get to see them play together during their one year at Jackson State. I was a poor college student at the time and could barely afford my free student pass to the MSU campus games. My loss.

As both Paytons starred in the NFL, though, I cheered proudly. I'll never forget when Eddie scored two touchdowns in one game in 1977, then returned a kick 99 yards in 1981 while with the Minnesota Vikings. As for Walter, well, I hosted a Super Bowl party in January of 1986 and arrogantly wore a No. 34 Bears jersey, rooting for Walter and his Chicago team in Super Bowl XX. I *had* discovered him in that all-star game, remember?

My first opportunity to meet one of the Paytons came years later with a chance seating assignment on a flight out of Miami in the late

1980s. I immediately recognized Eddie Payton seated in the window seat next to my aisle seat on a Delta flight returning to Jackson. Eddie was known throughout the area and was an SEC baseball umpire at the time who frequently called Mississippi State games. He was one of the best balls-and-strikes guys I've ever seen. Eddie had been playing in a celebrity pro-am golf tournament in the Miami area, and I'd been on a photo shoot in the Everglades. We talked mostly about hunting and fishing, which I quickly learned was a passion of both Payton men.

We promised to stay in touch…and indeed we did. I even wrote a feature magazine piece about the hunting proficiency of the Paytons. Eddie and I became good friends and huntin' buddies. Eddie likes hunting wild hogs, and I have a glut of that evasive species tearing up my property and competing with the native wildlife. So, Eddie comes over and "helps me out" from time to time. And the guy's not a bad fisherman either. As for golf, well, let's just say there ain't no way I'll play with him. Walter wouldn't either. At least that's something I had in common with Walter—neither of us could compete with Eddie on the golf course. One of several things Eddie and I share is an enthusiasm for the outdoors. Eddie Payton is colorful, energetic, and obsessed with his loves—golf, football, hunting, fishing, and family. We've shared many unforgettable moments on the water and in the field. And Eddie has shared so much more…

During the hours upon hours of interviews we conducted for this book, Eddie narrated tale after tale with cool candor, exposing his emotions and those of his late brother. Walter speaks clearly through the pages of this book by way of Eddie's empathic understanding of his little brother. Walter and Eddie were connected kindred spirits— two of a kind. In the coming pages, you'll find out exactly what I mean.

—Paul Brown

CHAPTER 1

Dyin' Ain't Easy

I t was late November in 1998, and Sweetness was on his way home. Momma, my friend Bubba Barham, and I were all at the Jackson, Mississippi, airport, waiting on Walter to walk off the plane. It had touched down just moments before. Daddy would have been there, too, had he not already passed on. The airport was busting at the seams with busyness, and with Christmas only a few weeks away, the atmosphere was full of good cheer. There were big ol' smiles all over the place and lots of laughter and chipper chatter as folks met up with loved ones, associates, and friends. It all paled in comparison to how I felt, though. I was more keyed up than anyone, that's for sure. It'd been about five months since I'd seen my brother, so I was really looking forward to jumping in a car with him for the ride over to Butler, Alabama. We were headed to our annual deer hunt at Pushmataha Plantation.

It seemed like forever until people started walking off that plane, so it was quite a welcome sight to see Walter among the first passengers coming through. There he was, a larger-than-life sports icon who doubled as my little bro. He had a bag on his arm and, once he saw me, a big smile on his face. But it didn't take long to see something was wrong with that normally electrified grin of his. It didn't match the merriness of the other smiles floating all around us. Actually, Walter's smile wasn't floating at all. It looked as heavy as that bag he was carrying. Maybe he'd had a bad flight. Did the other passengers hound him for autographs? Did the plane hit a rough patch and toss him around a bit? Did all that turbulence make him toss his peanuts?

I looked over at my momma, Alyne, and her face was like a ray of sunshine breaking through the clouds that had followed Walter off that plane. Her toothy smile was as wide-open as the great American South, and her eyes sparked up as bright as the stars out there in that clear Southern sky. She approached Walter with her arms open even wider than her smile and gave him the biggest Momma hug I'd ever seen. You know, the extra-long, uncut, extended version of what would have already been a pretty long hug. Walter didn't fight it at all; he just let it linger. About an hour later it was my turn. I looked deep into Walter's eyes before hugging him with all my might. The world knew him as Sweetness, but I knew him as something more. He was my brother, and I was his. We slapped each other on the back with that great-to-see-you-bro-but-this-is-gonna-hurt-a-little enthusiasm that only brothers can give each other.

As we pulled away, I looked at Walter's eyes again, only this time not so deep. I focused on the surface and noticed the color. Just like that, all the heaviness that had gone away came right on back. "Dawg, you feelin' okay?" I asked in a way that was more like a statement than a question. That color…it was definitely off. "You look a little yellow. Your eyes…"

Sweetness had grown accustomed to shaking defensive backs on the field, but when he heard my question, all he could shake was his head. "Nah, I'm good, dawg. I'm good. I just been drinkin' a lot of juice, takin' a lot of vitamins and stuff. You know, cleansin' my system and all that."

Despite his MVP-worthy effort, he sure wasn't shaking my concern with all his vitamin talk. I could just see something wasn't right about him, and Momma was starting to take notice, too. Her eyes stopped sparking like stars and started moving up and down with that patented Payton quickness that was passed down to Walter and me. She was scanning her baby boy as if examining him. "You losing weight, Walter?"

"Yeah, sure," Walter conceded. "This stuff I'm taking and drinking...I don't know, maybe I've lost a few pounds, but I'm fine. Really, I am."

I jumped back in. "Well, when you get back to Chicago, you need to get yourself checked out."

"I will, man, I will. Don't worry, I'm good." He put his hand on my shoulder to change subjects. "Let's go huntin'!"

I'd gotten so wrapped up in hunting for answers from Walter that I'd forgotten about all the real hunting we were fixin' to do. Walter's "let's go huntin'" snapped me back to it, though, and I decided to look past what was bothering me. Yellow eyes or not, I was ready to go hunting with Sweetness.

We visited with Momma for a little while longer there in the airport before Walter, Bubba, and I left for Alabama. When Momma finally said her good-byes, she walked away without saying another word about Walter's weight or how he looked. I thought I should probably do the same for the rest of the trip, so it was mostly small talk on the drive to Pushmataha. You know, just catchin' up and whatnot. He'd already assured us he would get checked out when he got back, so that was that.

When we got to the lodge that evening, we were sitting around, just chillin' in anticipation of our morning hunt the next day. I looked closely at Walter's eyes again. Contrasted against his dark complexion, they were as yellow as a Post-it note colored in full with a neon yellow marker and placed under a neon yellow light. Okay, maybe they weren't that yellow, but you get the idea. I was still disturbed by those yellow eyes, but I told myself I wasn't going to bring it up again on that trip, so I kept my mouth shut. Then I noticed his skin. Even with skin as dark as Walter's, I could see the yellowish undertones. Not as drastic as his eyes, but it was there. And that's when my mouth just had to open.

"Hey, dawg," I said as we sat there. He looked at me with raised eyebrows that said "what's up?" I responded to his eyebrows with a two-word accusation. "You're jaundiced."

Walter's eyebrows lowered quickly to form a scowl. "I told you not to worry. It's just the juice, man."

It wasn't adding up to me, but what did I know? I'm not a doctor, and I'd heard of that sort of thing happening before with vitamins and juice. Maybe he was all right, but I wanted to hear it from a professional. "Okay, okay, just get it checked out to be sure."

"I told you I will, man. I promise, okay?" It was a short conversation, but I could tell he'd had enough of it anyway. It was time to head to bed and start dreaming about all those deer we'd be hunting the next day. All that worrying and questioning about yellow eyes and skin must have worn me out, too, 'cause I was sleeping like a rock as soon as I hit the mattress.

We all woke up bright and early the next day ready to hunt, so we got right on out there. It was a good hunt, but Walter didn't seem like his usual energetic self; he seemed fatigued and lethargic, even for a normal person, but much more so for a world-class athlete. I tried to let it go and just have a good time, but when we got back to the lodge to clean up and rest a little, I noticed Walter as he got out of the shower. I was shocked at what I saw. It looked to me like he'd lost about 25 to 30 pounds since the last time we'd gotten together.

Now, again, I'm no doctor, but dropping that much weight over five months for a guy like Walter didn't make sense. The drastic weight loss plus the yellow eyes plus the yellow skin was all adding up quickly in my mind to one thing: Walter was a sick man. I had to express my concern once again and insist he really go see a doctor.

"Walter, man, what's up? You look pretty thin. I don't think those juices and vitamins are making you lose that much weight. And I don't think it's turning you yellow neither. I don't give a shit what you think is causin' it, you need to have it checked out. I'm serious."

Walter had a look of defeat on his face. It was very unusual for him. "Look, I'll go to the doctor if it'll make you feel better."

"Well, it damn sure will," I said, "and it'll make you feel better, too."

"Just promise me one thing, okay?" Walter said. "I promise I'll go get checked out right when I get back if you promise not to bring it up again for the rest of this trip." I agreed, and so we hunted hard for the next three days without a word about how Walter looked or any of that. When I took Walter back to the airport for his return flight to Chicago, though, I couldn't help myself. I walked with him to the gate and bit my tongue only until the boarding call. That's when I made him promise me one more time that he'd see a doctor when he got back to Chicago.

"I promise," he said with a wink and a grin, and just like that, he turned and was off again.

I tried to talk myself into thinking maybe it actually was just vitamins and all that, like Walter said. Maybe he was okay. After all, he was Superman, and I hadn't heard anything about any kryptonite where we're from. This was a man who had only missed one game in his entire NFL career. I had absolutely no need to worry. That's what I wanted to think, and that's what I tried to tell myself. But in the days following our hunt, I just couldn't get Walter off my mind. I kept thinking back to that week hunting with him in Alabama, and the same troubling details kept rising to the top of my head. Not only was he yellow-eyed, yellow-skinned, frail, and tired, but he also didn't eat much during the trip. He said he wasn't hungry, but that just wasn't Walter. He was always hungry, so something just had to be wrong. I felt a little better each time I remembered he was going to see a doctor. What I didn't know at the time was that a few weeks prior, he already had.

Walter was a big, big star, but he was a very private person. He kept mostly to himself, and if something was wrong, he'd often try to keep it even from his family. He didn't want anyone fussin' over him or worrying about anything. Looking back, my opinion is that Walter came to that deer hunt fully suspecting he was seriously ill. I think that's why he visited a doctor before the trip, and I think that's why he let Momma's hug linger for as long as possible. I think that heaviness around him at the airport wasn't something I imagined. I think that shadow coming off the plane behind him was something he knew was there. I think he also knew that what was ahead of him was the most difficult challenge of his life.

When I checked in on him just days after he got back, he told me he had visited a doctor already and that he had been diagnosed with "vitamin toxicity." Now, I have no reason to think he was lying to me. I think he did visit that doctor, and I think that doctor really did tell him it was vitamins. Of course, that's what Walter had blamed it all on during our hunting trip, but I felt a little better about it when he told me a doctor actually said it. I'm not sure why I didn't think to ask him why he didn't tell me before that he'd already seen a doctor. Maybe I was just too excited to hear that it was just because of the vitamins. Looking back, though, I think Walter may've talked the doctor into that diagnosis. He couldn't do it with me, but Walter had a way of talking others into saying what he wanted to hear.

As soon as Walter returned to Chicago from his trip, he picked up his regular schedule as best he could. And his regular schedule was anything but regular. It could usually be boiled down to three words and then three more: *hustle, hustle, hustle* and *push, push, push.* Before his illness, all that activity would have been because that's just how Walter Payton lived his life. After his illness, I think it was all a distraction so he could avoid dealing with reality. He was trying to act normal, but it certainly wasn't normal for Walter to go to the doctor. He couldn't keep the charade up for long due to one very inconvenient truth: Walter kept getting worse.

When he called me up to tell me things weren't going so well, despite what the doctor had said about vitamins, that's when I knew things were bad. That's when I really started to worry. And that's when we started to connect like we did back in the day, before we got pulled away from each other by life. For the first time in a long time, we started talking a lot. Every three days, in fact. And our days of talking weren't the only things coming in threes. He started describing three recurring symptoms: severe stomach aches, diarrhea, and exhaustion. Those things were hitting him harder than any linebacker ever did. Sweetness was hurting, and I could tell he was reaching out to me, his older brother, to push him to do something about it. He couldn't force himself to take the next step, so he was asking me to. And that's exactly what I did. I told him to forget all this vitamin stuff he heard from that doctor and finally get some real help. He stopped telling me nothing was wrong and agreed to do what I said.

In early December, Walter called Jim Sheridan, a business partner and one of his closest friends. I didn't know much about the guy, but I knew he had a lot to do with the Mayo Clinic in Rochester, Minnesota. That's to say, I knew he was legit and would be able to help my little bro. He was a very busy guy, but he got Walter worked in within a few weeks, which was fantastic. Still, I was worried. The fact that Walter listened to me and was going in there to get checked out had me thinking something very bad could be going down. I didn't feel optimistic about it at all. I feared the worst. I expected our world to come crashing down. Even so, I was stunned by the results. Superman had stumbled upon some kryptonite.

Walter was diagnosed with primary sclerosing cholangitis (PSC), a rare and chronic disease that attacks the bile ducts of the liver. In plain English, he was gravely ill, and the diagnosis hit me like a speeding bullet. I was dazed, trying to make sense of it all, and at the same time I was trying to keep up with my duties as golf coach at Jackson State. It was a tough, tough time and almost impossible to stay focused on my job. Primary sclerosing cholangitis didn't sound good, and not just because I couldn't pronounce it. Walter was dying. He wasn't just injured, he wasn't just hit a little too hard in the head, and he wasn't just "doubtful" for his next NFL game. My little brother was actually dying. He was doubtful to live.

Then I got a little bit of hope from Walter. He explained that the doctors said a liver transplant could save his life. I pumped my fist and instantly thought Walter was gonna make it. He'd be certain to get a transplant. I mean, he was a big football hero, so surely they'd put him high on the list, right? Well, in all my hope, I guess I forgot for a second that Walter is Walter. He told the doctors that just because he carried a football better than most people in the world didn't mean he deserved to get ahead of anyone else on the list. The Mickey Mantle liver transplant fiasco was still fresh on Walter's mind, I think. Some thought Mantle had jumped ahead of others since he got his donor liver in just one day, and Walter didn't want to be remembered as pushing folks aside to get his. He didn't think he was better than anyone else, and he didn't want to be treated that way. That was hard for his family to hear.

Us kids were always tops in Momma's eyes, though, and Walter was about to get the Momma treatment. She decided to make

Chicago her temporary—but indefinite—new home. She just had to see Walter through this and went to all the doctor appointments with him. I wanted to be there, too, but I knew he was in good hands with Momma by his side. It was at that point that I started getting most of my information about Walter's rapidly advancing condition straight from Momma. I knew Walter would try to give me the optimistic view with a wink and a grin like he often did, but Momma wouldn't. No, sir. She'd just lay it on me, unfiltered and with no candy coating. I was counting on her for that, so I called her right after they met with the doctor for the final results of all his tests. Good, bad, or whatever, I wanted to know the truth.

"Momma, what did y'all find out?" I asked, hoping for any sort of good news.

No good news came.

"They told him it was really bad, Eddie. The doctor said his only chance is to have a liver transplant."

"Yeah, that's what Walter told me before," I said. "He acted like it was no big deal, but it sounds radical to me. What do you think?"

"That's what I think, too," Momma continued. "And to have this surgery…you know…it could work, I guess, but they say sometimes they take and sometimes they don't, so who knows? Walter asked me what I'd do if I was him.'"

"What did you say?"

"I told him I wouldn't have it."

I was wishing Momma would have told him to do whatever it takes, but like I said, with Momma you always get the truth. "What did Walter say to that?" I asked.

"Not much. He just said he didn't want to be put ahead of anybody, that if he was going to do it, he'd wait his turn."

I was relieved to hear that Walter at least wanted to have the transplant, even if he'd insisted on waiting in line like everyone else.

There was hope again, but along the road of waiting for Walter's turn, that hope turned into despair. A few weeks later, New Year's Day 1999, brought with it a return visit for Walter to the hospital at the Mayo Clinic. He emerged from the hospital this time without his patented wink and grin. He'd been told he was no longer a candidate for a transplant and that he wouldn't be placed on the transplant list after all.

We were all stunned and couldn't make sense of what we were hearing. I didn't believe it. I mean, this guy had made all sorts of lists as a football player. He'd received the kind of recognition that other guys would die for. Yet here he was, actually dying, and he couldn't get on the one list that could save his life. I wanted to know why, so I started digging.

Though I may never know exactly what went down with all that, I suspect any hope we ever had that Walter would get a liver transplant was nothing more than false hope. After much research and talking with experts in the hepatobiliary field (liver, bile duct specialists), I've come to the conclusion that Walter was *never* a candidate for a liver transplant and was *never* on a transplant list. As I later discovered, by the time Walter got to the Mayo Clinic in mid-December, he already had bile duct cancer, so a liver transplant would've been pointless. So, why did the doctor tell Walter the only thing that could save him was a liver transplant? Why did he get his hopes up?

It could've been a few different things. Maybe the doctor told Walter a transplant was a possibility for PSC, not addressing the fact that it wouldn't help a patient with bile duct cancer. Or maybe Walter simply heard what he wanted to hear. The doctor might've said something like, "A transplant would be the best 'treatment' for PSC...," and then gone on to explain, in terms over everybody's heads and to a patient deaf to anything negative, that Walter wasn't a candidate for a transplant. Or it could just be that Walter pulled one over on me and Momma, simply telling us what he thought would make us feel better. Walter might've told Momma something like, "See, Momma, a transplant is all I need to beat this thing," knowing full well that a transplant was out of the question. Having known Walter like I did, it wouldn't surprise me at all had he done something like that.

No matter what actually happened with all of that, looking back, I wish all the doctors and such would've just told Walter to go fishing and enjoy the rest of his life. I can tell you I'd have jumped at the chance to join him out there on the water, bass fishing and finishing out his days in peace. Instead, we were there in a hospital together, and all I was joining him in was a state of devastation and depression. Even so, he didn't stay there with me for very long. Walter quickly accepted the hand he was dealt, and he resolved to move on. Just like when he was living in my shadow growing up as a kid, he never once complained, blamed, or bellyached about what he was going through.

Walter was so set in his acceptance of the situation that when our close family friend, Bud Holmes, wanted to send his plane up to get Walter and fly him to MD Anderson Cancer Center in Houston for a second opinion, Walter just flat-out refused the offer. Bud was in the room when the autopsy was performed on my daddy, Peter, after he died in Columbia, Mississippi, and I'll never forget what he told me when he saw Walter sick. He said Walter actually looked older than Daddy did when his body was in that autopsy room. He looked older than a dead man? That told me that in Bud's mind, Walter looked like a dead man walking.

Well, Walter didn't act like a dead man, that's for sure. He just kept trying to keep hope alive for his family, friends, and fans by continuing to assert that he was just waiting on a liver and that everything would be fine once he got on a list and the transplant had been done. But he knew the truth. Momma and I did, too. Momma had talked with the doctors one-on-one, and they didn't sugarcoat it like Sweetness tended to do. She knew there would be no transplant, and she made sure I was well aware of that fact, too. I wanted to believe it didn't matter. I was hoping Walter really was Superman and that he'd somehow find a way to overcome this kryptonite at the very last second, when all hope was seemingly lost. I imagined him as the Walter of 10 years earlier and tried to hold on to the dream that he would rise above and conquer his illness like he always conquered everything else in life. But down deep I knew it wasn't going to be. I knew he was the Walter of today and that right then and there, he was dying. No matter how powerful I liked to imagine him to be, he wasn't really Superman. Even with all of his otherworldly accomplishments on the football field, he was just flesh and bone like you and me.

The weakened flesh and aching bones of a mere mortal notwithstanding, Walter attacked his sickness with the same ferociousness he used to assault opposing defenses. There was nothing he could do about his physical condition, but his mentality never changed. As a mega-star athlete, he lived by the old "suck it up and play with pain" attitude, as well as his own personal motto of "Never Die Easy." He took all that to heart as he struggled against a foe that he had no chance of defeating. In truth, he'd only had to apply it before on a football field. It wasn't life or death when he was carrying that pigskin, but this was a whole new ballgame he found himself in. Others might have just crumbled, but not Walter. He still wasn't going to die easy, even if he knew he was going to die.

At times like that, you realize that relationships are the only things we take with us when we go, and I wanted desperately to be there with Walter every step of the way. My job as Jackson State golf coach prevented me from seeing him as much as I wanted to. We talked regularly, of course, but as Walter's condition worsened, that got harder and harder. He just didn't want to talk much at times, so I'd usually just be looking at a silent phone instead of that face I knew so well. And when he did talk, he'd make it clear that he didn't want the public to see him sick. One time he said, "If I'm going to have to leave here, I want them to remember me from my playing days." He didn't want to be remembered for a sickness. He wanted his fans and the generations that followed to remember him as Sweetness, with those bright white eyes sitting just below his ever-present headband and scanning ahead for an open running lane. To me, that says a lot about who Walter was. He didn't want his fans to be in despair about his condition; he wanted them to remember how much fun the ride he took them all on had been.

Another thing we talked about, when he actually felt like talking there at the end, was our Christian faith. We talked more and more about that as he approached death, in fact. Walter and I shared the belief that through God, all things are possible. Not that all things we desire will happen, but that all things are possible—and only according to His will. Only by His grace were we able to do the things we did and enjoy the talents He gave us. Walter was so very thankful to God for graciously giving him the life that he had the great privilege of living.

Some writers and others have said Walter wasn't religious. Jeff Pearlman wrongly, even recklessly, concluded from sources he interviewed that my brother would have "cringed" at all the religious expression at his funeral. Well, shame on Pearlman and his sources. In truth, Walter wouldn't have had it any other way. It's easier for writers like Pearlman to get attention if they just tell stories about the "big fish that got away" rather than showing real evidence to back up their sensational claims. You see, with "professional" writers and other members of the media, falsehoods and scandals often rise to the surface like dead fish. Now, I understand that a dead fish is easy to catch, but it sure don't make for good eatin'. You have to be patient and do some deep-sea fishing to get to the good stuff. That's where you'll find the truth about Walter. It's swimming deep under the surface with everything else worth catching. I promise it's there. You just have to fish for it.

There are all these surface-level "revelations" floating around out there about the "enigmatic life of Walter Payton," and we can have ourselves a debate about what's true and what isn't, but to say he wasn't religious is a flat-out unreligious thing to do. Walter often professed his faith during his speeches and gave credit to the Lord for his talent, in public, yes, but even more so in private. Make no mistake; Walter was a believer in Jesus Christ and a follower of our Lord. He wasn't Tim Tebow, that's for sure, but that doesn't mean he wasn't religious. Tebow puts it out there for all the world to see, and that's great. You can't miss it with him, but that wasn't Walter Payton. He was a high-profile person with a low-profile personality. He liked his business to be his business, and he'd stay out of yours, too. He revealed who he truly was only to those willing to take time to look. You can argue Tebow's way is better than Walter's if you want. I'll leave that to you. But whether or not Walter was religious and whether or not he's with the good Lord right now, well, that's not up to you. And it's not up to all those sportswriters, either.

There's another side to the story of Sweetness that has to be told. Guys like Jeff Pearlman can't tell it. They don't have memories of growing up with my brother. They didn't know him before he was a star. They don't have much more to give you than dead fish. The truth about Walter Payton can only come from those of us who knew him best, those of us who truly loved him, not just for a short time, but for his whole life.

I'll never forget October 31, 1999, Halloween night. Walter was at his home, where he wanted to spend his final days with his wife, Connie, and other family. None of us knew exactly how long he had, and we wanted to spend as much time with him as we could. I was there for a visit and had just walked into his bedroom. I didn't know exactly what we were going to say to each other, of course, but it turns out we were about to have a conversation that will stay with me forever. It was one of those special moments that comes once in a lifetime, and it was about to take place right there in that room between us Payton boys. I'll let you in on that conversation later in the book, but for now, just take in the scene with me.

At first, there were no words spoken. There was only the background noise of a television with the volume turned low. I tiptoed farther into the room, and before I broke the silence, I just looked at him. There was my baby brother, unable to move, just lying there, dying. I shook my head. It couldn't be. A million images of Walter and me ran through my mind. Our life together flashed before my eyes. I remembered us as children hunting in our neighborhood woods, as teenagers playing together on the field, as young men going out into the world. There was a hard conversation coming later in that room, but all I wanted to do when I saw him there was go back—back to the beginning of an era. Back to when the man you know as Sweetness was just my baby brother. Back to where you'll find the truth about Walter Payton.

CHAPTER 2

The Garden of Eatin'

'm not one to point fingers, but there's nobody to blame except
Adam for bringing pain into the world. And it makes sense to
me that it was his eating of forbidden fruit that did it. You see,
Walter and I endured our fair share of wrath and pain from a little ol'
"forbidden" fruit known as the plum. The plums I'm talking about
weren't growing in the Garden of Eden, of course, and they weren't
declared "forbidden" by God. Still, they were in Reverend Hendricks'
garden, and Reverend Hendricks was, as should be obvious by my
calling him "Reverend," a man of God. So, there you go.

Now, Reverend Hendricks wasn't just a man of God. He was also
a sourpuss. He didn't really speak much, unless he was speaking the
Word…then he could get going, that's for sure. He'd mind his own
business for the most part, and his physical presence wasn't much
more imposing than his personality. He was a thin man of average
height with a quiet manner and a noticeable limp. Of course, looks
can be deceiving, and he was tougher than he appeared. Walter and
I may've even used the word "mean" a time or two to describe him.
Some have the fear of God in them, but we had the fear of Reverend
Hendricks in us early on.

Reverend Hendricks lived in a big wood-framed house in the middle of our street, right across the road from our aunt's house. Two wooded vacant lots divided Reverend Hendricks' house and Miss Willie Mae's house, so you can imagine all the little feet that explored those woods over the years, seeking mischief and whatnot. A well-worn path snaked through the two vacant lots and connected our street to the next street over. Then another path forked like a venomous tongue off the main trail and led straight to Reverend Hendricks' garden.

That garden was the Reverend's favorite thing in the world. And his favorite thing in his favorite thing in the world was a row of lush plum trees, full of fruit. Such good-lookin' fruit, too. I knew I wasn't supposed to touch or taste, but every time I saw those plums as a kid, I just couldn't help but think about sinking my teeth into them... all of them. Right and wrong didn't seem to matter much. Neither did punishment. It was nine-year-old Walter, called "Bubba" at the time, and 12-year-old me, called "Edward Charles," up against that Serpent hissing in the trees, and we weren't trying real hard to fight the temptation. We were plum poachin'.

A four-foot-high chain-link fence surrounded the "Garden of Eatin'." Not quite cherubim and a flaming sword, but it was an obstacle nonetheless. In the middle of the garden were the finest plum trees you'll ever lay eyes on, so it didn't take long to see the "obstacle" as more of an obstacle course. You know, more fun than work. The diamond pattern wire of the fence was perfect for little barefooted brothers to grasp and climb right over.

In addition to plums, Reverend Hendricks raised green veggie things in his garden on the end flanking the path...and sunflowers, okra, tomatoes, and other unknown (at least to us kids) veggies and such. But the plums were what we had our eyes on. They were the objects of our desire, no doubt. Those big, ripe, yellowish-red plums might as well have been the apple that tempted Adam in the Garden of Eden. I mean, I know exactly what he was feeling. And I must admit that had I been there in the Garden of Eden, it would have probably been Edward Charles that brought pain into the world. And I even think I had it worse than Adam. I'd gotten a taste (legitimately) of those plums a time or two before, when the Reverend's wife had brought some to the house. I'm sure that made my will that much weaker than Adam's. Those plums were just plain delicious.

The taste of those plums from a week earlier was still in our mouths, and we had images of Reverend Hendricks' forbidden plums dancing in our heads. Of course, plums in our heads wasn't enough. We wanted those plums in our bellies, so Walter and I mapped out a military-style plan to get us some more. We were fixin' to take all the plums we could see…and no prisoners. Our plan was to go by Miss Willie Mae's house on the other side of the vacant lots, cut through the thick woods (which would provide cover), stay low, follow the path to the garden, and finally belly-crawl the last few feet. To make a quick escape, we planned to push the fence down. I didn't want us having to worry about climbing over the fence if something went wrong. We'd grab as many plums as could fill our pockets and our hands as we cupped them against our tummies. Then we'd take the plums home and eat them all in the backyard.

We even plotted Reverend Hendricks' moves, sort of like Danny Ocean and his boys accounted for the moves of Terry Benedict in *Ocean's Eleven*. They knew where Benedict would be, and we thought we knew Reverend Hendricks' moves pretty well. Like clockwork, the Reverend would walk to church every morning around eight and walk back at five. Our plan was to get home from school at four and then roll out "Operation Plum Poach." With only an hour window, we knew we had to move quickly. The whole thing was pretty elaborate for a nine-year-old and a 12-year-old, but like I said, those were some kind of wonderful plums! They could drive a boy to do things he shouldn't be able to do.

And so, the day finally arrived. Then the hour. Then the moment. It was time. The plan was a go. We were ready. I ripped off my T-shirt, and Walter seemed puzzled by that. It wasn't part of the plan, so he asked, "Why you takin' off your shirt?"

"Camouflage!" I said with the authority of a general. I suppose I trusted that our brown skin would make us less visible through the dark woods. It made sense to me and must have started making sense to Walter, too, because he stripped off his shirt and followed. We eased into the woods by Miss Willie Mae's house, and then hiked to the back as if we were going through to the next street. Then we slid back through the woods as planned, taking the path toward the garden, and got within 10 yards of the fence, stopping short of the well-manicured lawn with no cover. When the coast was clear, we commenced belly-crawlin' the rest of way, and finally reached the plums. We started snatching up the fruit that littered the ground on both sides of the fence.

We had plenty.

We were set.

We had more than enough.

We wanted more.

If we hadn't gotten greedy, we shoulda/woulda/coulda escaped unnoticed right then and there, but I spotted some beauties still clinging to the top of one of the trees. Those plums had our names on them, so I started shaking the tree at its base to get them loose. Plums started plopping all over Walter, and he got to giggling about it. It must have been the funniest thing that ever happened to him, because he started getting louder and louder. There was no hushing him up. Looking back, I probably should have just shoved a plum in his mouth. That would shut him up for sure. When he finally stopped giggling, we looked around to make sure no one was looking. Everything seemed fine, so we kept going.

The fence was stronger than I thought it was going to be, so pushing it down wasn't happening. Plus, we realized at about that point that we didn't want this to be a one-and-done poaching. No, sir…we wanted to come back for more later on once the trees recovered, so we didn't want to leave any signs that we had been there. I told Walter to get inside the fence with me to help pick up the freshly fallen plums.

I was feeling pretty good about life at that moment. We were little masterminds rewarded with the spoils of our conquest. Plums covered the ground inside and outside the fence. It was fruit galore! "Operation Plum Poach" was a success. Then a voice came out of nowhere…

"Have you eaten from the tree that I commanded you not to eat from?"

Okay, that isn't what the voice said. And it actually wasn't a "voice." It was more like a roar.

"Hey!" Reverend Hendricks shouted from the window in his house. "Boys, get out of my trees! I sees ya, I sees ya! I knows who you is!" Reverend Hendricks had obviously snuck himself home without our knowing and was just sitting quietly, watching us, waiting for his moment. Definitely an ambush…and it worked in scaring the living crap out of us.

Instincts kicked into gear, and I was gone. I shot over to the fence like a deer, bounced off once, and then hit it again, bare feet first, and two-toe crawled it over the fence and into the woods. I guess the whole "never leave a man behind" thing hadn't made it into our military-style plan, because I didn't even think of helping Walter, who was struggling to get his fat butt over the fence.

Now, y'all only know Walter as "Sweetness" and one of the best football players of all time. So you probably won't believe me when I tell you this, but at one time I was quicker than Walter. It's true. In fact, at the time of "Operation Plum Poach," you might have called him "Slowness." I was no doubt much faster than him that day, because I disappeared into the woods while he continued to climb over that dang fence. I would just tell him to stay on the other side if I had to do it over again.

Walter finally jelly-rolled himself over and crashed into the woods like a big ol' buffalo. Back in the cover of the woods, we took off together. It was like one of those Road Runner cartoons, with our legs and feet just circular blurs. Straight home and into the backyard we went. We could still hear Reverend Hendricks yelling in the distance, "I sees ya, I sees ya! I knows who you is! Just wait 'til your daddy gets home!"

Oh man, our daddy? It started sinking in when we heard "wait 'til your daddy gets home." That's when we were really scared and started thinking, *Okay, maybe we shouldn't have done that.*

By the time we got back home, we checked out pockets. All we had left was a couple of plums apiece, and they were squashed in all the frenzy of getting out of there. They were still edible, though, so we ate 'em. One thing we learned from hanging out with the older boys in the neighborhood was that if you're stealing food, you always eat the evidence.

There was this one man outside of Columbia, Mississippi, where we grew up, who grew watermelons in a huge field. The older boys would sneak into his field and eat the heart of the watermelons but leave the rest in the field to rot. That put the farmer on alert to the fact that someone was stealing his melons, so he started watching and caught those melon robbers red-handed. Well, Walter and I learned from that. We weren't going to get caught with any plums, so we ate them all up. Also, we just plain *wanted* to eat them all up. We hunkered down in our shared bedroom, savoring the taste of those juicy plums and hoping Reverend Hendricks was just talking when he said he saw us and knew who we were.

We tried to convince ourselves that we had pulled it off, but down deep inside, I think we knew the Reverend wasn't just talking, because we kept looking out the window to see if he was coming. It wasn't long before we saw the slim, well-groomed man of God limping his way up the street, straight to our house. He looked as dapper as could be in his suit, just like a pastor should. The only thing that didn't match his suit was that scowl on his face. We were all made in the image of God, I know, but on that day, Reverend Hendricks' image was definitely favoring the wrath of God. Every limp he took toward our door would send another surge of adrenaline through our bodies. And then the limping stopped. Was he healed? No, he was at our front door. There was a knock, and our daddy opened up.

"Hello, Reverend Hendricks, come on in," Daddy said, thinking (or maybe hoping) the fine Reverend was there for a social visit. "Can I get you something to drink? My wife just made up some lemonade. Would you like some?"

"Yes, I believe I would." Even angry, plum-less reverends couldn't pass up a glass of my momma's lemonade.

As both men walked into the kitchen, Walter and I eased on down the hallway toward the kitchen door to get a closer listen, as if we didn't know what the Reverend was about to say.

"Brother Payton," Reverend Hendricks said in a stern voice, perhaps only slightly less stern than it would've been without the taste of sugared-up lemons in his mouth. "I have a serious matter that I need to speak to you about."

"Yes, sir. I'll be glad to help if I can," Daddy offered.

"Now, Brother Payton, some boys stole some of my plums, got in my fence and was stealing plums," Reverend Hendricks began. I had a lump in my throat bigger than any plum we stole that day. The Reverend went on, "I yelled at them, and they took off running. It was two of 'em, but I only got a good look at one, and it sure looked like Bubba…your boy, Bubba. Worst of it, they broke one of my trees, limbs and things."

Daddy didn't seem too happy about that. "Are you sure it was *my* boys?" he asked.

"Well, I didn't get a real good look at 'em, but one of them was small and heavyset like Bubba. I'm not sure, but the other one looked a lot like Edward Charles."

"Well, I tell you what," Daddy stated, "if it was my boys, you can be sure they won't ever do it again!"

The Reverend nodded. He seemed a little too pleased to hear that, from my perspective anyway. "I wanted you to know," he said, pausing for effect, "because I could've shot 'em." And that had some effect all right. Get shot for stealing fruit from trees? Now, that would just be plum stupid!

Anyway, hearing all that, we ran back down the hall into our room to hatch a quick plan. And by "hatch a plan," I mean we were coming up with a lie. As the older brother with all the ideas, I took the lead. And I thought this idea was a particularly good one. "Okay, Bubba, here's what we're gonna do. When Daddy comes in here, he's gonna be mad! I mean, mad! He might whoop us to death. Since Reverend Hendricks only saw you, you're gonna confess. Then I'm gonna say, 'Daddy, it's my fault. I shoulda been watching Bubba closer. Don't whoop Bubba, whoop me instead.' Then Daddy won't whoop either one of us, 'cause he'll be so proud of me for sticking up for you that he just won't be able to whoop either of us."

Bubba bought in like a dumb little brother ought to when his smarter, older (and better-looking, if I do say so myself) brother presents a plan. So, now we just had to wait for Daddy to come through that door.

During all that listening and planning, I'd developed quite an urge to pee and was about to pee my pants, so I went to the bathroom to take a leak. While I was in there, Reverend Hendricks left, and I heard Daddy yell, "Bubba!"

Uh-oh. Better finish peeing right quick!

"Did you go into Reverend Hendricks' garden and steal his plums?"

Walter stuck with the plan even though I was still in the bathroom. "Yes, sir, Daddy, I did," he answered as instructed.

By the time I got my pants zipped up and made it back to the bedroom, Daddy had a belt in one hand with his other hand on back of Walter's neck, pressing him into the mattress.

Now, before you go judging my daddy, you need to understand something. In the Deep South where I'm from, corporal punishment is not only accepted as a way to rear a child, it's heralded as the *only* way. In fact, "rearing" a child has a whole different meaning where I'm from. Parents down there acted as if a whoopin' could only be felt (and therefore effective) if the bottom being whooped was a bare one. The butt had to be nekkid. Not "naked," as you might say it. N*e*kkid.

And it wasn't just us black kids getting whooped, either. Down south, the belt was an equal opportunity means of discipline. The white kids were getting it, too, and it sort of linked us all up together in that way. It created a sort of unspoken (perhaps even unrealized) bond that transcended skin color. Whether your skin was black or white to begin with, after the belt, everybody's skin was the same color—red.

Daddy was a God-fearing, sometimes-churchgoing man. He was a good man. He knew his Bible, and he believed in the King James Version. His favorite verse was Proverbs 13:24, which states, "*He that spareth the rod hateth his son; but he that loveth him chasteneth him betimes.*" Daddy's paraphrase: "Spare the rod, spoil the child." My daddy was not one to spare the rod. No, sir.

To us kids, Daddy seemed as big as Goliath. In reality, he was a slightly built, thin man of 5'6" or so. So, maybe he was more like David than Goliath. I know one thing to be true: he sure could swing a belt like David could sling a rock!

The sound of leather flogging flesh filled the house that day, along with my daddy's words. When he got going, it was sort of a conversation combined with the ass-whoopin'. A whack per word, if you will. My daddy was yelling and whacking on Walter, "I (WHACK) told (WHACK) you (WHACK) not (WHACK) to (WHACK) steal (WHACK)! We (WHACK) don't (WHACK) steal (WHACK)!" There was always one more WHACK after the last word for good measure.

At that point, Walter sort of got off script. He wasn't going down alone. During Daddy's string of sage words, Bubba was screaming, "Edward Charles was there, too! Edward Charles was there, too!"

After that, I had to pee again. And I was wishing right about then, too, that Reverend Hendricks would've just shot me there in his garden!

I didn't even have time to say, "Stop, it's my fault!" before our plan was ruined. It was my plan, I know, but I still felt like Walter ratted me out since he'd agreed to go along with it. Didn't really matter, though, because I knew that belt would soon be upon my nekkid butt, too.

Momma stood in the hall bawling and hollering at Daddy, "That's enough, Edward! That's enough! Stop now!" Momma was crying for what was happening to Walter. Walter was crying from the pain of child "rearin'." I was crying for what was about to happen to me. Everybody was crying. Everybody except Daddy.

Then Daddy stopped on Walter, turned, and grabbed me. He slung me to the bed, and it was on. "Get them britches down, boy! Ain't that plum juice on your pants?" Now, say that last sentence again with a WHACK between every word.

Those plums were good, but they weren't *that* good!

My only strategy during a whoopin' like that was to reverse the guilt, try to throw it back on Daddy. I'd always attempt to make Daddy feel guilty by bawling out things like, "Don't beat me no more, Daddy, don't beat me! I won't do it again, I promise!" The "please don't beat me" plan seemed to fail like all of my other plans on that day. Nothing was working right for me. To Daddy, this one wasn't a beating, and he wasn't going to feel bad about it. We had stolen (from a reverend, no less!), and this was a whoopin' we had earned. We just had to take it.

All bad things come to an end eventually, and that plum whoopin' finally stopped, too. The one-and-a-half-inch belt marks swelled into red welts that faded in a few days, but that whoopin' is still imprinted on my soul nearly 50 years later. I will never, ever forget it. That was a defining moment of growing up in Columbia, Mississippi, with my little brother, Walter "Bubba" Payton.

For those never receiving the business end of a deserved ass-whoopin', you won't understand what I'm talking about here, but Walter and I both had a great relationship with our father despite the pain of his belt. He cared about us. He got angry at us because he cared. Show me a father who doesn't get mad when his kids do something wrong, and I'll show you a father who just doesn't care about his kids. But our daddy? He was our hero. He was our nekkid-butt-whoopin' hero. Walter and I did everything with him. It was kind of like he was a sibling at times, an older brother to both of us. He taught us to fish and hunt, and he taught us how to appreciate the outdoors. That's a gift that is still giving to this very day.

Walter, Daddy, and I were about as close as father and sons could be. It was like he compartmentalized his roles as friend and disciplinarian, and we did the same. When he was hanging out with us, he was our homeboy, that's for sure. But when we were messing up, well, Daddy was definitely the enforcer.

Momma set the rules, and Daddy made sure the rules were followed. Momma would set a rule, we'd break it, she'd tell Daddy, and he'd make us pay. From the time I was about seven until my senior year in high school, I'd often go to bed fully dressed because we'd do mischievous things worthy of a whoopin', and I knew my momma would tell Daddy when he got home. Right before I started going to bed fully clothed, I noticed that sometimes, when my momma told Daddy we'd been bad, he'd wait until about 10:30 or 11:00 at night, when we'd be in the bed half-nekkid, to come in and whoop some behind. Many nights I thought I'd gotten away with something, when all of a sudden, Daddy would rip off the covers with his belt in his hand. Each of our beds was in a corner, wedged against the wall, so we were sitting ducks. Sitting nekkid ducks. So, anyway, after a while, I figured out when my momma was gonna tell Daddy I did something wrong, and that's the night I'd go to bed fully clothed. You know, so I wouldn't be nekkid and so that it hopefully wouldn't hurt as bad.

Of course, if Daddy was using a switch, it wouldn't matter if you had your clothes on. You'd need armor to not feel the sting of that thing! If Daddy had time to think through how exactly he was going to whoop us, he'd make us go get a switch from the "switch tree" growing in our front yard. That tree was a willow that we swore was planted solely for supplying whoopin' switches. Between the plum trees and our switch willow, it's a wonder I don't cringe every time I see a tree!

Now, I know all of this probably sounds bad to you. Whoopin' and pain and switches and nekkid butts and all. But I can tell you that if it weren't for my parents' heavy-handed discipline, there's a real good chance Walter and I would've been juvenile delinquents. There's a good chance the world would've never known Sweetness. We were curious little boys, always getting into trouble, and without discipline, we would've just gotten into more and more instead of less and less. Really, we were explorers, adventurers, and lovers of the outdoors and all it had for us, just like most boys, but we'd push it to the edge. We were always staying out too long, going farther than allowed, swimming in fordidden mud puddles, and yes…stealing fruit from trees that belonged to men of God. (What, you never did that when you were a kid?) And I guess we weren't very good at it, because we were always getting caught…and whooped. And as much as whoopin' hurt, it worked. It was exactly what we needed.

Dr. Spock wrote a book about talking to kids, making them understand what they've done wrong instead of whooping them, blah blah blah. Well, that's all fine and good and might work for some kids up north or something, but it wouldn't have worked for Walter and me. If my daddy had tried that, we would've figured out from day one that we could just play along, and we would've gotten no whoopin' and probably would've ended up criminals. Other kids might have remorse and all of that, but Walter and I didn't. That Dr. Spock stuff wouldn't have worked on us. What we needed was *Mr.* Spock's Vulcan nerve pinch.

Without pain, we would've figured out that touchy-feely stuff and thought, *I ain't gonna get nothing but a timeout.* A timeout? Really?

29

Shoot, timeout for us was that period of time right after Daddy whooped us. We'd go to our room with red welts on our nekkid butts, and we'd be in timeout. Maybe some other kids might go into the closet, sulk and think about it, and then they might come out and be sorry or whatever. Not Walter and me.

All kids need positive reinforcement, but positive reinforcement can mean different things to different kids. And you can't raise a black kid from the South with an instruction manual for a white kid from the North. It's just different. Walter and I needed positive reinforcement, that's for sure, but the best motivator you could've given us was pain. We remembered pain.

A lot of our activities (you know, to keep us out of trouble) involved pain. My mother figured the two best ways to keep us out of trouble were to get us in church and to keep us busy with yard work. Both of those things can be painful experiences depending on where you are spiritually or physically, but I have to admit the yard work was on a whole other level.

Every year, my momma would have a truck dump a whole load of topsoil in the driveway by the front yard. This started when I was about 10 (Walter was seven), and it continued for at least five or six years. I started playing Little League baseball when I was 10, but when I wasn't ballin', our job for the summer was to take that topsoil and level off the yard. The operation was sort of like when a prisoner moves a rock pile from point "A" to point "B," then back to point "A" again. It seemed futile to us, but we did it. Futile was always better than a whoopin' from Daddy, ya know?

All we had was one shovel and a really small, wobbly wheelbarrow. It would take all summer—every summer. Walter would load it; I'd roll it down and dump it. I'd push; he'd load. When it got wet, we'd lay down boards all the way to where we were going, and I'd push the wheelbarrow back and forth on the boards. It took all I had to push that heavy load, and the same for Walter to load it. And it got worse every year. In fact, after a couple of years, the shovel's wooden handle broke off near the blade. The broken shovel wasn't replaced, either. Oh no, Walter just had to make do with the stump of wood and the rusty old metal blade. It was hard, hard work.

Now, I said earlier that our momma would assign this work to keep us out of trouble, and that's true. We couldn't plan how to steal plums from a reverend if we were working hard in the yard, right? Well, we didn't know it at the time, but she was also assigning us that work to make us strong. During those summers, Walter developed a huge upper body, and I built up my lower body pretty good. Slowly but surely, we were becoming men. We were becoming athletes. We were becoming who we were meant to be.

When Walter and I finally got into organized sports, I understood what our momma was doing. It was kind of like *The Karate Kid*. Daniel-san would "paint the fence" and do "wax on" and "wax off" over and over in what he thought was an exercise in futility, but it turned out to be great karate training. In the same way, our grueling summer work gave us the bodies we'd need to compete in sports at the highest levels. Until then, I could never understand why my momma would have us build up that yard every year. I mean, every summer we'd be building up that dang yard by the sweat of our brow. It was like the curse of Adam playing out right there. And it was the front yard, too, so think about how that looked. By the time we stopped doing it, we had a yard halfway up the bottom of the house for all to see. Years of pain and sweat for that? No, it wasn't for that. And it wasn't for nothing. It was for us—her sons.

My momma wasn't just trying to keep us boys from poaching plums, and she wasn't trying to keep us from getting whooped by

Daddy. Momma wasn't just having us do all that work for nothing, and she certainly wasn't doing it to build up the yard. No, my momma never meant to build up the yard at all. She was building up Walter and me.

CHAPTER 3

Movin' On Up

Georinge Jefferson was one bad dude. But what do I mean by that? "Bad" is such an interesting word. You hear someone saying it these days, and they could be talking about something bad or something good. The one phrase, "I'm bad," can have two entirely different meanings. Makes no good sense. And even when you're actually talking about bad behavior when describing someone, there's further complication of the subject when you throw in acronyms like ADD, ADHD, or any other combination of letters that makes a kid go bonkers. None of that stuff existed back in the day. Or at least, we didn't know about it. I wish we did 'cause I'm sure I could've gotten out of a whoopin' or two by blaming it on some personality disorder or whatnot. But no, there was no confusion about the term "bad" when I was growing up with Walter in Columbia, Mississippi. If you were misbehavin' where I'm from, it had nothing to do with ADD, and it certainly wasn't anything good. When some kid was acting up, it was just "He bad."

Us kids weren't the only bad things back home, though. I can tell you this: we had some bad-ass grass in our front yard. Momma was keeping Walter and me out of trouble and building us up with all that topsoil work she had us doing, but there was another unintended benefit to all that. We had the best grass around. Period. I'd put our grass up against anybody's. Boatloads of rich topsoil over the years can do that to a lawn. I'm actually surprised our neighbors weren't coming around every day to offer Walter and me wads of cash to make their grass as lush as ours. In fact, if our careers hadn't gone the professional sports route, I bet we could've started Payton & Payton Landscape Contractors. Our motto would've been: "Bad-ass grass...with style and class." Or something like that.

Of course, all this talk about how good our lawn looked could give you the wrong idea. We didn't always live in a house with an ever-present "yard of the month" sign out front. Walter and I grew up on what the folks back home called "Korea Alley," which is basically an alley (go figure) that goes off Orange Street between Hilton Woodson's place of business, which was a juke joint, and about five shotgun houses lining the street. I was born in one of those houses.

What's a "shotgun house," you ask? Well, let me start by saying the shotgun house floor plan is, in my view, an important part of African American history, especially in the South. For a house to be a shotgun house, you should be able to open the front and back doors and fire a shotgun cleanly through from front to back without a single pellet touching anything but air, assuming nobody dumb or with a death wish is occupying the house at that particular moment. This was all in theory, mind you. Neither Walter nor I (nor Daddy, for that matter) actually tried to prove it, but our first house was a shotgun house nonetheless.

The long, rectangular floor plan of our house was one room wide and had four rooms in a row with doorways lined up on the same side of the house. The front door opened to the front room, my parents' bedroom, then another bedroom for the kids, and then to the kitchen. There were no indoor bathroom facilities. Houses nowadays are built with three, four, even five bathrooms. Seems we take indoor plumbing and shiny, porcelain toilets with easy-flush levers for granted. You'd be hard-pressed to find a house in America these days without a bathroom, and you'd be even harder-pressed to find kids who wouldn't mind living in a house without a bathroom. It didn't bother us none, having no bathroom in the house. That's all we knew and we thought nothing of it. We had the typical outhouse with two holes (one adult size and one kid size) situated about 100 feet behind the house. When the wind was blowing just right, everyone in the next neighborhood sniffed off a little more than they should smell, so to speak. In other words, they'd have a good idea of what we had for dinner that night. The greasier the food, the worse it was for the neighbors. And if Walter was heading out there, well, you'd better close your windows. "Shoo-wee, that ain't sweetness I'm smellin'!"

The smell from our outhouse wasn't the only dangerous thing about Korea Alley. There was also Hilton Woodson's juke joint just across the street. A bunch of seedy characters were always hanging around that place. Lots of drinkin', fightin', and commode huggin'. I remember most of those cats drinking beer, but I also saw a lot of brown paper sacks concealing who knows what—probably not beer. There were good people running the place, and some of the people going in were good, too. But it didn't matter much if the people entering Hilton Woodson's joint were good. Good people plus good alcohol equals "He bad."

My aunts and uncles who lived in Smith Quarters, next to the Pearl River, now they were some good people. My Aunt Sister owned a duplex out there, and one day that duplex provided a chance for us to move out of Korea Alley and away from the bad influence of Hilton Woodson's joint. My aunt told Daddy that her tenant in the duplex had moved out. I was only four or five years old at the time (Walter was a toddler), but I still remember how quickly Daddy jumped on that. I know it must have taken longer than this, but it seemed like the very next day Daddy had packed up everything and moved us to Smith Quarters. We were like one of those old cartoons, impossibly folding up all of our belongings into one suitcase in a matter of minutes. We were also a lot like George Jefferson with his bad self, movin' on up!

The duplex was an upgrade for sure. Looking back, it probably wasn't as big of an upgrade as it seemed. Basically, being a duplex, it was just a bigger version of a shotgun house. Kind of like two shotgun houses in one. A double-barrel shotgun house, if you will. There was a group of shotgun houses leading up to our double-barrel shotgun house. My other aunt lived on one side of our place, and we lived on the other. My uncle was in another duplex on one side, and my land-lady aunt was on the other. Another aunt was on the hill right behind us. I guess it was an "aunt hill."

Our double-barrel shotgun house had a front room, two bedrooms, a kitchen, and a bathroom. Though it was still nothing compared to the bathrooms most folks have today, it was a big step in the right direction for us, being that it was indoors and all. Well, sort of indoors. To get there, you had to go out the back door and cross the porch, but at least it was attached to the house. And it had a real toilet. Like I said, big step in the right direction. Still, it was a community bathroom for both tenants of the double-barrel shotgun house, and it wasn't heated in the winter or cooled in the summer. I'm not sure where the waste went after flushing, but at least you could flush it. As long as it didn't sit there and bake during the summers, we didn't care much where it went.

We were living the life in those days. We had chickens, a pig pen, and yes, an indoor bathroom. We'd come a long way, baby! Or so we thought. Walter and I actually had no idea just how little progress we'd made. We had no clue that this big step up was only a big step from the perspective of little toddlers with such little legs. We thought we were out of the ghetto, but looking back, we were really just in a new ghetto with new things to do.

The facility at the top of the hill was a place locals went to get a job. It was a processing plant for the neighborhood cucumbers, and it had some official name, I'm sure. To Walter and me, it was simply the pickle plant. Right across the tracks that ran in front of the pickle plant and across from our new front yard was an old abandoned brakeman's hut. It lured Walter and me in a time or two (or a hundred) to play. We'd build fires and roast marshmallows in that old building. No one would bother us in there, and we had the time of our lives. That brakeman's hut wasn't but 30 yards back from the house, so it was Momma-proof, too. That was the best part, actually. When she'd get home, it was close enough that we'd know it and could get back before she'd have to come out calling for us from the front porch.

That old building must've been an eyesore to all the adults who could see it. Thinking back on the view from our front porch, it was something awful. In addition to that abandoned brakeman's hut, the city dump was a measly 80 yards away. We traded the smells of an outhouse for the smells of the city dump. Eighty yards! Shoot, I've returned footballs in NFL games longer distances than that (in fact, I returned a kickoff and a punt for touchdowns in the same game once, both over 80 yards). So, basically, we'd go out the back door, down the hill, and BAM…we'd be in the city dump, right there with all the smelly and unsightly mess that goes with it. Ironic, too, that right up next to the dump was the Pearl River. It was only about 200 yards or so from the backside of the house and seemed to press right up against the dump. The EPA would have a fit over anything like that today and rightfully so. Walter and I played down there all the time, and we even saw a bulldozer push garbage right into the water. And you know, I'm not even sure it was wrong to do stuff like that at the time. Funny how some types of "right and wrong" ("black and white," too, maybe?) can change over time.

Anyway, the Pearl River is where Daddy took us fishing, so we'd catch a little junk to go with our fish. Still, even the junk and nasty smells of the dump are fond memories in my heart. Actually, as a kid, the whole area was amazing. To Walter and me, it was sort of an oversized playground and the perfect place for playing hide-and-seek, army, or any other active, outdoor, crazy-fun game that kids just don't play anymore. A lot of kids these days have much nicer things than Walter and I had growing up, but they don't have any good places to play. That's the truth.

Walter and I had no time as kids to think about what we didn't have. We were too busy running around and enjoying what we did have. There were certainly other families back then that had more than we did in terms of material things, and the kids in those families had nicer toys and such, but Walter and I never noticed the difference. Today kids have to have the latest gadgets, video games, iPads, etc. They don't seem to care much anymore for trees, mud holes, old abandoned buildings, and yes, even city dumps. "The best things in life are free" is a cliché for a reason. Walter and I didn't spend time wanting what the other kids had, because we just wanted to have fun, and we had the most fun with all the free stuff outside our back door.

Another uncle of ours lived a few houses down. Between our uncle's house and the city dump was a little pond that seemed like Toledo Bend Lake to Walter and me. It was huge in our little eyes, and we just knew there had to be a world-record bass swimming under the surface. Though we never found that elusive giant fish in the water hole, I can tell you a couple of things that for sure lived there: leeches and snakes. Saw plenty of those. Or were they slimy blood-sucking monsters and man-eating anacondas? Well, that's what "Edward Charles" would've said, so let's just go with it.

Walter and I were blessed to grow up when playing outside was all a kid could do to have fun and stay out of trouble. There was no Internet, no cell phones, MP3 players, no Xbox, or any other electrical doodads kids are distracted by today. Even television wasn't a distraction back home growing up. It was a while before we even got a little black-and-white unit. And when we finally got that, it wasn't like there was a whole lot on the thing to pull us in from the outdoors. When I was allowed to spend time in front of the TV, all I really wanted to watch were the Ole Miss football highlights. I'd sit there and dream of playing for the Rebels. Looking back, it was appropriate that those highlights were trapped in a box…and even more appropriate that they were in black and white. The reality was that I wouldn't be able to play for the Rebels in Oxford, Mississippi, because of the color of my skin. I knew it, too. Playing for Ole Miss was a dream I had that couldn't be realized until Dr. Martin Luther King Jr. realized his. Perhaps that should've bothered me, but as a kid, I guess it didn't. Back then, things were just how they were, and that was that. We could focus on what we couldn't do in Oxford, or we could focus on what we could do in Columbia. We chose the latter.

Our momma and daddy likely had no idea just how much they had given Walter and me by moving us all to Smith Quarters. Their goal was to provide something better. They simply wanted to give us the best they could. As should be clear, they gave us so much more than that, and it took me a while to realize just how much they sacrificed, how hard they worked for us. And it truly was for us.

In the current day and age, it seems a lot of parents work two jobs out of want rather than out of need. Some mothers say they would love to stay home, but that they have to work to make ends meet. Make ends meet? Really? I think that phrase has lost its meaning a bit. As a society, we now have all these things. All this nice, expensive stuff. Phones, cars, TVs, cable, houses, two- and three-car garages, multiple indoor bathrooms, you get the point. A lot of families need two incomes, not to make ends meet, but to maintain the current American lifestyle of having too much stuff. But back in the day, in Columbia, Momma and Daddy worked day and night, two jobs each, for a much greater purpose. It wasn't to maintain a lifestyle of want; it was to provide a step up (however small a step up) for our family and to give us kids what we needed. Momma and Daddy each worked two jobs, not so we could have three TVs and 400 channels, but to get us out (and to keep us out) of Korea Alley.

It's important to point out, too, that the two-income family in the Payton house didn't start until all of us kids were in school. A step up was important, but not so important to allow a step back in our connection with Momma. She wanted to build a very strong bond with us while we were small, and it sure worked. We definitely felt close to her in a way that we wouldn't have had she worked outside the home and let someone else watch us during those years. There's no way to replace time spent with family, especially when we're talking about a momma who could cook.

Momma baked up the best-tasting, from-scratch, hand-squished Southern biscuits ever! Walter and I chipped in for breakfast, too. Momma would have us hunt a wooded area at the end of the street for some squirrels to go along with her biscuits. We loved doing that so much that sometimes we'd get up before Momma, walk to the woods, kill us a mess of squirrels, get back home, and have 'em cleaned and ready for Momma to cook before she even got out of bed. I'll always cherish those memories of hunting with Walter and helping Momma with breakfast, memories I wouldn't have if Momma hadn't been home when we were kids. And though the squirrels were tasty, it was those handsome, orangey-brown, candy-crispy, crunchy, firm-but-tender biscuits from Momma's oven that we savored in the morning. And that just set the stage for a day with her.

Momma didn't leave the house to work when we were kids, but looking back, I think those were actually the years she worked the most and the hardest in her life. Walter and I weren't exactly easy to raise, as you might've guessed. Along with my fond memories are the times Momma had to say, "Wait 'til your daddy gets home." We required plenty of "child-rearing" from Daddy, as you already know. I'm just thankful we at least had a break from that during the day while Daddy was away!

Daddy worked as a custodian and a maintenance man at the Pioneer Recovery factory, where they made parachutes. That was his main job. Once we were all in school, Momma started working at that factory, too, as a seamstress. When Momma was ready to take on other jobs, she picked up a sponge and a fryin' pan. She cooked and cleaned at the country club and at the homes of many prominent white families in Columbia. Some might read that last sentence and think of my momma as "the help" and feel sorry for her, but she actually loved that work. She never once complained about her "second job." And if you asked me as a kid what my daddy's second job was, I'd probably respond by saying "everything." He had a truck he used to haul stuff for people and help them move. Basically, he'd use that truck in any way he could to bring in some extra money. He also would cut grass, shine shoes, whatever. Like I said—everything.

Daddy was a proud man, but he wasn't above swallowing his pride if it would put food on the table for his family. He always did what he had to do for as long as I can remember, even back to our days on Korea Alley. I say this with great shame now, but Walter and I weren't always proud of Daddy's work. In particular, we'd try to make sure the other kids didn't find out Daddy shined shoes. Not sure what it was about shining shoes. Perhaps it was too much like servitude, I don't know. All I know is, Walter and I would try to avoid Daddy when he was shining shoes. And we'd do that on the way to church of all places.

Walter and I always walked to church. We had two paths we could take: (1) the long way or (2) the point-A-to-point-B way. The long way required us to head out the back door, cross a log over a ditch that was always full of water, walk up the road, and then go straight ahead to Orange Street. The short way was to go down Orange to the corner and cut across directly to the church. Though the short way was obviously the better choice for two kids trying to get to church quickly, Walter and I would take the long way, because on Sunday morning, Daddy could be seen shining shoes along the short way. We didn't want the other kids to make fun of us, so we just avoided him altogether. Shameful, I know. Daddy swallowed his pride to shine shoes and provide for us, and if I could do it over again, I'd give him the respect he was due.

The adults in our neighborhood knew better than Walter and I did. Our parents were very well-respected in our area, and that included over at the local bank. When Daddy was ready to move us all up from our double-barrel shotgun house, he went to the bank for a construction loan. Let's just say he didn't need a shotgun to get them to give him money. He secured a construction loan and mortgage based on his reputation alone and soon started the project of building us our third house. Looking back, I'm amazed at how shrewd a negotiator Daddy was. Plain and simply, he was a "can-do" kind of person. When he wanted to do something, he found a way, whether we're talking about securing money to build a house or actually building it.

When Daddy started building our new house, he went to the high school shop teacher and made him an offer he couldn't refuse. Daddy presented him with the generous opportunity to use the construction of our new house as a project for the kids in his class. Brilliant. The shop teacher quickly agreed, and his students worked alongside Daddy and his subcontractors to build the house. A "learning experience" for the kids, a fulfillment of job requirements for the teacher, and free labor for Daddy. Win, win, win. That's what our daddy did.

That new house Daddy built for us is still standing to this day. Though I was only eight years old at the time, I remember feeling a little uneasy about moving into the house, not because high school kids had helped Daddy build it, but because I had grown to love our place in Smith Quarters, despite (and maybe even because of) the less than desirable surroundings. Saying good-bye to the city dump, the abandoned brakeman's hut, the pond, and the Pearl River was difficult for sure, but I also knew we were moving on up to something better once again. The excitement of moving to a new house that was built just for us began to grow as we got closer to the moving date, and I knew it was a step up, because others were wondering why we built ourselves such a "big house."

Well, not only did Daddy build that big house, but somehow Momma figured out a way to buy the house next to it, too. She had a vision to make us some extra money on the side, and she ended up renting that other house to a couple of school teachers. Momma had a real good sense about how to make money, how to save money, how to invest, how to spot opportunity, and even how to borrow when needed. She developed all of this because she wasn't too proud to work jobs others might look down on, and because she was always on the lookout for what she could get out of a job.

One of the prominent white folks Momma worked for was W.E. Walker, who was the founder of Bill's Dollar Stores, a discount variety store with locations mostly in Mississippi, Louisiana, and Alabama. Momma cleaned Mr. Walker's house and cooked for his family, starting from the time Walter went to school, and she still cooks for their family to this day. She did her best for Mr. Walker and consequently won his respect. He began to share some of his business sense with her, and Momma would listen and learn, taking it all in. Most importantly, she wasn't scared to ask questions and to seek specific advice from him. She'd be doing her job well, all the time picking Mr. Walker's brain and gathering pearls of business and money-related know-how. Over the years, Mr. Walker shared a lot of information with Momma, teaching her how and when to borrow money, how to buy property, and how to put people in it and cash flow it. And Momma wasn't gathering this info to just sit on it, either. She put it to work. At one time, she had about 13 units that all made money. Not too bad for "the help," don't ya think?

So, there we were, owning houses other people lived in, and living in a big ol' house of our own. But please don't think for a second that having a big house meant Walter and I could just sit around in it. No, sir. Our parents didn't just care about providing us with a good place to live; they were set on making sure we got out of the house and actually did live. There was a time to be in the house, and there was a time to be outside. Monday through Friday, your ass better be in the house when the streetlights come on. But between school and the streetlights coming on, you better be out there working, playing, or doing something. When we weren't working, Walter and I were mostly out there playing football in the front yard with other kids or basketball in the backyard using a bicycle tire rim tacked up to a tree. Mostly just staying busy, having fun, and passing time.

As kids, we weren't allowed to just play sports, either. Momma was all about broadening our horizons, so Walter and I had to take music at school and piano after school before we were allowed to play any kind of sports during our outside playtime. We played other instruments, too, and all three of us kids were in the marching band. I played trumpet,

Walter played drums (makes sense with all that rhythm, don't it?), and my sister, Pam, played clarinet. Thanks to marching band, Walter and I even mixed sports and music together from time to time.

I was in the concert band for football and basketball in the winter and for baseball in the spring. Walter was also in the band for football when he played, though we were never on the field together in high school (whether running the ball or marching in the band). When I started playing football, I just marched with the band at halftime in my football uniform. When there was a parade for homecoming, I'd march in uniform during the parade. Walter did the same when he started playing football. And Momma would always be out there watching whenever Walter or I would be marching in the band. I think she liked that part even better than watching us play football. Looking back, I can see why. I mean, it must've been a sight to see a football player in a wet, smelly T-shirt and cleats out there marching and playing his instrument with a bunch of other kids dressed up like toy soldiers. Regardless, from Monday to Friday, whether it was sports, work, or music, Momma was behind it in some way.

And on the weekends, well, that was family time. On Saturday, there was always a family outing of some sort. And that usually involved work, of course. We'd sometimes visit our relatives out in the country. When we were there we'd help them pick greens and work in the garden before having supper and visiting with them. My parents knew the importance of strong relationships and helping others when they needed it, whether in times of emergency or just when a little work around the yard was in order.

Then came Sunday.

Sunday was for church. And I'm talkin' the whole day was for church, okay? We went to Owens Chapel Missionary Baptist for Sunday school, regular church service, and then the evening service.

No one dared complain about being there all day, and I wouldn't have complained even without the threat of a whoopin'. I actually liked being there because I got to see a bunch of kids I didn't get to see during the week and sing songs with family and friends.

Walter, Pam, and I were all in the church choir. That's until they realized I couldn't sing and had no business being in the choir. The powers that be soon viewed me as a "congregational singer," and then it was just Walter and Pam representing the Payton kids. Walter had quite the voice, too. He often sang solo, and I'll never forget the time he just kept repeating the same verse over and over. There he was, belting his little heart out....

"Bringin' in the sheaves, bringin' in the sheaves, we shall come rejoicin', bringin' in the sheaves!"

Again and again with the "bringin' in the sheaves." Even as his older brother, I couldn't help but think Walter was sweet up there, repeating the hook, because he didn't know the rest of the words.

Our church was the typical Baptist church. Everybody knew everybody, and that meant everybody knew everybody's business. Sunday school, vacation Bible school, choir, life. We did it all together. That's how church was, and that's how it should be. Church where I'm from was nothing like some of the churches I see today, where you have a faceless and anonymous churchgoer who can't be bothered to smile at anyone else, let alone get to know others in the church and be held to account for their spiritual walk. It seems walking into some churches these days is no different than walking into a Walmart. Everyone just comes in with their heads down, going about their business and leaving as soon as possible. That wasn't our church. There was no way for that to happen with us. I got to know everybody. And I got to know the best part of "everybody" when we had revivals.

At the revivals, another church pastor would come in and preach. The sermons were good and all, but it wasn't usually the sermons that got my attention. You see, along with the pastor came his congregation. And with his congregation came an unending flow of pretty girls. It never failed, and I could hardly contain myself when they'd all file in. I'd pay attention to where the pretty girls would go to sit, and yep, I'd sit my little butt down right there with 'em. You can bet I was never going to miss a revival.

The only problem I had with all of that was that Walter was there, too, hanging around like an albatross around my neck. Our parents made us all go to church, of course, and being the older brother, Daddy put it on me to kind of look after my little brother and sister. What Daddy didn't know was that, when it came time to put a move on a girl, I'd pass Walter off to Pam and let my sister be the babysitter. I didn't even think twice about it despite Daddy's hyperactive belt. I guess I figured if he ever found out, he'd understand that a guy just can't get with the ladies if there's a little brother hanging around. Also, I suppose I didn't care much if Daddy wouldn't understand. I mean, we're talking about girls here. *Girls.* The best thing God ever created. And I mean, come on…I was just admiring God's creation, and in church after all. Nothing at all could get my eyes off the girls. Not the safety of my little brother and not the fear of Daddy's whoopin'. Nothing.

Okay, maybe not nothing. There was this one thing. If girls were queens to me in those days, baseball was king. God made girls, but it sure seemed like Zeke Bradley made baseball. Mr. Bradley was a well-known and great athlete from back in the day. He'd moved away from Columbia down to the coast for a while, but he moved back when I was nine or 10 and started organizing youth athletics in the area. He started Columbia's first Little League baseball team and the "Babe Ruth" league for teenagers.

And that was it. I was hooked. I had my second love—baseball.

Mr. Bradley and his volunteers, along with the city of Columbia, built a pool, a recreation center, and baseball fields for the area. And like everything else in those days, it was segregated. The athletic complex Mr. Bradley brought to town was all black. And though it didn't live up to the ideals of Dr. King, at least it was something that I, as a black kid, could use. The only problem: it was five miles away from where I lived, on the other side of town. Well, I was going to be playing baseball, period, so five miles without a car wasn't going to get between me and the recreation center. Walter and I had to walk or jog down there every day to practice. And it only seemed worth it once we got there. That place was a refuge for Walter and me; it was a haven. Mr. Bradley taught us about discipline and being part of a successful team. And it worked. We were successful. Heck, our team didn't lose a single game in Little League in the first three years I played.

When I reached the ripe old age of 11, I was bumped up to the Babe Ruth league. I could've played in Little League until I was 12, since that was the cutoff age, but Mr. Bradley saw I was ready for Babe Ruth a little early. And it didn't take me long to progress from there. When I finally reached 12, I moved on from Babe Ruth and was playing semipro baseball. Then when I was 13, I began playing in what we all called the Negro League, obviously for black players only. I played for the Hattiesburg Black Sox and the Laurel Black Cats. No matter how you sliced it, I guess I was a black sox. And I was getting paid to play baseball. At 13 years of age. Black sox, white sox, whatever. I was seeing green!

Walter didn't take to baseball like I did. He played with me in Little League, but he didn't stay long. Since he wasn't a starter like me, he got bored real fast. He quit after I moved up to Babe Ruth and never played Little League baseball again. I really missed the time we spent together traveling to practice and games, but as it turned out, that wouldn't be the last time we played baseball together. Walking away from Little League didn't mean he would be able to walk away from who he was. And when someone is as gifted an athlete as Walter was, people eventually find out about it. So, despite quitting Little League, Walter did end up eventually playing a little semipro baseball with us, based solely on his raw, God-given, athletic talent.

Now, when I say "semipro," you're probably thinking of something better than it actually was. We had athletes, no doubt, but we didn't have much more than that by today's standards. Some guys, like Walter, didn't even have gloves at times. And our days in semipro baseball could've easily been called "pasture ball." We literally played in cow pastures, complete with dried cow patties. So, we had a little something extra in our cleats from time to time. Still, we had a place to play, and we were thankful to Kurt Jefferson (no relation to George) for providing it. Kurt was the manager of an opposing team, and he owned the pasture we played in. Kurt also provided the umpire each week. And though we appreciated having a place to play, we didn't always appreciate the umps.

Kurt had this one ump named D.D. D.D. was an ex–Negro League baseball player and, as they say, he was kind of a homer. No matter your perspective, though, D.D. had a tendency to make some terrible calls. Everyone agreed on that. He also apparently had rabbit ears because he could hear us players talking about his terrible calls.

One time Walter and I were in the dugout laughing and picking on ump D.D. He seemed to always have bad days, but he was having an unusually bad day, even for him. D.D. seemed to just be alternating between calling "strike" and calling "ball." It was "strike, ball, strike, ball" all day long, and it didn't matter where the ball was. One pitch would be chest high, and he'd call "strike." The next pitch would be in the exact same location, and he'd call "ball." Walter and I picked up on this pretty quickly and started yelling, "Strike! Ball! Strike! Ball!" Well, that didn't sit well with D.D. No, not at all. He got crazy mad…and then he was running over to our dugout. *Uh-oh.*

"I don't care who you are, I'll kill both of y'all right here! Y'all don't know who you're messin' with!"

We just sat there, expressionless while he spewed—perhaps even spat—forth the above words of insanity. Crazy-mad D.D. had to be restrained. The older guys in the league held him back, and we heard a lot of, "They're just kids, they're just kids, man!" They had to pull on him so hard that I'm surprised he didn't end up shirtless. Even so, Walter and I were scared shitless. Let's just say we never messed with crazy-mad D.D. ever again. We just kept our mouths shut around him and played ball.

Walter just played because he could, but I absolutely loved the game. Baseball dominated my summers as a kid, all through junior high. There really wasn't much else in terms of sports or extracurricular activities at the time (unless you want to count my other love, of course). But even though I knew I wouldn't be able to play for Ole Miss, the idea of playing organized football began to creep in on baseball a bit. As I was getting ready to move on up into the ninth grade, I decided there was room in my organized sports life for more than baseball. I was going to go out for the high school football team, and I knew Walter would soon be movin' on up right behind me.

CHAPTER 4

Flirtin' with Football

Sleigh bells were ringin', carolers were singin', and Santa Claus was bringin' something new for Walter and me that Christmas. I was nine and Walter was six. I'll never forget looking under the tree to find two single-bar helmets and some shoulder pads that just never seemed to fit us right. Not top of the line stuff, but for two little boys, it was like hitting the jackpot. I just couldn't figure how we pulled it off. I mean, Santa sees you when you're sleeping. He knows when you're awake. But he must not have known about all the whoopin's we got from Daddy that year, for goodness' sake. Walter and I looked at each other and knew what the other was thinking, but we were keeping our mouths shut about it. Santa done screwed up. But that gear was ours, and we were gonna play us some football.

Walter and I were pretty small when we started playing football, but that Christmas gear made us feel like Goliath. In reality, we must have looked more like little David in his oversized armor, but it was good enough for the front yard where we mostly played as youngsters. Nothing organized with coaches and refs and such, just playground ball. We'd get out there with some of the other neighborhood kids, divide up teams, throw the ball up over our heads, and it was on.

From age nine all the way up until I was 14 and heading into high school, whenever we played football, it was pretty much only out there in the front yard, except for when we were playing in the school yard at recess. Playground ball was all there was for Walter and me. We didn't play organized football together until we were in college (more on that later in this book). There was no Pee Wee ball where we're from, no junior high ball, nothing organized until high school—at least for black kids. As an adult, I often found (and still find) myself wishing Walter and I would've been two years apart in school instead of three. Walter didn't play until he was a junior in high school, and I was already in my sophomore year in college. With Walter and me in the same backfield at Jefferson High, we'd have been unstoppable.

Even though Walter wouldn't be there, I still wanted to play high school ball pretty bad. And if you wanted any chance of playing in high school back then, you had to either get so big in stature or so good on the playground that head coach Charles Boston had no choice but to take notice of you before you even got there. I wasn't very big as a kid, so I figured I had to tear it up in my front yard and hope Coach heard about me through the grapevine. I also figured I'd get an edge if I helped tote helmets, towels, and stuff for the high school team, just to show Coach I cared. Well, Coach noticed, but that wasn't the only benefit I got from carrying their equipment. I also learned a lot from the team by just being around. I'd do my duties and then sit and watch practice, and I'd take all of that with me back to the playground. We'd play touch football from time to time, but we mostly played tackle, so what I was learning from the high school boys translated perfectly. And I was starting to get pretty good, if I do say so myself. I'm sure all the boys I knocked around at the time would say the same thing.

We'd mostly play a game called "You It." It was a simple game, and I absolutely loved it. You'd take the ball, throw it straight up as high as you could, and the guy who caught it would try to score or, if we didn't have a clearly marked goal line that day, just run until he got tackled. That was it, and it was beautiful. I'll never forget the first time I played. The game had started and some guy was running with the ball. I hit him with everything I had, and the ball popped up into the air. Everyone got up off the ground to catch the ball (except the guy I clocked, of course), but it landed it my arms. That thing could have been a bolt of lightning, because I definitely felt juiced. I took off running, cutting this way and that. One guy missed, and I flew on by. Then another tried to grab me, but I shook him, too. Then a third guy. Then a fourth. No one could touch me. I made it to the other end leaving nothing but footprints and wannabe tacklers behind me. Touchdown!

From then on, football was easy. I could always just make 'em miss. And once I did that, it was over. There was just no way one of them cats was going to catch me. I was too fast for them, and they all knew it. They started telling me I should go out for football in high school, and I knew that the playground wasn't the only area where I was way ahead of them. I already knew I'd be going out for football in the fall during my freshman year. There was no question about that. The one question I did have was, would I make the team? Well, all my playground shakin' and bakin' had me convinced the answer was "yes." There wasn't a shadow of doubt in my mind about it. But that's not to say there wasn't a different sort of shadow hanging around the Payton house. The day I made the high school football team, I became the big man on campus, and Walter was now the little man in my shadow.

I felt good about my upcoming first season in organized football. I felt mature and ready to take on the world. I was practicing at a high level, and the stage was set for opening night of the "Eddie Payton

Show." When I imagined my family beaming with pride as I took the field, I'd practice harder. When I closed my eyes, I'd see everyone going nuts as I waltzed into the end zone, and I'd practice harder still. I could hear all of my soon-to-be fans telling me to break a leg out there on the field, and that's exactly what I did. I practiced so hard one day that it ended with a nasty fracture about an inch above my knee. Just like that, my imaginary stardom came crashing down. My freshman season was over before it started, and the shadow Walter was in started to engulf me, too. It was a dark, dark shadow…not at all like my doctor.

Frank Fortenberry was his name, and he was one of the few white doctors who'd take black patients. I wasn't really worried about whether my doctor was black or white, though. I was worried about whether his news would be good or bad. And it wasn't good. After looking at my X-rays, he came to my room trying to explain to me that if he set the leg, with a break so close to the growth line, it would probably stop growing. In short, one leg would be longer than the other, and I knew that would make it nearly impossible to keep playing running back and linebacker, especially at the level I'd planned on playing. No more shakin' and bakin', no more fakin' and quakin'. There would just be breakin' and achin' for little ol' me.

Momma and Coach Boston were in the room when I heard the news, and they could tell I was devastated. But Doc Fortenberry wasn't done talking. He had something else up his sleeve, and he was fixin' to pull it out on us.

"I've been toyin' with this idea," he said to my mother. "I've seen it done before, but I've never done it myself. If we put a pin through Eddie's leg to hold it still, and then place his leg in a pulley with weights while it grows together and heals, it might reduce the chance of one leg being shorter than the other."

Momma and Coach didn't seem too happy to hear all the "I've never done it myself" stuff, and the idea of using pulleys and weights to reduce the chances of one leg being shorter than the other didn't give any of us much confidence that I would ever play ball again, much less have two legs that were the same length. But we didn't really have much of a choice at the time, and we agreed we wanted to try anything that could work. Anything at all—even pulleys and weights and a white doctor who'd never done any of it himself.

So, we reluctantly agreed to a six-week stay in the hospital. Still, Coach in particular was pretty worried that Doc Fortenberry was going to ruin my leg. Coach was probably angrier at the message, but he directed it toward the messenger. Good thing for Doc Fortenberry that he was such a huge man, or I think Coach might've put an ass-whoopin' on him right then and there. Momma wasn't exactly all warm and fuzzy about it either.

I think the less-than-enthusiastic response Doc got about the whole thing from Momma and Coach made him nervous. When he started his treatment and got me all set up in that leg-pullin' contraption of his, he'd come in the room, look at me and Momma, not say a word, and then he'd leave without doing anything to me. Momma's face must have been sayin', "You better not do nothing to mess up my son's leg!" It's only when Momma wasn't in the room that he'd work on me. He must've been hidin' and watchin' from just outside or something, waiting for his small windows of opportunity to do his thing without a mad black woman in the room, 'cause whenever Momma would leave for whatever reason, Doc would walk right through the door. Most of the time, he'd just come in, look at my leg, and then pull and twist it a little. The only thing I remember clearly is that I was in some kinda serious pain. Doc wouldn't give me any kind of anesthetic or nothing. I think he was too worried about the pain my momma might inflict on him to mess around with taking time to limit mine. Looking back, I guess I don't blame him. I mean, my momma would do anything to help her kids, and Doc got that message loud and clear. Momma could've come on back through that door at any moment, so yeah, I probably would've moved in and out as quickly as possible, too.

Pain or no pain, I didn't feel like it was working. I was starting to think Coach and Momma were right—that Doc might be messin' up my leg and that I might not ever walk again, let alone run with a football. I stayed in traction, flat on my back with my leg twisted up in Doc's painful pulley system and my mind wrapped up with worry. There was nothing to numb the pain, and nothing could take my mind off the situation I found myself in. That is, not until I was introduced to my nurse.

I didn't even catch her name, but I saw enough when she walked in to know that her name didn't matter. Whatever her name, it definitely was not her best feature. That nurse was the most beautiful, brown-skinned, fine-lookin' woman I'd ever seen. She was probably something like 23 or 24 years old (a true woman to a high school kid), and she was all legs. I was in love. You know, that instant, knock-you-to-the-ground, bust-you-up-with-lust kind of love. She would come by to clean me up, and it was just the best part of my day. My pain went away whenever she walked in, and my worries were wiped clean with each stroke of her sponge. All of a sudden, being in that hospital room didn't seem like such a bad deal. I'd look forward to that visit every day and would get so worked up and excited about it that, most of the time, I'd have to ask her to wait a few minutes before pulling back the sheets. Hey, I was a high school kid. What can I say?

Coach Boston would come by and visit me every day, too, but I just didn't like his legs as much. I did appreciate all the fresh fruit he brought along with him, though. I ate most of it, but I had other plans for the grapes Coach gave me. I'd throw 'em at the only thing in the room that was sweeter. A grape would hit that nurse in the thigh, and she'd throw it right back at me. Every once in a while, I'd earn a giggle or a flirtatiously raised eyebrow. The only thing better would've been getting her to feed me those grapes.

Thanks to my nurse, my six weeks stuck in that hospital bed and chained to that pulley system flew right by. Would you believe that when the day came for me to go home, I asked if I could stay another couple of weeks? You'd believe it if you saw that nurse. Coach, Momma, and Doc all knew what I was up to, though, and they made me leave. I imagined the nurse sitting in the middle of the room, cryin' hysterically over my departure as she threw grapes against the wall. I guess it just wasn't meant to be.

I traded a broken leg for a broken heart there in that hospital room, and I still came out of there with a cast on my leg. There was good news, though. At least I didn't have a limp. In fact, I could tell my leg was going to be perfectly fine. Doc Fortenberry had done it! Momma and I were thrilled, of course. And then it was Coach Boston's turn to fall in love. He turned to the good doctor with a look that said, "You just have to be mine." That's when Doc Fortenberry became the Jefferson High School football team physician. If only they would've also brought Miss Thing along to be the team nurse! Oh, well. I was on the road to full recovery, and it didn't take me long to start focusing on what was ahead of me instead of what I left back there in that hospital room. My leg was going to be fine, and I was going to play football again.

Then came Momma's words, like the scratch of a record.

"I don't know if we're gonna let you play that ball anymore."

Okay, so no nurse, and now no football? My teenage heart couldn't take it. "Momma," I protested, "I'll be ready in the spring!"

"I don't think so, baby."

Calling me "baby" didn't soften the blow, but I tried to be optimistic. I just thought I'd wait and see how she felt once the cast was off my leg and I got through rehab without any issues. Well, I got the cast off in late October, and though I obviously wasn't playing any football that year, I thought the leg felt good enough for me to start looking forward to playing the next season. It was time to rehab.

After football season was over, Coach Boston decided to take me bird huntin' with him almost every day. I think he wanted to kill two birds with one stone, so to speak. We were able to spend some time together doing something we both enjoyed, but Coach also knew it was good for my leg. We walked the fields, following the dogs up and down hills, and the leg got stronger and stronger. Coach also had me spending some time with Quitman Lewis, a former Jefferson High fullback who also played at Alcorn State. Quitman showed me what weightlifting was all about. He was straight-up ripped, and I couldn't have had a better guy showing me how it's done. I followed his lead and really started to develop physically, and my leg just kept getting stronger. It wasn't long before I felt like it was even stronger than before I broke it.

I was ready. Spring rolled around, and I wanted to play. It was time to see if Momma felt any different about it.

She didn't. Momma said I still couldn't play, despite all the great progress I'd made. I wasn't sure what else I could do to make her feel confident enough about my leg to allow me to start taking handoffs again. Then she surprised me and handed off the decision to Doc Fortenberry. "Okay, how about this…? If the doctor writes me up a note saying you can play," Momma offered, "then we'll talk about it." Good enough for me.

I eagerly headed to Doc Fortenberry for a follow-up so I could get his blessing and finally get back on the field. It was a quick check-up, as I knew it'd be, and he told me everything looked fine with my leg. I was thrilled and ready to put that mess behind me.

"So, about football…I can do spring training in March, right?" I asked, trying to take him to the right answer.

"No, I don't want you playing football for a while."

That was not the right answer. I felt like I'd just been blindsided and was heartbroken yet again. And this time, I didn't know what I was going to do. I didn't have anything to look forward to. There was no looking on the bright side with this. No light at the end of the tunnel…. Then a light turned on in my head.

"Well, how about baseball in the spring?" I asked with the slightest of hesitancy. I thought he'd be okay with baseball since it wasn't as strenuous as football, and I was right.

"Sure, I guess. You should be all right to play baseball."

My plan was coming together. "Great, but here's the thing. Momma's worried, and she said I need a letter from you that says it's all right to play baseball."

Doc didn't see what I was doing. He didn't suspect a thing. "Okay," he said, "I oughtta be able to do that. What do you want the note to say?"

Music to my ears. A symphony, in fact. "It should just say something simple like 'I've examined Edward, and it's all right for him to play *ball* this spring.'" I repeated it slowly for the good doctor to write it down, and he did just that. Word for word. The note said I could play "ball," and I ran that thing back home like I was already back on the field.

"Momma! Momma!" She could tell I had good news. "Here's the note from the doctor! See, it says right here that I can play football!"

Momma quickly scanned the note and sort of turned one side of her mouth up into a half smile. Did she notice the word "ball"?

Would she question it? *Oh, no, she's on to me....* She handed the note back to me and said, "All right, you can go back out there."

Hallelujah! Hallelujah! Hal-le-lu-jah!

I'm not sure angels were singing that chorus, but it was sure running through my head. I felt bad about my little trick for a second, or at most until I was out on that practice field in the spring. The next fall, I was ready for two-a-days and felt like I was close to all the way back. I just had to avoid a run-in with Doc Fortenberry out there on the field and I was home free. The missed time put me pretty far behind, though, so when my sophomore season came rolling around, I wasn't getting much glory under the Saturday night lights (the white school had the field on Friday nights). None, to be exact. Plus, though the running back spot was okay, I had originally played running back *and* linebacker, and there just wasn't a lot of demand that year for a 5'5", 145-pound linebacker. I wasn't thrilled, but this time there was a light at the end of the tunnel. The next two years would be all mine.

Heading into my junior year, having still not grown, I was starting to develop a classic Napoleon complex. I started to feel like I was being overlooked because of my size, and I became determined to prove that size doesn't matter. The goal became to do the only thing I could: knock the hell out of everybody. During spring training, I compensated for my size by being overly aggressive, especially on the defensive side of the ball, where my size mattered most. My kill-'em-all mentality seemed to be working just fine, and then I got what I'd been praying for all along. That's right, I hit a growth spurt.

I got serious about weights, and Momma found me some nutriments, too. She'd seen me lose 10 pounds just lying there flirtin' with that nurse in the hospital, and she started giving me nutriments to put some of that weight back on. I also started eating everything I could. I guzzled down a gallon of milk a week, and I started packing on the pounds. In addition to growing out, I starting growing up. And boy, did I ever grow. By the time my growth spurtin' and weight gainin' were done, heading into my junior year, I was playing middle linebacker at a whopping 5'7" and 160 pounds. Okay, fine, so it wasn't such a great growth spurt, and I didn't gain that much weight. But hey, for a kid as small as I was, growing an inch was like growing a foot, and putting on 15 pounds was like putting on a ton. So, there.

All of my aggressiveness and extreme growth paid off and catapulted me to great heights during my junior year. In addition to earning the starting middle linebacker spot, I earned the starting running back spot (and even served as the backup quarterback). So, there I was as a junior, finally all the way back (and then some) from that terrible broken leg. The only problem was that now other bones were breaking. Not mine, but bones of other kids. I was so aggressive that I had a hard time staying in games. Penalties were common, and I got thrown out of three or four games that year.

Have you ever seen *The Waterboy* with Adam Sandler? Well, on defense, I was kind of like that. Whacking people left and right. Making them pay for having the nerve to step onto the field with me. My first ejection was for throwing an elbow. I wanted to inflict pain and punishment, so I got it in my head that I needed to start leading with an elbow. It got worse and worse…until I got ejected. Coach wasn't very happy about that. He placed me at the end of bench and calmly, yet firmly, said, "You sit down right there."

Later on that same year, I got ejected for throwing a knee into some poor kid. I'll never forget it. While playing middle linebacker, the center had his head down, and when he snapped the ball, I grabbed him by the shoulder pads and went straight up with my knee into his facemask. Stuff like that will get you tossed every time, but I guess I didn't care. Well, Coach sure cared, and he once again placed me on the end of the bench, saying, "You sit down right there."

Now, Coach Boston was a very nice coach. He never cursed at us. I mean, never. He was just a different sort of cat that way. He was a great teacher with simple ways about him. He was a do-it-right, do-it-again, play-as-hard-as-you-can kind of coach. And did I mention he didn't curse? At the time, I thought he was just a calm guy and a little soft in the verbal abuse department. I thought he didn't know how to curse when needed. Turns out I was wrong. He knew exactly what he was doing.

Later on that same year, Coach had had enough of my getting ejected and playing dirty and all that. We were playing the game that ended up getting us into the conference championship, and we were dominating early when I high tee'd a guy—elbow to the chin—which brought with it a 15-yard penalty. I wasn't ejected on that play, but it was headed that way, and a penalty hurts the team, too. Coach called me over to the sideline and I was expecting him to place me on the end of the bench with another calm yet firm, "You sit down right there." I got a little more than that. Coach grabbed me by the jersey with all the force he could muster, looked me square in the eyes and yelled, "You ain't gonna fuck me up tonight, Chief!" I was shocked. In fact, that one sentence from Coach was so effective that it calmed me down for the rest of my career. And you know what? I think it was so effective because Coach didn't overuse curse words like Rex Ryan and some other coaches famously do. Now, I realize this was high school and all, but I can tell you from experience that, while curse words can be powerful motivators, they're most powerful when rarely used. That's when they pack the most punch.

Fully motivated by Coach to get my act together on the field, I was the complete package heading into my senior year. I was finally starting to reach my maximum potential, and Walter was slipping ever more into the shadow of his older brother. I had come back from my broken leg to be a star football player, and Walter wasn't even playing football during my junior and senior seasons. That was his choice. And looking back, I think he was showing me some sort of unspoken, adolescent, sibling type of respect, letting me have my time in the spotlight even it if meant I was casting a shadow on him.

If Walter was living in my shadow by choice, I'm grateful, because my senior year was something special. We were such a good team that year. We opened up against Jim Hill High of Jackson. They were in the North Big 8, and we were a couple of divisions below them in the Tideland conference. Jim Hill High was the largest school we'd play ll year. The previous year, they really beat up on us. I think I scored a touchdown, but they won the game something like 30–14. It was embarrassing, but my senior year was our chance at a little payback. We knew it, too. It was opening game, and we were ready to roll. Coach Boston tells it best:

> We really had no business playing a big school like Jim Hill. I'd been trying to drop them from our schedule, but my principal wouldn't let me. We didn't have film and everything like they do now, but I'd ease up to Jackson and try to catch them practicing. Usually when I'd go up there, I'd first stop by Jackson State College and visit a friend who worked there. Then I'd go scout Jim Hill High, and on game day, I'd see different players than the ones I saw at practice. I didn't know what was happening until before the last game we played against them with Eddie. The coach at Jackson State and the coach at Jim Hill High were buddies, and as it turns out, the Jackson State coach would find out I'd stopped by the college

and would let the Jim Hill High coach know I was coming over to scout, and he'd have a different set of guys out there for me to see. So, during my last visit to Jackson, I didn't go by Jackson State first. I went straight to Jim Hill's practice that time. When I walked up, people were just standing around, so I mixed right in. I didn't have a notepad because I knew they would've noticed that, so I just had to try to make mental notes. The first thing I noticed was their center. He was a small guy. I saw that he kept his head down after he snapped the ball, so I thought, *I'm going to tell Eddie to attack him.* And you know he did—he did a marvelous job on that guy. We beat Jim Hill High that day 35–12, if I remember correctly. They dropped us from their schedule after that game. My, oh my, how roles reverse sometimes.

That game against Jim Hill High defined my senior season. We ripped through the schedule and made it to the championship game, which we lost to Heidelberg. To this day, I say we didn't lose that championship game because of talent; we lost it because of their level of experience. They were grown men over there. We'd never lined up against high school players who had beards and mustaches before, so we thought something funny was going on. Who knows? All I know is it was a great year, and it flew by. Before I knew it, and perhaps even before I was ready for it, the college recruiting process was on.

It was all sorts of surreal, with people calling and coming by to talk to us. Our team had seven or eight top-notch prospects, including me, all of which would be recruited today by Division I programs from all over the country. At the time, opportunities were a bit limited. Recruiters were in and out from places like Cal State, Long Beach, West Virginia, and Wisconsin. Those seemed like the only schools recruiting black players. The SEC didn't recruit black players at the time, so we could only talk to who'd talk to us.

I was all-conference my senior year and was told over and over again that I was one of the most versatile athletes in the state of Mississippi. I was being recruited by Wisconsin, Cal State, Xavier of New Orleans, and Dillard. But despite my junior-year growth spurt of a full inch, I was still too small for most schools. Again, I was only 5'7" and 160 pounds. Maybe a little taller and a little heavier soaking wet with mud stuck to my shoes, but even so, I was just too little for a lot of coaches. Too small even for friends of Coach Boston.

Coach was an Alcorn alum, so Jefferson High had become a pipeline for players to Alcorn. Also, Alcorn was a historically all-black school, so I had no problem there. I was all black, that's for sure. On top of that, Coach Boston specifically told Alcorn's coach, Marino "The Godfather" Casem, that he needed to take me. Though it seemed like a sure thing, it wasn't enough for Coach Casem. He still said I was too small, so Alcorn was a no-go. Funny thing is, looking back, it's good that I didn't go to Alcorn. Not necessarily because Alcorn would've been a bad place for me, but as it turns out (as I'll get into a little more later), Walter would've followed me there. Who knows how things would have turned out for him had he gone to Alcorn? All we know is how things turned out at Jackson State, and I'm sure we'd all agree that we wouldn't change a thing.

Jackson State wanted two guys from Jefferson High: Ray Holmes (the other running back) and me. Holmes had scored 30 touchdowns as a senior, and I had scored 28, so we were pretty even in terms of scoring. He was bigger than me, though. At 5'10" and 200 pounds, Ray was considered a big back by any standards back in 1969. I guess you could say we were like thunder and lightning, and Jackson State wanted the whole storm. They certainly seemed to want us more than the other schools that were recruiting us from far away places. Perhaps it's just that they were closer than the other schools, and head coach Bob Hill could come visit more.

Coach Hill would come down to Columbia to meet with me and Ray, and it all seemed just fine to us. During one of his visits, he must've cut a deal with Mr. McLaurin, the Jefferson High principal at the time. Ray and I were called to Mr. McLaurin's office one day, and he told us how our football dreams were going to come true. "This is what we're gonna do the night before national signing day," he said. "I want you guys to stay here in my office after school, and Coach Hill will be coming down to pick y'all up. He's gonna take you up to Jackson. If you need anything, clothes and stuff, he's gonna get it for ya, and they want you to sign with Jackson State."

I guess you could say I was pretty damn naïve back then, because I just went right on along with what I was told and didn't think nothing of it. Ray and I were called from our last class on the day before national signing day and taken to Mr. McLaurin's office. I say "taken," but we went willingly. We were told to just sit there in the principal's office to wait for Coach Hill, and Mr. McLaurin said he'd let our parents know where we were. When Coach Hill got there, he took us to his purple Impala, and we shuffled on in for the ride to Jackson. On the way, there wasn't much conversation between Coach Hill, Ray, and me. Just small talk about how Ray and I were going to be featured backs in the Jackson State offense. Sounded good to us, I guess. What did we know? It was kind of like all that "be all you can be in the Army" stuff. Speaking of which, when we arrived at Jackson State, we were ushered into a military-style barracks on campus with about 15 other guys we didn't know. Seemed the principals of their high schools had apparently cut the same deal with Coach Hill. We were all a little uneasy about the whole situation and didn't really say much. Coach Hill and others then took us to what was the Penguin Restaurant at the time to feed us hot dogs and hamburgers, and then returned us to the barracks for the night, where we slept on fold-out cots lined up in a row. The next morning we all signed a letter of intent in the coach's office, and that was that. I'd like to say I was offered a bunch of money to sign, but the fact is I signed for the hot dog special at the Penguin Restaurant.

Hot dog special or not, I was officially a college football player, and I was ready to go for Jackson State. Other colleges had their chance, but I was at a place that wanted me. Along with Alcorn, Mississippi Valley State was a historically black college and should've been an option for me. But being all black wasn't the only thing they had in common with Alcorn. Like Alcorn, they thought I was just too small for their program. The Mississippi Valley State coach, "Redskin" Weathersby, was sure I couldn't produce there given my size. He'd come to regret his decision. I wouldn't come to regret mine.

The offense at Jackson State fit me perfectly. We ran a lot of traps, a lot of quick pitches, and a lot of screens. I ran those really well, because we had huge offensive linemen, and the opposing defense could never find me. Turns out I was so good, precisely because I was so small. Go figure. Once I got out in the open, I just brought the funk, as they say, and was gone. During my sophomore season at Jackson State, I scored five touchdowns against Coach Weathersby and Mississippi Valley State. It was just one of those days, you know? I was in the zone, and I got it in my head to let Coach Weathersby know all about it. After I scored my third touchdown, I ran across the field and up to Coach Weathersby and said, "Coach, am I big enough yet?" He frowned. I smiled. But that wasn't the end of it.

When I scored my fourth touchdown, I went back down the Mississippi Valley State sideline and asked Coach Weathersby the same question. I thought I was pretty good and pretty funny all at the same time. On my fifth touchdown, I scored on the same end as the Mississippi Valley State bench, and I was all set to give Coach Weathersby some more grief about it. I was really going to rub it in this time, too. I mean, five touchdowns from a guy too small to play on their team? Come on, now, I just had to have some fun with that. But as I ran down the sideline, Coach Weathersby was nowhere to be found. He didn't want to hear it again and was hiding from me. I later heard from other players that he was pretty pissed off about my taunting. Scoring five touchdowns was good and all, but hearing that was even better.

Jackson State fans loved it, of course, but I became a bit of a legend around Mississippi Valley State, too. They all talked about the little guy they could've had but turned away. The guy they said was too small and then scored five touchdowns on them! The tiny dude with a huge shadow. I thought I was on my way. Everyone in the area knew my name. I was flirtin' with football stardom and wasn't going to stop until I got there. But I had no idea what football stardom was. I couldn't yet see what I and the rest of the world were getting ready to witness. During my glory days there at Jackson State, I had no idea that the true legend was forming back home in my shadow.

CHAPTER 5

Can't Buy Me Sweetness

Columbia is way down south in Marion County, Mississippi. I mean, way the hell down there. If someone up north asked me for directions, I'd be right to say, "Just keep goin'." Do that, and eventually you'll run into lots of heat and some good people. That's when you'll know you're in my hometown. Nowadays, people say the name Payton put that place on the map, but in the 1930s, the name to know around there was Bascom. I've heard we had a couple of cowboys back then who bore that last name. Folks called them Earl and Weldon, I think. Those two cowboys made Columbia the historic "Home of Mississippi Rodeo." That was our claim to fame for a little while. The Bascom boys brought with them many a wild ride for the folks of Columbia. They just had no idea that it'd all pale in comparison to what was coming up behind them. Columbia hadn't ever seen nothing like the wild ride my little brother was going to take it on. Walter wasn't no cowboy like the Bascom boys, but what he'd do would make him a Bear one day.

Walter didn't start playing organized football until I left high school, but his recruitment to play on the high school team actually began during my senior year. As you know, in order to play in high school, most of us kids had to first be noticed on the playground. That might seem like a crude way to recruit kids for high school football, but in a segregated small town at a small all-black school with a small amount of resources, that's how it was done. Like I said earlier, we black kids didn't have a feeder program like junior high football or even organized youth leagues. You had to show you could run with the wild horses in the playground before you'd get your shot at taming them in the arena. Welcome to our rodeo.

Coach Boston would go out to the playground after school, or he'd sometimes watch the kids play football at recess during school. He was always on the lookout for boys who stood out from the crowd. One day, he got more than he bargained for. Walter was a "little husky kid," as Coach remembers. I was already playing for Coach when he spotted Walter on the playground, so Coach pretty much knew the Payton name. It helped that I was having a great high school career, too, if I do say so myself. I guess you could say Coach was a bit predisposed to thinking Walter would be good based on what he had already seen in me. Still, Walter took it to a whole new level and did his own impressing. He didn't need to ride my coattails when he was out there dragging his own through the dirt just fine. But it wasn't Walter's speed that impressed Coach the most. Coach often recalled the time he saw young Walter, not out there making fools of the other boys, but just sitting on the side, holding his arm and crying as he watched the other boys make fools of themselves.

Coach walked over and asked why he was crying, and Walter told him he'd hurt his shoulder. Walter wanted to get back out there, pain and all, but Coach made him sit tight. After checking his shoulder out in an untrained poke-it-and-say-if-it-hurt sort of way, Coach thought it seemed bad enough to require professional attention. He helped Walter away from the playground and used his van as a temporary ambulance to take Walter to the Marion County Hospital. After the drive, Walter's shoulder wasn't the only thing hurting. From what I've been told, Coach's head was hurting, too, on account of all of Walter's "drumming" on the way there.

Before he took the name "Sweetness" in college, Walter was known around school as "The Little Drummer Boy." He became world famous for beating linebackers to the hole, but he could also beat a drum with the best of them. Before he mastered the art of running up the middle, Walter was perfecting his double paradiddle. Before he made the Pro Bowl, he was practicing his slow roll. All right, enough of that. Point is, he was an excellent drummer. It's just that he didn't play drums on only the drums. He'd play on just about anything he could get his hands on. Coach drove Walter to the hospital, and I think Walter drove Coach a little crazy. Coach says he was beating on everything in the van. He rat-tat-tat-tat-tatted on the roof, the windows, books, the dashboard, whatever was in reach and would make a sound. It was the same way in school. The teachers were always getting on him for beating on his desk during class. The thing is, I don't even think he could've helped it. No one could stop Walter when he was running with a football, but even Walter himself was helpless to stop the tune that was always running through his head. It was just there and had to come out, even in a van on a drive to the hospital to get his bum shoulder checked out.

Now, I can only imagine what was running through Dr. Fortenberry's head when he saw yet another Payton boy with yet another broken bone. That's right, Walter's "hurt shoulder" turned out to be a broken collarbone. And that, my friends, is what impressed Coach Boston on that day. Though Walter had been crying when Coach walked up, Coach could tell he wanted to get back out there on the playground. He saw a toughness in Walter that he couldn't help but like. Had Coach not come around that day and said something, Walter probably would never have said anything about his collarbone. He'd have just gotten back in there. He'd have played hurt, and Coach had no choice but to respect that. Also, I think Coach knew that, hurt or not, Walter would've still made a fool of those other boys out there.

So, why did it take Walter until his junior year in high school to join the football team? Why was he wasting all that fool-makin' talent out there on the playground? Well, you know what I think about that, and Coach Boston agrees. "My theory as to why Walter didn't come out for football earlier is, he didn't want to compete with Eddie," Coach says. "So, he waited until Eddie graduated, and that's when he came out for the team, his junior year."

I was older than Walter, of course, and I was an established star athlete at the high school. I may've been smaller than Walter, but I was definitely still casting a shadow on him. Maybe he had to bend down a little to get in it, but he was there nonetheless. Looking back, I think bending down is exactly what he was doing. Seems to me that he stepped into my shadow by choice. As his older brother, he looked up to me and respected me. He was content to let the light shine on me. The thing is, high school is only four years long. That meant it had to end for me eventually, and I was going to have to leave for Jackson State at some point. Well, "some point" came like a flash, and I'm no Peter Pan. I'm just Eddie Payton, so my shadow sticks with me. It goes where I go. When I left high school, Walter no longer had a choice. He couldn't stay in my shadow, because my shadow was no longer there. It was following me to Jackson, and Columbia was all his. With no older brother's shadow to step into anymore, the only stepping he could do was onto the football field. All he needed was a little coaxing from Coach.

Twisting his arm just a tad (don't worry, his collarbone had healed by then), Coach Boston convinced Walter to join the high school football team during his junior year. And Walter took to it like a shark takes to eating. You know how a shark is born in the water, don't you? A baby shark just comes out along with a puff of blood in the water, and the next thing you know, that shark is swimming and feeding on its own. It doesn't need other sharks to show it what to do. It just does what it does. Well, Walter was like that shark. He just popped out onto the high school football field, and before long, Coach Boston had a maneater on his hands. When they tossed him the pigskin, Walter's arms chomped down on it like Jaws, and his legs took over from there. He didn't just make people miss, either. I could do that, but Walter could do a little more. He'd juke 'em left and right, of course, but he'd also plow right over them if he had to. He could leave them in the dust or return them to the dust, depending on whether they decided to get in his way. Can you hear that eerie *Jaws* theme song playing in the background yet? It's getting closer....

Walter's first game as a high school player is the stuff of legend. It's the kind of stuff that will make folks forget about an older brother's shadow in a heartbeat. Walter stepped onto the field for the first time, and just like that, my shadow was replaced with his spotlight. He was the starting running back, and the offense had taken the field. The ball was snapped, and they handed it off to Walter. That was all they had to do. Walter took his very first official carry in an organized game, and he ripped off a 65-yard touchdown. The boys on that high school field trying to stop him looked no different than those poor kids back on the playground. When it comes to God-given talent like my brother had, it just didn't matter who he was up against it. They all looked like fools.

With that first run to the end zone, a bright and shining star was born. As a junior in the fall of 1969, Walter came out of nowhere as the clear leader of the Jefferson High School football team. He was a young, talented black kid just picking his victims at will in the waters of the all-black Tideland Conference. But a tidal wave of change was coming. In 1970, mandatory integration was instituted for the schools in Mississippi. "All black" and "all white" was turning into just plain "all." That's how it was supposed to look on paper, anyway. Coach Boston led his group of 20 excellent black football players over to Columbia High in January of 1970, where they were to merge with 16 white players who were already there. White or black didn't really matter to Walter and his teammates, though. Individual talent would rise to the top, and Walter's individual talent was undeniable.

Coach Boston explains that the integration actually came at a good time for his football team in general. It just so happened that he would've had a hard time putting together his full team that year. He had Walter and some other standouts, but he was short on linemen. When they got to Columbia High, he had but one tackle, a tight end, and maybe a guard or two. And Coach always said, as far as football teams go, "What's up front is what counts. You got to have some linemen if you're going to have success." Columbia High provided a few more solid linemen, so Coach saw that as a good thing. And Columbia High eventually saw the good things that Coach Boston was bringing. Jefferson High had all the running backs. They had Walter, Edward "Sugarman" Moses, and Michael "Toby" Woodson. So, they were definitely set and still all black in the backfield. Coach Boston also provided Archie Ray Johnson, the young man who would be the starting quarterback.

When the Jefferson High and Columbia High teams came together, there was all this nervous talk about how there would be all these fights and unrest and whatnot. But it never happened. Hell, Coach Boston even said there were more fights at Jefferson High *before* they integrated. The football team seemed to come together just fine, probably because each side filled in well the needs of the other. Columbia High's linemen rose on up to the surface, and the running talent of Jefferson did the same. If only the same could be said about the coaching talent.

Coach Boston wanted the head coaching position when he took his team over to Columbia High for the integration, and he should've gotten it. Of course, there are a lot of "should'ves" in this world that don't happen, and I get that. All I'm saying is that Coach Boston getting the head coaching job at Columbia High was one of those should'ves. As Coach Boston said, "I felt I was qualified and had proven myself at Jefferson, but the school district named the Columbia High coach as the head man. He was white, and maybe the community just wasn't ready for a black head football coach. I wasn't happy about that, but I accepted it. I had to put Walter and those kids above myself. It wasn't about me. It was about the team, and I just wanted Walter and my boys to shine."

That integrated Columbia High team sure looked like it was ready to shine. All the pieces were in place, from the top on down. Then suddenly, for whatever reason, the man appointed to be head coach stepped down. That's when Coach Boston decided it might be his time to shine. He applied for the open position. Turned out, though, that the junior high head coach at Columbia applied, too. Coach Boston thought again they'd just pick the white guy. Well, that didn't happen. But they didn't pick Coach Boston either. Coach was called in and told that he wouldn't be getting the job because two people from the same district applied for the job, so they were going to bring someone in from outside of the district. As Coach recalled, "That didn't sound right to me; sounded like a lot of shuckin' and jivin'."

Were they just trying to avoid the appearance of racism that would come from picking the less qualified white guy over the more qualified black guy? Again? Well, I suppose no one knows for sure. All I know is Coach said it right when he told them, "Look, all you need to do is pick the right person, just who you think is the best." That didn't happen when they didn't pick Coach Boston, I can tell you that. Coach was disappointed, of course, but he's not one to sit around and bellyache about things. He accepted it and moved on, yet again. The only thing was, he wasn't sure exactly what he'd be moving on to. Would he have a job? Would he need to find a new line of work? Coach Boston was dealing with a lot of uncertainty, and then he met the new head coach of Columbia High.

"It was strange," Coach Boston said, "I saw this man on campus, and someone told me, 'That's going to be the football coach.' I saw him coming toward me; he called my name and asked if we could talk. How'd he know my name? Did it even matter? I said, 'Sure.' He then said, 'I'm Thomas Davis, and I'm going to be the head football coach, and I was wondering if you would work for me.'"

Now, some of you might think Coach Boston should've told that guy to go screw himself, yada yada yada. Well, it's easy to think that having not actually been there, but Coach Boston knew what he was doing given the situation he was in. He was supporting three kids at the time, and he knew they were the most important things, but he also didn't want to just be walked on either. Coach said, "I had to feed them and get them through school; I knew I had to have a job. I said, 'I will work for you, but I'm not going to be in the press box.'"

Coach Davis assured Coach Boston that if he joined the Columbia High coaching staff, it wouldn't just be for show. He promised Coach

Boston that he wouldn't just be a token appointment. He knew Coach Boston wanted to actually coach, and more importantly, he knew Coach Boston *could* actually coach. He knew Coach Boston was a qualified coach who'd be a valuable member of his team, and that's why he asked him to join. Turned out Coach Davis knew what he was doing, too.

So, the team had come together, and Coach Boston was on the coaching staff at Columbia High, back with his boys. With the leaves of fall came team practices, and that's when the team identity really started falling into place. All spots were filled nicely, and they had a very solid unit. The kids were all getting along great with no problems at all. No fights or anything like that. They were gelling and moving quickly toward the opening game. Coach Boston was coaching receivers and punters, but he still knew where the real talent was. He knew how they were going to win games. He knew which guys would take them to victory. He knew the team needed to rely on the stud running backs that came over from Jefferson High. He just hoped the other coaches knew it, too. Then it was déjà vu all over again.

"We get up to the first football game, and we were playing Prentiss," Coach Boston remembered. "I had heard on the radio that Prentiss would be a pretty tough team for Columbia. There was some smack going around out there about how they'd beat us. Well, they came in, and we beat them, if I remember correctly, something like 13–6. We scored two touchdowns and an extra point. Walter scored the two touchdowns, both over 60 yards."

If they hadn't already, the rest of the Columbia High coaches knew after that game who should be getting the ball. It was all running backs all the time, and Walter and Sugarman were the two studs. Columbia High's second game brought yet another victory, only this time, it was Sugarman who took the spotlight. Seems the coaches were doing that on purpose, because in every other game, one of the stud backs would stand out while the other took the back seat. Because of that, Walter and Sugarman were pretty much even in the race for the conference scoring crown. Think about that for a second…the two scoring leaders of the Little Dixie Conference were on the same team! That was one heck of a backfield. But I know the question you're asking now: did Walter or Sugarman come out on top as the scoring champ? I'll let Coach Boston fill you in on the results.

"We were playing Franklin County, and Sugarman was having himself a great football game. He was leading the conference in scoring heading into that game, and then he got it in his head to punch a guy. Well, you can't do that. Refs don't like that sort of thing. So, they threw him out of the game. Walter came in and didn't miss a beat. After Sugarman's one punch, Walter came in and punched in two touchdowns. With those scores, he took the lead back from Sugarman for the conference scoring crown. That's when us coaches just decided to push Walter to get the scoring title from that point on. And that's exactly what he did. We won seven straight ballgames because of our conference scoring champ, and man, Columbia was sure buzzing about that young man!"

Like I said, Columbia was once known for rodeos, but it hadn't seen nothing before like Walter Payton. And that's true in more ways than one. Columbia High hadn't even seen black players until Walter's senior year, so there you go. But the color really didn't matter. Black, white, red, orange, whatever—Columbia High had never before seen a player of any color that could do what Walter could out there on the football field. He could pretty much score at will. Columbia was witnessing a man among boys. Guys would try to grab him as he darted by, but all they'd be left holding was their jocks as Walter sprinted down the field.

Eyes from outside of Columbia started taking notice, too. College scouts would come to see Walter play, and what they'd find was about 5'10" and 185 pounds of supreme coolness. I think Walter was starting to figure out just how cool he was, too, because sometimes he'd act just a tad too cocky out there. P.W. Underwood, the head coach from Southern Mississippi, came over once to scout Walter. In that game, Columbia ran a little toss sweep, and Walter got outside. He was gone. The other team had a defense out there, but they were defenseless against what Walter was bringing. They were chasing him down the sideline with absolutely no hope of catching him. At about the 20-yard line or so, Walter turned around and started back-stepping. He ran the ball in backward for the touchdown, watching those kids try to catch him. He was also holding the ball high over his head as if to ask, "Why are y'all even trying?" Today, something like that would bring a 15-yard unsportsmanlike conduct penalty. Back then, with the way Walter was running on that team, it just had to be done.

Coach Underwood didn't see it that way. He couldn't deny Walter's undeniable talent, of course, but he told Coach Boston after the game that Walter would never amount to anything as a football player. "He's just a hot dog," Coach Underwood said, dismissing the obvious game-changing talent of my baby brother. Guess he didn't care much for hot dogs unless they came with white buns. And that was too bad for Southern Miss, because they could've had the upper hand in recruiting Walter, being only 25 miles from Columbia. In fact, any of the predominantly white Mississippi colleges could've landed him. Ole Miss, Mississippi State, and Southern Miss were all considered "big time" programs back then, but none of them recruited the "big time" playmaker who was Walter Payton. None of them—other than Southern Miss coming to watch him play that one game—so much as even called. And it wasn't like they didn't know about Walter. He wasn't some undiscovered talent, hidden away in Podunk, Mississippi. Everyone knew who he was as a senior, and if only those schools could've looked past the hot-doggin' (and with some of them, I think they needed to look past his color), they could've had themselves a stud.

If Walter was playing today, he'd have offers from all the schools in the South and every single SEC school, no doubt. But he's not playing now. He played his senior season in 1970, the first year of forced integration, and the fact is that he graduated high school in 1971 with no offers from any SEC schools. I don't know, maybe it wasn't so much that Walter was black. Maybe those schools just didn't have "room" for another one. I mean, Southern Miss and Mississippi State had one black player each on their teams at that time. That's a whole lot, you know? They were probably at their self-imposed limit or quota for black athletes, and Walter would have put them over that.

Mississippi State became the first of the predominantly white schools in the state to accept a black football player when they signed Frank Dowsing in 1969. Like me, Dowsing was a return specialist, and he also played defensive back. He became all-conference, All-American, and graduated with honors. You'd think they would've wanted more than just one guy like that, right? I guess one was enough, because they didn't want Walter.

In 1970, Southern Mississippi signed Willie Heidelburg as their first black player. "Wee" Willie Heidelburg was a wee little guy like me at 5'6" and 145 pounds, probably "soaking wet" like they always described me at my heaviest. In 1970, Heidelburg was a major reason Southern Miss beat fourth-ranked Ole Miss 30–14 in what's considered one of the biggest upsets in college football history. Heidelburg scored two touchdowns on reverses to lead the way for Southern Miss in that historic game. You'd think they would've wanted more than just one guy like that, right? I guess one was enough for them, too, because they didn't want Walter either.

Walter graduated high school on June 18, 1971. That was the year Ole Miss signed James Reed and Robert "Ben" Williams as its first two black football players. The following year, Ben (a Yazoo City, Mississippi, native) became the first African American football player to take the field for Ole Miss. Williams became a star defensive lineman and went on to a great career in the NFL with the Buffalo Bills. Reed had a huge career for Ole Miss as well and was drafted in the ninth round of the 1976 NFL draft by the Cleveland Browns. Now, I know two black guys are twice as many as one, but you'd think they would've wanted more than just two guys like that, right? I guess two were enough for them because they, like the others, didn't want Walter.

So, all of the predominantly white schools could've recruited Walter but didn't. That's the point I'm making here. It seemed the college world in the South was going to sort of ease into the integration thing, and most of the historically white schools had committed their allowance of black scholarships to the guys mentioned above. Of course, that's not to say there weren't plenty of others that were quite willing to go after and sign Walter.

College recruiters outside of the historically white schools knew Walter was good, but no one really knew exactly how good he was until the Mississippi High School All-Star Game. That's when they found out what he could really do. Walter put on a show in that game and opened a lot of eyes. Made a lot of folks color-blind that day, I think. Playing for the south team, Walter blew up. It was like the recruiters were watching a highlight reel from the entire year. Now, Walter had already informally committed to Jackson State, but that meant nothing to non-racist Division I recruiters and colleges looking for a running back who could be a game changer, which Walter made clear he was in that game. The offers started coming in and, before long, they were catching up with his touchdowns.

Lots of schools from the North, the Midwest, and the West Coast now knew exactly what was waiting for them in Columbia. Anyone who saw Walter as just a football player, rather than a black one, came to try to claim their prize. Some of the schools wanted Walter a little too bad, in fact. One particular school from Kansas had an interesting way of trying to win the Walter Payton sweepstakes. The way they handled it is the reason why to this day there remains some confusion about exactly which Kansas school recruited Walter. Was it the University of Kansas, or was it Kansas State University?

Most of us thought it was the University of Kansas because Gale Sayers' name kept coming up from the recruiter. Sayers, known as the "Kansas Comet," played for the University of Kansas Jayhawks and would eventually star for the Chicago Bears, but Coach Boston remembers the guy who was talking about Gale Sayers to be "a young black recruiter named Frank Falks." Well, though Sayers played for the Jayhawks, Falks didn't recruit for the University of Kansas. He worked for the Kansas State University Wildcats. So, did Falks inappropriately use Gale Sayers' name to try and recruit Walter for Kansas State University? I say maybe. Momma says yes. She remembers being told by Falks that Walter was going to be the next Gale Sayers if he'd come to (the state of) Kansas. Today it'd be hard to pull off a trick like that, but back then, I can see it happening. Neither the University of Kansas nor Kansas State had any TV exposure in Columbia. Nowadays, if Sayers was playing for Kansas, kids in Columbia could tell you his stats, jersey color, number, shoe size, and probably what he had for breakfast. In 1970, we only knew he was good and played somewhere in Kansas. We were literally in the dark on more than just race back then.

I can't say for sure that Falks intended to make us think Sayers had played at Kansas State and that Walter would be following in his footsteps by going there, but I can tell you exactly how Walter's recruitment by Kansas State went down otherwise. Again, Walter had made it clear that he wanted to go to Jackson State, where I was a junior at the time. When we were in high school, he didn't want to compete against his older brother, but with both of us now a bit more "mature" as college kids, he wanted to play alongside me. And I wanted him to go there, too. In fact, he had all but committed to Jackson State during his senior season, before those other schools coming to get him even knew where Columbia, Mississippi, was. But by the time the cat was out of the bag on his talent, he was being pulled in every direction, and he just wasn't sure anymore. Or they all tried to make him think he wasn't sure.

The historically black schools were telling Walter, "You can play here, be a part of the tradition, and be close to home." The historically white schools were telling him, "You can bring change, you're going to be on national TV, this is a stepping stone to the next level, and we're going to give you the type of publicity and exposure you deserve." The white schools also pitched their education as being the best, telling Momma that her boy would get schooling that is second to none.

Now, listen, before Walter became a big star that could do no wrong in the eyes of the public, he was just a kid trying to figure out which way to go. Walter was confused by all the schools telling him this, that, and the other. All of a sudden, he was this hot commodity, and he wasn't sure what was what. Most of the recruiting would happen at Walter's games, and unfortunately I couldn't be there for him, because his games normally took place when I was practicing at Jackson State. Today it'd be easy to just text him, but without cell phones or much of a way to communicate back then, I wasn't able to help him through the recruiting process as much as I would've liked. I'd go home on weekends and whatnot, and he'd tell me about the schools that were coming at him and show me all the letters coaches were sending. I was starting to get confused, too, and just wanted to know one thing. I dismissed all those letters and all that attention and asked, "You coming to Jackson State, ain't ya?" He just sort of nervously laughed and said, "We'll see, we'll see."

Turned out that "we'll see" meant he wouldn't be in Mississippi anymore. He was going to be in Kansas. Of all the schools going after Walter, Kansas State did the best job tricking—uh, sorry, I mean convincing—Momma, Daddy, and Walter that they were gonna take care of him while away from home and that they'd give him a quality education. Of course, they weren't ready to just rely on their Northern charm to woo the Paytons. To sweeten the deal, somehow money got transferred here or there or somewhere. I'm not sure exactly what happened, but I know I came home one day, and there was central air and heating in the house. Felt good and all, but I was wondering where that came from. What hadn't changed was where Walter came from. He was a Mississippi boy through and through, and he really just wanted to go to Jackson State the whole time, because he'd never been that far away from home. The idea of going to Kansas State really wasn't appealing to him at all, but Falks was as good a pitchman as the late Billy Mays. Mays could make you buy OxiClean whether you wanted it or not, and Falks had ways of convincing Walter to come to his school just the same.

Falks was so persuasive that he actually talked my parents into letting him stay at their house to recruit Walter. Falks pretty much moved in for days and harassed Momma, Daddy, and Walter, trying to get my little brother to sign with Kansas State. Falks decided he'd just camp out and keep all the other predators away from Camp Payton until Walter was signed, sealed, and delivered. The suitcase full of money that Kansas State was throwing around only added to the pressure.

The counselor for Columbia High and Coach Boston found out through the grapevine (I wouldn't be surprised if it was Reverend Hendricks who spilled the beans) that Falks was holed up in the house with Walter, and they weren't happy about that at all. They went to the house and had themselves a little sit-down with Falks and told him that if he didn't leave, they were going to contact someone with the NCAA and report him for illegal recruiting. After that, Falks left the house so fast that someone might have thought *he* was the Kansas Comet. The only problem was, though he left without his suitcase of money, he managed to walk away with Walter's signature. Their lies, their pressure, and their throwing around of money had all added up to a signed letter of intent for Walter to play at Kansas State. And that was that, right? Wrong.

I'll never forget the day Walter was supposed to report to Kansas State. He'd taken the long bus ride from Columbia to Jackson and then later was planning on flying to Manhattan, Kansas. There was a long layover for him in Jackson. With time to kill, Walter decided to come to the Jackson State campus to hang out with me. I'm sure glad he did.

When I saw him, I could tell something was up, but I didn't even have to ask. He came right out with it, like he'd been holding it in his whole life and just couldn't anymore. "Man, I don't really want to go to Kansas," he said to me as if it was not his decision to make. I think he truly thought it wasn't.

When he told me he didn't want to go to Kansas, I jumped all over it. It was music to my ears, and I offered a simple solution. "Well, don't go," I said. "Leave your stuff here, we'll work it out."

Walter seemed worried. "I don't know if I can do that. Not sure how it all works, and I think there was some money involved or something like that."

Money? They tried to buy my little bro? "Let's go talk to Coach Hill," I said, with a big ol' grin on my face. I knew there had to be some way out of it for Walter, and I was sure Coach Hill would know what to do. Walter agreed we should see him, so we quickly went to his Jackson State office. We walked through the door and you can imagine what he thought when he saw my brother walk through with me. Let's just say he was happy to see us.

I started in right away with the most important part of what we had to say. "Coach, Walter don't want to go to Kansas. He wants to stay here and play at Jackson State with us, but he signed something with Kansas State. And there may have been some money involved somewhere." Coach Hill jumped out of his chair like he'd sat on a porcupine and then promptly shuffled on around his desk like he actually was one of those pointy little creatures. He wanted to be face to face with Walter for this.

"You want to come to Jackson State, son?" he asked.

"Yes sir, I do," Walter replied.

"Okay, then, let's go up to Dr. Peoples' office. He's our president, you know, and if anybody can fix this, it's him." Coach Hill ushered us through the maze of buildings on the Jackson State campus and eventually to Dr. Peoples' office. Dr. Peoples was mighty happy to see us, too.

"Dr. Peoples," Coach started, "this boy here, Walter, he don't want to go to Kansas State. He wants to play here. We recruited him fairly, and I didn't come to him or nothing. He came to me. And we're not bound by Kansas State's letter of intent anyway, because we're a different division. He just don't want to go. What do you think?"

"Well, I reckon the boy ought to play where he wants to play," Dr. Peoples said, in a "that's just how it is" sort of way. They talked a little about the alleged money Kansas State was flashin', and a plan was hatched.

Dr. Peoples went into action and got the athletic director at Kansas State on the phone. I figured that the AD said "hello" on the other end of that phone, but all I heard was what Dr. Peoples said. "I have a young man here in my office, Walter Payton, and he has decided he wants to stay at home and play football with his brother here at Jackson State," he explained in his signature calm, but firm voice. "We haven't tampered with him or changed his mind for him or anything like that. He came to us out of his own free will, and we'd like to have a release from you as a courtesy."

Both sides knew Jackson State wasn't obligated under NCAA rules to honor the Kansas State letter of intent that Walter had signed. Jackson State was a Division II school at that time and had a set of rules and regulations separate from Division I schools like Kansas State. Still, Dr. Peoples wanted to handle the matter in the right way by asking for a release, so he gave them that chance. They didn't take it.

What the Kansas State athletic director took was a hard line. He was none too happy about being asked to release their prize recruit. I could now hear him on the other end of the phone because he was barking. "No! We signed this kid, we recruited him, we have plans for him, and we want him here at Kansas State. We're not willing to release him. He made a commitment, and we're expecting him here tonight. Understand?"

Dr. Peoples was expecting a response like that, but he was willing to give them one more chance. "That's fine," Dr. Peoples deadpanned. "We understand and respect your decision. We'll send Walter on his way. And oh, one more thing…would you like us to mail your money back or just go ahead and send it up there with Mr. Payton in the suitcase it came in?"

There was silence. Beautiful silence.

"Hold on a second," the AD finally said. More silence. Even more beautiful than before. Several minutes passed before the AD returned to the line. He wasn't barking anymore. "You know, we reconsidered. We're not going to force anybody to come to Kansas State who doesn't really want to be here. If Mr. Payton wants to stay down there and he'll be happy, well, then that's what we want, too. We're going to let him go."

"Well, okay then. We appreciate you working with us," Dr. Peoples concluded. He hung up the phone, and that was that. Walter was coming to Jackson State. I guess you can add Sweetness to the list of things money can't buy.

Some say Walter's decision to come to Jackson State was the best decision of his life. That's debatable, but I'd say it was certainly the best decision of his life that he almost didn't make. At the time, I wasn't even thinking about all that. I didn't know what the future would hold and didn't really care, I guess. I was just thrilled that on that day, I found out Walter would be coming to play with me. We'd finally be on the field together. Oh yeah, and we'd both be getting a college education, too. I just had no idea what sort of education the world was about to get. Neither did the world, but we were all getting ready to find out. Recess was over.

CHAPTER 6

Keepin' It Real

Feathers had surely been ruffled at Kansas State when Walter didn't show up, but there was nothing they could do. Someone over there even tried to play chicken with Coach Hill after the fact, threatening to call the NCAA to report Jackson State's "kidnapping" of Walter, but none of that mattered. The rooster they wanted was still coming home, not to roost, but to give Jackson State a boost. And that meant Payton & Payton was back. Only this time we weren't just bringin "bad-ass grass with style and class." No, sir. We were just going to be bad-ass on the grass—style and class were optional.

It truly was Payton & Payton again there in Jackson. I know y'all are reading this book through the "Walter was a superstar" lens, but it wasn't just going to be about Walter right away at Jackson State. In fact, it wasn't even going to be about Walter and me, despite all my Payton & Payton talk. It was going to be about Jackson State. It was going to be about *team*. They weren't signing up for The Walter Payton Show. They wanted to win, and he was going to help them win, but it wasn't going to be all about Walter when he came to town. There was no parade or nothing like that. No one laid down palm leaves for him. In fact, though Jackson State recruited him and wanted him in a bad way, Walter enrolled with little fanfare or celebration of any kind. At least not from the football team. My baby brother was still a baby in our eyes. He was no longer a hotshot recruit who needed pursuit. He was now just another member of the football team, and he'd now have to be the one in pursuit—of playing time, just like the rest of us. And you know, he didn't really take to that whole "pursuit of playing time" thing at first.

After about two weeks of two-a-days to start out his college career, Walter decided Coach Hill had to be a little crazy. Now, those two-a-days upon arrival were akin to visiting the slums for your honeymoon. Having already gone through them myself, I knew exactly what Walter was feeling. Compared to Coach Boston, Coach Hill actually *was* crazy. Okay, maybe that's being a little too hard, but calling Coach Hill a mere disciplinarian would be far too soft. That man didn't pull punches. Coach was a hard-ass guy who was demanding, punishing, and humiliating. He was kind of like the Army, in fact. You might show up a boy, but you're leaving a man. Nonetheless, Walter decided early on he wasn't going to take any more of Coach Hill's military-style bullshit. My brother packed his stuff, left it all in the room so he could come get it later, and he walked to the bus station to catch a Greyhound out of there.

By the time Coach Hill found out about that, Walter was already halfway to Columbia. My brother had gone AWOL, and Coach went after him like the meanest drill sergeant you've ever seen. He was extremely upset, even a little like a rabid dog foaming at the mouth. He was spittin' and fittin', and he came looking for the closest thing he could find to Walter, which was me. He grabbed me by the arm and said, "Let's go!" I had no choice but to follow his orders, so we drove on down to Columbia together.

In the car, Coach Hill kept shaking his head and saying, "I can't believe Walter left, just up and left." Over and over and over...and over. It was only interrupted occasionally by the hurling of blame in my direction. He asked me why I hadn't been watching after Walter. If I hadn't been able to see the big picture and known better, I might have thought my main role on the team was to keep Walter with us. That wasn't my main role, of course, but it sure felt like it on that night.

We finally arrived at my parents' house in Columbia, and Coach just parked the car, left the keys in it, jumped out, and headed toward the house. He couldn't get inside fast enough. Coach didn't want to talk to Walter, though. He wanted to talk to Momma and Daddy. And boy did he talk. Coach just sat in the living room and rambled on and on and on, really putting on a show for my folks. He talked about what he and Jackson State were going to be able to do for Walter and how he wanted Walter back with no questions asked. It was like he was recruiting Walter all over again. He just couldn't say enough nice things about Walter and what great character he had and all that mess. He even mentioned how he thought Walter had "surely" gotten his great character from his parents. I couldn't believe it. I just sat there without so much as a peep, but I'm sure I rolled my eyes.

Walter must not have liked it either, because he rolled right on out of the house. As Coach continued laying it on thick, oblivious to anything else going on around him, I noticed Walter tiptoeing out of his room and then sneaking through the kitchen door. I thought he was just annoyed and was going to walk around the neighborhood or something, but he had other plans. That kid got out there and hopped right into Coach Hill's car. But that wasn't all. He started Coach Hill's car and drove off! You can say what you want about Walter, but you can't say he didn't have balls. And on that night, you couldn't say he didn't have wheels, either.

Now, it would've been bad enough for Walter to just drive around town for a bit, but he wasn't done. Get this—he drove Coach Hill's car the 90 minutes from Columbia back to Jackson, loaded all of his stuff into the car, and then drove back to Columbia. The funniest part is that he got home and unpacked his stuff before Coach Hill even finished talking with my parents. No joke. And you know, I'm not sure what's more impressive: Walter driving roughly 180 miles in two and a half hours, or Coach keeping up his snow job on my parents for the same amount of time.

Coach sure did shovel a helluva lot of snow on my folks, because Daddy was convinced. And let me tell you, when Daddy was convinced of something, we kids were usually convinced of it, too. That was true whether we were truly convinced or not, if you know what I mean. After the talk with Coach Hill, Daddy found Walter and said, "Listen, Coach Hill's going to help you, okay? And I gave him my word—just like I gave my word about Eddie—that you'd be there to play ball and do the right thing. Now, you go back up there and you stay this time." Though Walter obviously didn't want to go back, he listened to Daddy and did what he said. He was now bigger and stronger than Daddy, but Walter still knew who his daddy was. My brother went back to Jackson State…again. I don't think anyone said a word on our drive back. Though if Coach would've looked down at his odometer, maybe some words would've been said then.

Daddy made the decision for Walter to return to campus, but Daddy couldn't be there with him. Seeing Walter through the tough transition to college sports, well, that was my job. I had to step up and teach him how things worked. I had to be his friend and mentor. Walter needed his big brother.

I began by teaching Walter how to block and how to set up blocks, and he was a very good listener. He took it all in. I was just passing down the blocking technique I'd learned from Coach Hill, which was basically how to set people up, how to get to them before they even got started, and how to attack an opponent at his most vulnerable spot. I filled Walter in on how most big guys seem to worry about their shins, not their knees. I told him if you hit those guys on the shins, you don't have to worry about them anymore. "If you make it look like you're going for the shins," I offered, "they'll just stop and go down."

During games, well, I kind of had to go with the flow a bit. If Walter got tackled for a loss, or if he fumbled, we'd go over to the sideline together and just sit and talk it out. I'd try to get Walter to see what he could've done differently to turn that loss into a gain or to hold onto the ball. Lost yardage and lost fumbles were two things that could get you on Coach Hill's bad side, so I wanted Walter to minimize all that. I also let Walter know about two things he could do to get on Coach's good side: shut up and score.

We were playing Grambling at our stadium on a Thursday night, and it was on TV. Grambling had their own TV network, and they were covering the matchup. Some of our players must've been nervous about that or something because we didn't play too well in the first half. Coach Hill was definitely coaching a good ballgame, though, because the game was still close. At halftime, the score was Grambling 7 and Jackson State 0. It was really all Coach Hill that first half, scheming and keeping us close. He always brought his best against Grambling's legendary coach, Eddie Robinson. In my opinion, Coach Hill and Coach Robinson were two of the best head coaches anywhere, black or white, north or south, or however you sliced it up. So, it was always a good matchup. Still, Coach Hill wasn't patting himself on the back at halftime for keeping it close, and he certainly wasn't praising his players.

A score of 7–0, bad guys, will always leave the coach of the good guys wanting more. When the coach is Coach Hill, it'll leave him wanting someone's head on a platter. He was ranting and raving on an elite level, really laying into us. It was one of those times at half where we all kept our helmets on. We knew it was coming. You see, Coach Hill had this reputation of being a bit of a hothead in certain situations. If we were down at half, he'd likely be throwing things, kicking chairs, punching walls, just pitchin' an overall fit. It could get pretty dangerous in there, so we'd just keep our helmets on. Oh, and we'd keep our eyes on the ground. No eye contact. We never dared look at him while he was in the middle of one of his episodes. We all knew that if we looked at him, he'd take it about as well as a crazed dog might. That's to say, not well at all.

We were sitting still and bracing for impact while he was screaming some mess about lying down out there and ankle tackling, basically playing like a bunch of wimps. Then he goes, "Guys, if you don't play a better second half, I'm gonna kick your ass in person, okay? I mean, I'm gonna kick your ass personally. I don't care who you are, who you know, or who knows you."

Walter and I were sitting together, and the next thing you know, Coach Hill walked over close to us and threw his clipboard against the wall. Walter hadn't fully learned the ways of Coach Hill yet, I guess, because he responded to that with a "What?" I don't know if he was just startled and that came out or if he was taking the "I'm gonna kick your ass" comment a little too personally. It didn't really matter; I knew I had to stop him from saying anything else. I was sitting down with my helmet-protected head pointed straight to the floor and whispered out the side of the mouth toward my little brother, "*Shut up!*" There was no telling for sure, but with Coach so close to us and throwing his clipboard against the wall right by our heads, there was a pretty good chance he was talking to and about Walter and me the whole time. I didn't want Walter pushing him, and despite the whisper, Walter heard me loud and clear. He didn't say another word. So, now that we had both mastered the art of shutting up in the middle of a Coach Hill tirade, we were ready to do the second thing that will get you on Coach Hill's good side. It was time to score.

We went back out for the second half and scored 13 unanswered points, winning the game 13–7. Walter and I scored every one of those points. I had our only touchdown of the second half, and Walter kicked the extra point and made two field goals, too. Yep, that's what I said. Walter scored seven points in that second half, not as a tackle-shedding runner, but as the kicker. And I know exactly what you're thinking right now. *What?!*

Try to keep up with me for a second. Despite all the stuff he did in high school carrying the ball, Walter didn't come to Jackson State and just take over as our running back. We had some pretty good running backs before he got there, if I do say so myself, so he wasn't needed right away. He came in as a kicker. And I know exactly what you're thinking right now, too. *Yeah, but he was Walter Payton, so he was at least the starting kicker, right?* Well, no. He was the backup kicker, and then he was the starting kicker, and then he was my backup running back, and then he was the starting running back alongside me. Okay, okay, I know, it's all terribly confusing. Here's how it happened…

During Walter's freshman year, we lost our first game to Prairie View on the road. Only two freshmen made that trip, Walter and a guy named Jimmy Lewis. Jimmy was a backup quarterback out of Jackson. Walter came to that game as the backup kicker. We had a lot of penalties that night and had a couple of touchdowns called back, so there was a lot of blame to go around for the loss. But the thing is, we lost the game 13–12, so what really stood out to the coaches was the fact that our starting kicker missed two extra points. Those two points would have given us 14 points and the win. Unforgivable. And so, just like that, Walter became the starting kicker. He didn't take it lightly, either. He even had a square-toed shoe that he used when he kicked. Of course, his stint as the Jackson State starting kicker lasted about as long as the short distance of those two extra point attempts that the other guy missed. He'd soon move to another spot. His number was about to be called at his natural position.

Jackson State's record in 1971: 9 wins, 1 loss, and 1 tie. Walter missed a field goal in the one game we tied, which was against Texas Southern down at their place. After he missed that field goal, he suffered the same fate as the other guy. The coaches were upset (naturally) and decided to once again make a change at kicker. Somebody else started kicking field goals, and they put Walter in the backfield full-time. Maybe they thought they were making a good move by removing him as kicker, but as it turned out, the fact that it moved him to the backfield made it the best move they ever made. And I was excited. It was finally going to be Walter and me in the same backfield. Now, everyone would know what Payton & Payton was all about. At some point, anyway. Some time soon. Eventually. Not right away, though.

A little time had to pass before Walter and I would get a chance to take the field together. When they moved Walter to the backfield, he was serving as my backup. A kid named John Ely and I were the starters. But come on, you know it was only going to be a matter of time before Walter took one of the starting spots, right? Well, I bet you didn't know that it was John Ely and not Walter who made it happen.

Walter and Ricky Young were the backups, and Ely and I were the starters. After the first two games (and despite losing that first one),

I had a total of four touchdowns and a two-point conversion. We were ripping through defenses and running up and down the field just fine. Ely was playing at a high level, too, and really feeling his oats, as they say. The problem with him was that, in his mind, he was more valuable to the team than he was in reality. Coach Hill was the law, and Ely thought he was above it. He tried to pull me into that, too. Ely decided that he and I were so good, in fact, that we didn't need to practice. He told me we could bypass practice and that we'd still play because, well, the team just flat-out needed us and couldn't win a game without us. "Let's take the week off," he suggested.

But I hadn't forgotten what I was trying to teach Walter about Coach Hill. That is, you just don't mess with him. "I don't think that's such a good idea," I said. It went in one of Ely's ears and out the other.

"We'll go to the health center," he continued, "and we'll tell them our backs are hurting, and they'll give us some stuff to take, and we'll take three days off, go back to practice on Friday, and play on Saturday. They can't win without us." I was totally freaked by what he was saying. No way was I gonna do that. No way.

"You know how Coach Hill is," I tried to reason. "He'll come up to the health center and pull us out and make us practice. And if we're lucky, that's *all* he'll do. So, no thanks, man, you can go ahead if you want to, but I'm going to practice."

Ely dismissed my warning and rode off into the sunset like the Lone Ranger. He thought he had it all figured out, so he set off to the health center to carry out his plan. He told them his back was hurting, and they put a heating pad on it, just like he thought they would. They gave him some pain medication, just like he thought they would. They told him to take it easy for a few days, just like he thought they would. But he came back on Friday to find out things weren't going to go exactly like he thought they would. Coach Hill's "if you don't practice, you don't play; if you're too hurt to practice, you're too hurt to play" policy was for everybody. It applied even to the "can't win without 'em" guys. There were no exceptions. So, on that Saturday, Walter got his first start. Ely never played again. You don't mess with Coach Hill.

Though I didn't mess with him, Coach must've seen the starters as a unit because I didn't start either. Guilt by association, I guess. That's what I'm blaming it on, anyway. Coach didn't like Ely at the moment, and I started with Ely, so he didn't like me none either. He probably figured I must've known about Ely's little plan (which I did) and wasn't too happy that I didn't let him know about it. So, I sat, and Walter and Ricky were the lead guys for that next game. They ran up and down the field like rabbits. We were playing some directional division NAIA school from Texas, and they didn't even know what hit them. Though I didn't start because of my link to Ely, Coach Hill eventually let me up from "time out" and onto the field for a little mop-up duty in the third quarter.

Thinking back on it and breaking it down, the way Coach Hill handled all that "too hurt to practice, too hurt to play" stuff was actually sort of brilliant. For those guys who were really hurt, well, they were really hurt and had no business playing. For those guys trying to pull one over on Coach or who just couldn't cut it, well, they had no business playing either. Coach came out with the better team no matter what. So, you see, brilliant. Of course, there was a downside to it as well. Did this old-school approach to coaching cause us players at Jackson State to play with injuries that should've had us in the clinic instead of the huddle? Sure. But really, nobody knew any better back then. With all the discussions about concussions on top of the sports section these days, coaches are changing the way they teach technique and the way they treat injuries (more on that later as it relates to the way Walter played the game), but back when we played, if you got knocked down, you just had to get back up or you may never get back in. And if you got knocked down without even getting hit like that shit Ely tried to pull, well, you were definitely not getting back in.

Though Ely's move even landed me in the doghouse for a game, I'm kind of glad he did it. It's what set into motion the pieces that would end up bringing Walter and me onto the field at the same time—for the first time ever. I'm glad Ely did it, because when it finally happened, when Walter and I were finally in the same backfield, well, it was exactly like we'd planned all along. Bad-ass on the grass.

Let me tell you, when it comes to the running back position, there's nothing like blocking for your brother or having your brother blocking for you. If you're the one running the ball, it's almost like blocking for yourself, but without having to actually do the blocking. When we were out there together, Walter saw the same things I saw in the same way I saw them. It was like having two of me or, from his point of view, two of him. I knew what Walter liked to do, and he knew what I liked to do. I knew exactly what he was good at doing, and he knew the same about me. If I was blocking and hit the outside linebacker straight up—BAM—and he didn't move, I would just stick him there, and I knew Walter would want to bounce it outside, so I'd grab the outside part of the linebacker's jersey, then I'd kinda turn him inside just enough so that Walter could jump out there and run. When the roles were reversed, he knew I'd want to go inside, so he'd try to move his ass around and lead his man to the outside, and then I could take off up the middle. It was that easy. It was that simple.

Jackson State ran a pro set and split backfields. And when I say that's what we ran, I mean that was *all* we ran. It didn't really matter much, either, because we executed the crap out of that simplicity.

With Walter and me, we could run a sweep either way, quick pitch either way, trap off the quick pitch, and lead off the tackle. All those years of waiting were worth it. Payton & Payton was a thing of beauty.

Walter didn't really find his groove as a starter right away, though. Maybe he should've retained the nickname "Spider-Man" from his high school days rather than switching to "Sweetness." I mean, the kid was a little high-strung at times. He wanted to be a starter, of course, but when he became the starter, he'd get all worked up before a game. We all got butterflies from time to time, but Walter seemed to have something closer to pterodactyls flying around in his stomach. We'd always have to figure out some way to calm him down. The coaches knew he wasn't quite ready at first to carry the ball, so they put him out there to block for me.

In the first game we started together, Walter didn't get a whole lot of carries. Or I should say he didn't get a whole lot of carries until the game was well in hand. I scored five touchdowns before the beginning of the fourth quarter, so we were rolling. That's when Walter got his first shot as the primary ball carrier. And it was a shot in the arm to me. I got a chance to watch him from the sideline in that final quarter, and it was like, *Wow*. They ran the basic off-tackle stuff, but I'll never forget it. I just stood there and watched as my little brother gave me a blast from the past and a glimpse into the future all at the same time. He was breaking tackles, running through guys, cutting on a dime, and just doing his thing like he did on the playground and like he'd later do at Soldier Field. He was just making fools of those kids all over again, looking like a future NFL star. I was like, *Damn*, and I beamed with pride. That was my baby brother out there.

Despite his amazing display of talent during that fourth quarter, Walter still mostly blocked for me in the games that followed. As that first season progressed, he really turned out to be an outstanding blocker.

He'd stick his head in there and rip through those guys, opening holes for me that guys twice my size could have run through. He didn't mind not getting the carries, either, because he just wanted to be on the field and play. And he wanted to win above all. In the meantime, I was benefiting from his blocking, leading the conference in rushing and scoring. I did so much of that during Walter's freshman year that now people say there just ain't no telling how many yards and touchdowns my kid brother would've gotten during his college career if I hadn't stolen so many while I was there. They think he could've had the best college career ever if it hadn't been for me.

But here's the thing…I was there. That's the way it played out. For one season, Walter and I played together. That can't, won't, and shouldn't ever be taken from us. People can say this or that or whatever about "What if Eddie hadn't played and stolen those yards and touchdowns from Walter?" But I can say this: that season Walter and I played together wasn't for those people. That season was for the Payton brothers. At the time, we were dubbed the best running back combination in the South by the *Atlanta Constitution* (this was before the paper merged with the *Atlanta Journal*). They said that it was impossible to defend us because we lined up in the pro set, and when you tried to take something away from one, you would give something to the other.

People don't seem to realize that we were just brothers playing a game the best we knew how. We didn't have a crystal ball. We didn't know there would one day be sports nerds looking back and drooling over what might've been instead of reveling in what was. We were just living in the moment, having fun, and winning games. That's it, and that's all.

Still, I get blamed for single-handedly screwing up the fairy tale. To a lot of people, I was the reason Walter didn't break every rushing and scoring record in NCAA history, because he was mostly blocking for me as a freshman while I lead the SWAC in rushing and scoring as a senior. They give me my first three seasons, but they say my final season should've belonged to Walter. Now, Walter, of course, ended up smashing all the stuff I did anyway (it didn't take him long), but that wasn't what it was about when we were together. Whether you get that or not, Walter sure did. He understood that the Jackson State Tigers were a team.

As good a back as Walter was in high school, and even in light of what he was able to do throughout the rest of his college career, there were other good players on that Jackson State team when he showed up. It wasn't "Walter and the Jackson 10" from day one. It was the Jackson State Tigers. Like I said earlier, Walter arrived with little fanfare. He was a Tiger, not a superstar. He was just another great member of a great team.

When Walter and I were both running backs at Jackson State, we had three of the best receivers in the country: Jerome Barkum, Alfred Clanton, and Jimmy Ellis. They were ballers and a big part of what we did at Jackson State. They kept defenses honest and spread the field like nobody's business, making it easy for Walter and me to do our thing out there. It wasn't just "Give Walter the ball because he's our offense and the rest of y'all are gonna watch." It was "Walter's a part of this offense just like everyone else." Now, he was a big and productive part of the offense for sure, but what I'm saying is that he wasn't the whole offense like you might think. Coach Hill wasn't going to have that. He demanded team over individual and preached that all day, every day. No one was thinking at the time how many yards one guy was going to get. Nobody tried to figure out which cat was a future Hall of Famer, so he could get the ball and all the stats and break all the records and get all the glory. We all only cared about one thing and one thing only: winning. That was it. That was everything. Well, it was everything right up until Walter's senior season, anyway.

Walter's senior year became the first time, as far as I know, that he was even concerned about the numbers. In fairness, at that point in his career, after having done what he'd done, the numbers were kind of hard to ignore. He was a candidate for the Heisman Trophy, and let's face it, you gotta chase that if it's right there in front of you. Jackson State started pushing him to get it and they focused on getting him the ball. But really, even that was about the team, with all the attention the trophy could bring to the program. That's what made Jackson State so successful. That's what made us so great. No one guy was bigger than the team. And to me, that highlights Walter's exceptional accomplishments all the more. Nowadays they try to put kids in situations that will make them shine as individuals, but Walter made it happen in a system and within an offensive framework that was all about the team. That's the mark of a true champion right there. A truly great player can do what Walter did without being the only great player on a team. In fact, he had plenty of great players around him.

Despite what you might think, Walter wasn't the fastest player on the field at Jackson State, although he certainly wasn't slow. He ran a 4.43 40-yard dash as compared to my 4.39. Still, the real trouble Walter had wasn't his speed, it was his stamina. Walter had exceptional quickness and front-end speed for sure. He could go from zero to 100 in a hurry. His problem was that after about 50 yards or so, he started to fizzle out a bit. A lot of the other guys on the team, after about 50 yards, well, we were just taking off. I used to pick on him about that, too, even when he got to the NFL. Walter led the NFL his rookie year in kickoff returns, but his longest ones were like 65 yards, and the defensive backs always seemed to run him down. I once said to him,

"Shit, I ain't never been ran down, dawg. What's up with that?" So, if that's what I thought even when he was in the NFL, imagine how it was that first year at Jackson State.

Now, don't get me wrong, okay? Walter was awesome at Jackson State, even as a freshman. It's just that the standards for him coming in there were so high. He was great, but he started out as part of something even greater. You may only know about Walter, but he wasn't the only guy from that era of Jackson State football to go to the next level. We just had so many great athletes there during those years, and I've got proof. There was, of course, Walter, who had more success at the next level than any of us (round 1, pick 4, 13 NFL seasons, Hall of Fame), but we also had guys like Jackie Slater (round 3, pick 86, 20 NFL seasons, Hall of Fame), Jerome Barkum (round 1, pick 9, 12 NFL seasons), Robert Brazile (round 1, pick 6, 10 NFL seasons), Don Reese (round 1, pick 26, 6 NFL seasons), Roscoe Word (round 3, pick 74, 3 NFL seasons), Leon Gray (round 3, pick 78, 11 NFL seasons), Rickey Young (round 7, pick 164, 9 NFL seasons), Ed Hardy (round 7, pick 175, 1 NFL season), John Tate (round 8, pick 183, 1 NFL season), Bill Houston (1 NFL season), Ernie Richardson (1 NFL season), Rod Phillips (6 NFL seasons), Emanuel Zanders (8 NFL seasons), and finally, that other Payton guy, me (5 NFL seasons). Did you know that we had all those great players who went on to the NFL? Take a look at that list again. Yep, that's what Walter stepped into. And now think about how none of the SEC teams had recruited any of those guys, even when they were right under their noses.

How about Oxford, Mississippi, native, Bill Houston? Could he have helped his hometown Ole Miss Rebels win a couple more games and gotten them to a bowl game? Something to ponder. But that's okay. It all worked out for the best at Jackson State. I loved my college experience and my teammates, and so did Walter. Coach Hill's tactics were tough at times, but we still wouldn't have changed a thing. Walter and I knew how much talent we had as a team, and we loved the way Coach kept it simple. With guys like we had, Coach knew to just let us go.

Coach Hill didn't see any use in making things complicated for all of his talented guys. To him, football was a simplistic game anyway, so why not just keep it that way? It's sort of like all those basketball players who get interviewed after a game. The reporter might ask, "So, how'd you guys get the victory tonight?" The player might say, "Well, we were better than them tonight, we brought our 'A' game, we ran when we could and got baskets when we needed them." You hear that kind of stuff over and over from the winning team, and it's really not any more complicated than that. The easiest way to become a millionaire is to get a million dollars, and the easiest way to win a game is to score more points than the other guys. You just have to figure out the best way to do that. For us, the best way was usually our running game.

Coach Hill thought that if we would run, block, and tackle, we were going to beat the bad guys every time. If we were better at it than them, we'd beat them. Coach Hill had a very basic philosophy that football is a game of runs, blocks, and tackles. That's it. And he figured the best way to get good at runs, blocks, and tackles was to run, block, and tackle every day. So, practice was pretty simple, too, even if it was a little hard. Every single day we went out there and scrimmaged, blocking and running and tackling. We did it over and over. Practice makes perfect, as they say, but it also perfects the team. It brings the best to the top. All those who were left after the hard push of practice were the real players. Those who got hurt or quit, they were the weaker ones. When it was all said and done, we had the guys who were gonna give us the best shot at winning each game. Like I said, simple. Coach Hill even liked to refer to our program as KISS (the Keep It Simple School). But with all that weeding out of the weaklings, the guys who remained were more like the kiss of death for anyone who faced us. And I think it would've been the same for all the teams we never got to face.

Take Ole Miss, for example. They were a big time program, right? Everyone just knew they were the best team in the area. Well, the Jackson State team with Walter and me would've beaten Ole Miss easily. For all you Rebels fans out there, I'm sorry if that upsets you, but it's the truth. Back when Walter and I were playing together, Ole Miss was a three-yards-and-a-cloud-of-dust team. They'd line up with two tight ends, and we'd have known exactly what they were going to do. And when we knew what a team was going to do, we were going to win. It didn't even matter that the Rebels would've probably known what we were going to do, too. They would've likely known we were just going to run it down their throats, but they would've been defenseless against it anyway. We had the superior fire power. With us, it was lights, cameras, JACKSON (STATE)! Compared to the wave of the future we were bringing, calling them "Ole Miss" would've been right in more ways than one. We had men; they had ladies.

The SEC teams like Ole Miss didn't have receivers of the caliber we had in our league. There's no question we had better runners, but we also had receivers who could flat-out fly and catch anything delivered anywhere close to them. The SEC had a bunch of possession receivers, so they couldn't spread the field for their runners like our receivers could spread the field for Walter and me. The SEC schools didn't throw to the tight ends, either, like we did, so they didn't have as many threats in the passing game to account for. We threw to our tight ends a lot, probably eight or 10 times a game. The SEC teams would've had to adjust to that while also trying to cover our elite wideouts. You can imagine the room we runners would've had. It would've been like that all day long, too. And, without being able to stack the box on us, they just wouldn't have had the speed to match up with ours. Not a single team in the SEC could match up with our speed, period. They had the "better" programs in the eyes of many, but we had the better players. I don't care whose eyes were doing the looking.

If you disagree with that, then name me one team in the SEC—or in the South for that matter—in 1972 that wouldn't have wanted four first-round draft picks and 10 future NFL players on their team. What's that? Come again? I can't hear you. The fact is, we looked good to them on paper, but just not in person. We were the wrong color. We were stacked with elite black athletes who'd been overlooked. As I said, not a single one of us was recruited by any of the top-flight white schools, and that's more than just a shame. It was downright stupid. Without even talking about Walter, a few of the guys we had, like Rickey Young, Don Reese, Robert Brazile, John Tate, and Emanuel Zanders, could've been the difference makers for Alabama (10–2) or Auburn (10–1) in their failed quests to win the national championship. Yet those schools didn't even see those guys standing right there in their own backyards. Either that or they saw them and just looked the other way because they couldn't get over the color of their skin.

You probably don't even think of mentioning Jackson State when you talk about the great teams of yesteryear, because being all black, we weren't part of the history. But let me tell you, our team had so much speed up and down the lineup and so much pure athletic ability that I don't know of any team anywhere who would've been able to match up with us. Not even legendary Alabama would've been up to the task. We would've done the same thing to them that USC did when they pounded 'em 42–21 in Birmingham in 1970. USC's Sam Cunningham was historic that night and ran all over 'Bama. The world remembers what Sam the Bam did, and they remember how Bear Bryant reacted by reaching out to black players after that game. But there were lots of unnoticed black kids who could've done that. Not to take anything away from Cunningham, but it could've easily been any of us Jackson State guys had we played that game. Change came to college football not because Sam Cunningham was Sam Cunningham, but because Sam Cunningham was black. It wasn't that Sam Cunningham couldn't be ignored anymore; it was that black kids couldn't be.

I've heard before that after the USC/Alabama game, Bear Bryant said something like, "We got to get some of ours to keep up with some of theirs." What he meant was, they had to start looking at the black kids. Bear Bryant gets credit, but only for seeing that first. In Sam Cunningham, Bear saw what he was missing out there, so he wanted to start recruiting blacks. Cunningham changed Bear's mind in the same way Elmo Wright and Warren McVea of the University of Houston convinced Johnny Vaught that Ole Miss needed to take this integration thing a little more seriously, too. They hadn't before seen anybody that big and athletic and with that kind of speed. Our color kept those white schools from recruiting us for so long, but hey, at least they finally came to their senses. All the white schools started to want us black kids around the end of my college days—but let's be real here. They didn't want us because they wanted us. They wanted us because they needed us.

Of course, if I am really being real here, I have to say it wasn't just white folks who saw some of us black kids as too dark back then. Some black folks did, too. Take, for example, the parents of a black girl Walter took a liking to. During his first year at Jackson State, he found himself this little number that turned into his girlfriend. Walter was completely infatuated with her, and she was infatuated with him. Then the girl's parents got all up in their business and started fussin' about Walter dating their daughter. The problem there was that, though the girl's mother was dark-skinned, the girl's father was fair-skinned. The two of them coming together produced a daughter who was also fair-skinned. Amazingly, the girl's mother disapproved of her fair-skinned daughter's relationship with Walter and ultimately ended it because she was concerned about the skin complexion of her grandkids. Walter was too dark, and they didn't want to risk having dark-skinned grandbabies. Can you believe that? The mother wasn't worried about her daughter's happiness or anything like that. She was worried about the color of her daughter's potential offspring. I shake my head about that even to this day.

That was all pretty hard for Walter to deal with, as you can imagine. In fact, it crushed him. What made it worse was that the girl went right along with it. Walter bounced back from hits on the field all the time, but that girl's rejection really leveled the poor guy. He couldn't get his mind off that girl, and it put him in a real funk. If it had been me, I might've just said "good riddance" and moved on to all the other pretty girls out there waiting for me. I mean, I've been out of the dating game for so long now that I don't know if this is still the case, but I don't remember ever seeing an unattractive black female back then, whether fair-skinned, dark-skinned, or whatever. They were all beautiful. I couldn't understand why some black people didn't see it that way.

It's gotten better over time, I guess, just like the whole "white schools not recruiting black kids" thing got better, but it's still there in some places. In a state like Louisiana, for example, the biggest racial issue doesn't exist between blacks and whites. The biggest problem is between light-skinned blacks and dark-skinned blacks. One group says they're Creole Cajuns, and the other group says they're black. Each group sees the other group as different. There are still some black people out there who'd prefer their daughter or son marry somebody who is fairer-skinned than they are. Even when I was growing up in Columbia and going to an all-black school, the fair-skinned black males and females were always class president, prom queen, Miss this, Mr. that, etc.

Walter and I were roommates, and we talked a lot about that kind of stuff. We talked about how backward that girl and her parents were, and I tried to push Walter to just move on to other things. Prettier things. Like I said, there were plenty of beautiful black girls out there, and I knew most of them wouldn't care how dark he was. In an effort to get him to explore a little bit, I showed him "the tree."

There was this tree right outside our dorm room window. It was a towering old oak tree with lots and lots of big sprawling limbs, and I showed Walter how to slip down it so we could get out and see some girls. Of course, Walter mostly just wanted to go into town and hang out. So, we did that, too. We'd just slip out to go down to the Penguin Restaurant to get a fish sandwich or the hot dog special (which brought me back to what got me to sign with Jackson State in the first place). Anyway, though the food seemed to be the main thing on Walter's mind, I was usually scanning the place for girls. Actually, one girl in particular. Her name was Mary.

Mary's daddy had a big Cadillac, and she'd often get to drive it out and would park it in the parking lot adjacent to Jones Hall, the football dormitory. I'd climb down that tree with Walter, but once we were down, Mary was mine and Walter was on his own. You would've done the same had you seen Mary. I'd climb down the tree and go down the side of the building where it was dark, and I'd sit there in the car with her. And don't worry about how Walter was doing out there on his own. The kid was good-looking, and he was doing just fine. He finally found this one new girl he kinda liked (and who didn't mind his dark skin), and that girl's roommate had a place in the apartments right behind Jones Hall, right across the tracks. So, when we climbed down that tree, I'd go off to see Mary, and if Walter didn't head into town for a burger, he'd go around back, go through the fence, jump the track, and go across the street to the apartments where that girl would be waiting for him. Looking forward to going down that tree was often what got us through Coach Hill's crazy hard practices. Coach would push us to the limit, and Walter and I would talk about how crazy he was, and then we'd start talking about who was going down the tree first that night and what time we were coming back. Those were some damn good times. Then Coach Hill found out about that tree.

Word got to Coach Hill that players had been seen climbing out the window and on down that oak tree. He found out that Room 201 was the room with the window right by that tree, and he knew Walter and I were in that room. Well, Coach put two and two together and came up with 22, which was my number. That's right, he blamed me for the whole thing and said I put Walter up to it. So, he wanted to kill me, probably because I was a senior and all, but he didn't want to piss off Walter. He'd already had to chase Walter down once before, and he wasn't about to set him off again.

So, what Coach did, besides lay into me a little, was get out the saw and start cutting the bottom limbs off the tree. He figured we wouldn't have enough to hang onto at the end of our climb. He was wrong. Cutting down those bottom limbs didn't bother us at all. We discovered that we could hang from the top limb, catch the tree, shimmy down the tree, and use the cut off stumps to get back up to the upper limbs and get back in the room. I suppose the coaches at the white schools weren't the only ones underestimating our athletic ability.

Coach found out we were still getting up and down that tree about three weeks later, so he had maintenance cut off all of the limbs on the tree. So as not to kill the tree, they left a stump about five inches long where each limb had been and then painted the ends white. It looked an awful lot like steps to us, and that's what we used them for. Seemed every time they'd cut the limbs, it just got easier to climb up and down.

We started staying out longer and longer and didn't even really fear Coach Hill when it came to sneaking out down that tree. Coach could have the day, but the night belonged to us. Curfew? Not for the Payton boys. We snuck out every night, even if it wasn't exactly "sneaking out" anymore.

As you can imagine, Coach was getting frustrated because he knew what we were up to, but he just couldn't stop us. I think he didn't like two knuckleheads flaunting it in his face right there for all the other players to see. He called a team meeting and tried to make it seem like he wasn't going to take it anymore, but didn't yet know who was doing it. "I know some of y'all are slipping out at night," Coach said to the team. "If I catch you slipping out, I'll send you home to your folks." Walter and I knew better. We knew Coach knew who it was, and we knew he didn't want to catch us.

We kept going up and down that tree, thinking it would never end. Then Coach Hill finally won out. He didn't just cut more of the limbs off this time. That crazy man had the entire tree cut down. We were like, *Well, I guess that's it then.* No more tree meant no more tree-climbing, so we knew we were finally beat. The stump is still over there today, a very short but amusing monument to the antics of Walter and Eddie Payton. That's one bad-ass tree stump.

Coach cutting down that tree was probably the first time I realized that all good things come to an end eventually. And just like that tree, Payton & Payton would have to come to an end, too. Funny thing is that sometimes, when something good comes to end, something even better begins. Walter was fixin' to break out during the rest of his days at Jackson State. But the question is, was it because I left, or was it because a girl named Connie showed up?

My momma, Alyne, and my daddy, Peter.

This is a picture of me and my sister, Pam.

Walter was the youngest Payton child, born in 1954. Here we are with our momma in Korea Alley in Columbia, Mississippi.

Yours truly, upon graduating from high school.

Our high school coach, Charles Boston, who had an enormous impact on both Walter and me. (Getty Images)

Before my brother joined me at Jackson State, I was the big man on campus (even though I was 5'7"). (Jackson State University)

Walter ended his college career with 3,563 yards rushing and set the Division II scoring record with 464 points. (Jackson State University)

Walter and our coach at Jackson State, Bob Hill. (Jackson State University)

Walter, seen here with Ed "Too Tall" Jones, was selected to the first Black College All-America team in 1973. (AP Images)

I broke into the NFL with the Cleveland Browns, and later played for the Lions, the Chiefs, and the Vikings. (AP Images)

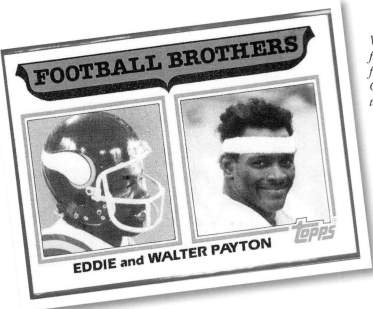

EDDIE and WALTER PAYTON

Walter and I were football brothers, from high school in Columbia, Mississippi, to the NFL. (TOPPS)

Walter flew over opposing NFL defenses throughout his career, and retired in 1987 as the league's all-time leading rusher. (Getty Images)

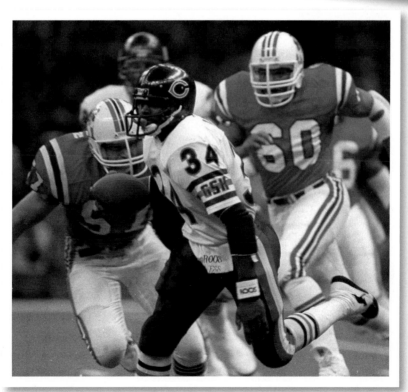

Though he didn't score a touchdown in the game, the Bears' victory in Super Bowl XX was one of the high points of my brother's career. (AP Images)

Following Walter's passing, a memorial service was held at Chicago's Soldier Field. The Reverend Jesse Jackson and I tried to console my momma. (Getty Images)

A statue of my brother now watches over the field that was named in his honor at Columbia High School in Columbia, Mississippi. (Getty Images)

CHAPTER 7

Throwin' Out the Old

Have I yet told you that Coach Hill was a hard-ass? Well, he was. Have I mentioned he pushed us football players a bit too far at times? Well, he did. Did you think I would miss Coach Hill's brutal ways when I left Jackson State? Well, I didn't. Not in the least. Still, I was hoping that he might miss me, at least a little, on the field. I guess it's hard to miss someone when someone better comes along. As it turned out, he still had my little brother, and Walter was about to explode. Coach knew Walter was fixin' to turn into the best player he'd ever seen. The best player to ever put on a Jackson State uniform. The best player the state of Mississippi had ever produced. Coach just had one problem: Walter was distracted. He wasn't sure how to get his mind off that girl who rejected him. Walter wanted to move on from all that mess, but he just didn't know how. Lucky for Walter, our hard-ass coach was a softie with the ladies.

Coach Hill didn't have any problem getting women to like him. Once he was divorced, it was open season. He'd been dating a woman from New Orleans named Betty, and that woman had a niece who Coach thought was a pretty cool girl. Coach had met her a few times on trips to see Betty, and in his eyes, she'd be quite a catch for some lucky young man. Well, one day Coach saw Walter on campus moping around, dwelling on the fact that he'd been kicked to the curb on account of his skin being too dark. He was always wallowing in despair over that situation and would sometimes even go around trying to be in the right place at the right time so he could "run into" that girl on campus. Coach looked at his depressed star running back and he thought about Betty's niece. Then he put two and two together. The best way to get Walter out of his rejection-induced funk was to introduce him to someone new. Someone with personality. Someone pretty. Someone who had it all. Someone who could make Walter forget all about that other girl. Coach introduced my baby brother to someone named Connie.

It might've taken Connie a little while to warm up to the idea of meeting Walter (especially when she first saw a picture of him), but once she did, the two of them really hit it off. Coach Hill knew exactly what he was doing. He had picked a good one for his prized player. Perhaps a perfect one. Connie proved to be an instant Payton funk eraser, and Walter was back to being happy. He now only had eyes for a girl from New Orleans, and he only had two words for that girl who had rejected him: "Who dat?" And you know, I think that other girl turned out to be heartbroken by Walter's sudden change in direction. But hey, what goes around comes around, right? And Connie was coming around more and more as she and Walter started developing their relationship. She was pulling on his heartstrings, and Coach Hill was pulling some strings of his own. He talked to someone who talked to someone, and they all agreed they wanted to keep Walter happy. It wasn't long before Connie was enrolled at Jackson State.

With that other girl off his mind and Connie on campus, Walter was out of his depression and back to giving Coach Hill what he had wanted all along: a focused stud running back. And not only was

Connie now Walter's one and only, but with me gone, the football field was all his, too. What wasn't gone, at least for me, were the great memories of our one year playing football together. Perhaps Coach Hill and Walter didn't think much about it at the time, but I was picturing plays from the previous year as if I was still on the team. I often thought about how Walter and I, depending on the formation, had the freedom to switch places. The thing is, I'd rather run to the right and then left, and Walter would rather run to the left and then right. There was a play we ran that was designed to originally go right, but if we saw the defense cheating toward that side, our quarterback could read it and change it to a sweep the other way. Since the play would be going left, Walter would want to run it, so we'd sometimes just trade places. Walter would holler, "Switch!" and he'd take the pitch and run it out. The quarterback didn't even need to know who was going to run the ball or which one of us he was going to pitch it to. It was no worry to him. He just knew it was a sweep and that he'd pitch to the trailing tailback, whether he was 5'7" or 5'10". If it was me, it was me. If it was Walter, it was Walter. Either way, it was gonna be good.

I often found myself thinking about how that Jackson State team with Walter and me was about as cohesive a group as you will ever see in college football. When you take a good look along the offensive line we had, you can't help but be in awe. I mean, we had guys like Ed Hardy (who was drafted by the 49ers), Emanuel Zanders (who played for the Saints), and Leon Gray (played 11 seasons in the NFL). Another kid on that line was Otis Stricklin, and he was probably even better than Leon, in my opinion. He just wasn't big enough to get attention and play in the NFL. Still, I think he was better. Or maybe I'm just partial to little guys. I often found myself looking back at it then. It was a year and a time in my life that meant a whole lot to me, and I'll never stop thinking about that. You know, I think that season meant a whole lot to all the other guys on that team, too, Walter included.

When I left Jackson State, a part of it came with me, and a part of me stayed behind. That part of me, the spirit of a young and cocky senior back who just knew he could conquer the world, will always be running the fields at Jackson State. What I didn't leave behind, though, was my shadow. When I was gone, Walter was out of my shadow once again—once and for all, in fact. The Jackson State Tigers were no longer *our* team. It was now Walter's team. And for a time there, it looked like he *was* the team.

With me gone, Walter became the lead running back, the punter, the place kicker, and even threw the halfback pass several times. And everything he did, he did top-notch. While Walter was engaging in what was the opposite of a sophomore slump, I was out there giving the Canadian Football League (CFL) a shot with Ottawa. And calling it a "shot" is just about right. I only lasted three months or so and decided to come back to Jackson State to work on my bachelor's degree, which I didn't finish when I ran out of football eligibility. So, there I was, back at school, and I wasn't going to be on the field. It was very different for me, that's for sure. I wasn't casting a shadow anymore, and I even started to notice that Walter's shadow was creeping its way toward me. Maybe I tried to ignore it, but that didn't stop it from moving ever closer. During his first year without his big brother, Walter was the second leading scorer. And I'm not just talking Jackson State. And I'm not just talking the SWAC. And I'm not just talking Mississippi. And I'm not just talking the South. I'm talking the whole nation. Walter scored the second-most points in all the land. He also managed the highest single-game scoring total in college football history when he scored 46 points in a single game. Now, just pause for a minute and do what I like to do. Close your eyes and just think about that. Okay, wait, don't close your eyes. I want you to keep reading. So, just keep your eyes open, stop for a bit here, and think about what an amazing thing Walter did. 46 points. From one man. In one game. And now think about how ironic it is that in the Super Bowl that Walter helped bring to Chicago, the Bears scored 46 points just like Walter did in that one game at Jackson State in 1972. Only Walter didn't get a single point in that Super Bowl.

Whether Walter should have gotten a shot at a touchdown in that Super Bowl is something I'll let you all talk about. Maybe we'll touch on it later in this book. What I want to get back to right now, though, is how Walter was nothing short of unstoppable the rest of his time at Jackson State. He was like a runaway train without the confinement of tracks. His insanely quick plant-and-cuts allowed him to change his direction faster than he took to Connie. His nuclear explosiveness let him tear through the line of scrimmage, steamrolling would-be tacklers like they were still a bunch of little boys on the playground. His power in the open field enabled him to outrun most anyone in pursuit, as if he was still stealing plums from the Garden of Eatin'. All of that added up to define Walter's style as a running back during his second year as a Tiger. He was so instinctive, so automatic, so natural, so in the zone. He didn't have to think about it or reason it out. He just was. My little brother quickly became the most intuitive runner I'd ever seen or would ever see carrying a ball. Anywhere. Any level. Ever.

He was so good the rest of the way at Jackson State that fans could've simply called him "The Best." That would have been fitting, but that didn't become his nickname. Too obvious, perhaps. Well, he had long left "Bubba" behind, and just calling him "Walter" wasn't sexy enough for what he was doing out there, so he needed something else. Sometime soon after I graduated, he somehow picked up one of my old nicknames, "Little Monk." The thing is, that really fit me much better than Walter, since I was the little guy. Plus, he was just becoming too good to follow in my footsteps. So, he was only "Little Monk" for a little while. Then something as sweet as Connie rolled his way once again. It was a nickname that would stick like honey. More heroic than his high school nickname "Spider-Man" and somehow more decadent than "Sugarman." It was a name unlike anything before used to describe a football player. "Sweetness" may've started out as something the other guys called Walter as a way to pick on him for his soft, high-pitched voice, but it soon developed into a moniker of pride for my brother. It was a nickname that matched his voice, yes, but it ended up matching the way he played even better. As a reporter once said about Walter, "He runs so sweet that it gives me cavities just watching him." I think there was a boom in business for dentists around Jackson State at the time, because Sweetness was there to stay. Walter embraced it, he loved it, and he never shied away from what would become one of sport's greatest and most-recognized nicknames.

Another reason the name "Sweetness" fit Walter so well was that he started leading the Tigers in their pregame prayer. Before each game, Walter would bring the team before God, and this wasn't something Coach Hill told him to do. Walter took over the pregame prayer out of choice. He wanted to do it. Now, remember, of course, that we're talking about the same Walter Payton that some folks in the media have been saying was not religious at all. Well, Walter was obviously religious at Jackson State, and I can tell you for sure that in the same way he didn't lose many games there, he also did *not* lose his religion anywhere along the line. Sweetness never wavered as a believer and follower of Jesus Christ, and I'm confident that if you believe in Jesus Christ, too, then you'll one day see for yourself that I'm right.

One thing I wasn't right about, I have to admit, was what I was going to do after leaving Jackson State. I expected to go off and create yet another shadow for Walter to one day step into on the next level, but that turned out to be more of a wish and a prayer, I suppose. And God had a different answer for it than I did. I thought I'd end up in the NFL or at least would light the CFL on fire. Well, when the NFL didn't call me for a workout and the CFL just plain didn't work out, I soon found out that God's answer to my prayer was a blessing I didn't even ask for. Though I wasn't yet living my dream, I got to watch Walter finish his last two years at Jackson State. I gave him his space while I was there, of course, but I still got to hang out and work out with him. And yes, I had a front row seat to witness him break all of my records. Okay, "break" is too soft of word. He smashed what I did. During his junior season in 1973, Sweetness rushed for 1,139 yards, led the country in scoring with 160 points, was voted the most valuable player in the SWAC, and was named to the Black All-American team. You're reading about it now, but I got to see it with my own eyes.

And you know, being right there and being his brother, I got to see more than football from Walter. I wasn't playing with him anymore, but I was still living life with him. And let me tell you, the football field wasn't the only place where he could play. In fact, he could've easily been the captain of the All-American team of off-the-field mischief, had there been one of those teams. Walter knew how to have fun and get into some serious trouble all at the same time. One of his favorite pranks was going around campus and letting the air out of two tires on a vehicle. He'd find a car that was parked, just sitting there, minding its own business, not hurting no one, and just waiting for someone like Walter to come along. Once he was sure there was nobody around or watching, he'd approach the car all stealth-like. He'd quickly bend down out of sight and release the air from the front right tire. Then he'd move around to the other side without standing up and let the air out of the back left tire. He'd then stand up, walk away, and find a spot close enough to the car to see it but far enough so as not to be seen. He'd sit and watch and wait for the owner to come back. Once that poor soul came strolling along, Walter would chuckle at knowing that in a matter of minutes, he'd be watching that car waddle away.

Some other parked cars suffered worse fates than that. If Walter could find a couple of teammates to help him (and he always could), they'd walk around until something teeny-tiny on four wheels was staring right at them. Those guys would pick up the smallest car they could find, like a Volkswagen or something, and they'd set it somewhere it didn't belong. They'd put it on a sidewalk, in front of a fireplug, between two trees, or somewhere like that. When the owner came back, he wouldn't be able to find the car at first. When he did finally locate it, he could at worst have a ticket for parking in front of a fireplug, but at best he'd be scratching his head about how the damn thing ended up where it was. And the whole time, Walter and his teammates would be—yep, you guessed it—chuckling like little kids. Walter would do anything to get a good laugh.

Now, there are some stories that went a little beyond just good ol' laughter. We can't talk about all of those stories. Or I should say, I won't talk about them. Some of things we did—uh, I mean, some of the things *they* did—will go with me to my grave. But there are enough funny stories that we can talk about, so sit back, relax, and enjoy the show. The main character in this next one is Sugarman. Remember him? You know, Edward "Sugarman" Moses, who played alongside Walter in high school. Well, he came to Jackson State with Walter, as you know, and they put him in a room with me and Walter during their freshman year. He got to go up and down that tree with us from time to time, but being in that room with Walter and me wasn't all good for Sugarman. I'll never forget about how Walter and I'd wait for him to fall asleep. He'd always go to bed earlier than us, and…come on now…in a room with Walter and me, that's just a big mistake. A few minutes after he was off in dreamland, we'd go to work. On more than one occasion, Sugarman woke up with his bed soaking wet on one side and his blanket on the floor. He would scramble to get it cleaned up, and I don't think he was ever completely sure whether he actually wet the bed or the two Payton boys had done it.

Sometimes Sugarman's bed would be a little more than wet. Like it'd be missing. He'd come in from a long, hard day of classes, and his mattress would just be gone. It'd be nowhere in the room, and he'd have to spend the rest of his day looking for it. We'd also do things like take all the clothes out of his closet and just stuff them in his drawer. After a few weeks of that sort of stuff, he started telling us he'd be sleeping with one eye open. Well, Sugarman must've have been blind in that one eye because we always got him.

Of course, Sugarman's going to get the last laugh on us Payton boys. I'm sure of that. You see, he went and became a minister. I'm thinking Walter and I will one day have to answer directly to God for a thing or two we did to Sugarman. Then again, I think even God has to think some of that was funny, so who knows? Maybe we'll get off easy. Regardless, and in all seriousness, Sugarman is one of the top 10 good guys I've ever been around in all my life. I'm sure Walter would agree. Wait, what am I saying? I'm sure Walter *does* agree. Sugarman was a hell of an athlete and a heaven of a man. He answered a higher calling when his playing days were through. He kept Walter and me in balance (as best he could, anyway) while we were at Jackson State, and he prayed with us all the time. We Payton boys sure needed that with all the crazy stuff we were doing.

Most of Walter's mischief back in the day was all in good fun, like in science class when he found out he could mix this and that together to give off the smelliest smell you ever done smelled. Let me tell you, when Walter got a hold of knowledge like that, everyone around him would pay through the nose for it. He stole some "this and that" from the lab once and stunk up the girls' dorms and even the coaches' offices.

But not every trick he pulled was just in good fun. Sometimes he and the guys would take things just a tad too far.

The popular swimming hole for a lot of us was Barnett Reservoir, just north of Jackson. Folks would go there to swim and to just have an overall good time. They'd park their cars up on the hill, and they'd head down to jump in the water. Well, Walter and his friends knew all about it. Sometimes they'd drive by, and if there were some cars parked up the hill, they'd park their own car down a bit and walk back to where the swimmers were. They'd check the cars, and if one of them had an open window, it was on. Walter would get inside the car, put it in neutral, and the guys would all push it from behind so that it started rolling down the hill. Once the car was on its way, Walter and his teammates would take off running and chuckling. The car they pushed would eventually hit the water and proceed to partially sink. Or it might sink all the way. Either way, some poor sucker had his car ruined, and all for a good laugh. Of course, now I must confess that it wasn't always just Walter and his teammates. I went along with 'em a time or two and might've participated in a "car drowning." Or two. Or more. But who's counting?

I wasn't involved in everything they were doing, and Walter was sometimes counting on me to be a confidant of sorts. He liked sitting down with me and talking about some of the stuff they did that no good person should ever be getting caught up in. Since I was still hanging around campus as a student, Walter knew that he could come to me and unload some of the crazier shit he and some of the guys on the team were getting into. I couldn't believe my ears on more than one occasion. Still, I can say that most of the time, Walter knew when to stop...even if his teammates didn't.

Sometimes, when you're hanging out with friends, things can get out of hand. A group of young guys hanging out night after night will sure enough get into some trouble even if they don't mean to. Walter found himself in one of those "sho' nuff" predicaments one night. He was just chilling with some of his teammates, and one of them followed another one who followed another one to a place they shouldn't have been. From what I was told, there was this girl who decided one night she wanted to take on three or four guys from the football team at once, so one of the guys found his way to that girl and led the others there, too. Well, Walter was hanging with that particular group on that particular night, so you know where he ended up. Before he could do anything about it, there he was in a room with his teammates as one after the other had their way with that girl. It was all consensual, mind you, but still not right. Walter knew it wasn't right, too. He was kicking himself for being there and, even worse, staying there. Well, a few weeks later, that girl said she thought she was pregnant and was going to sue them all and have 'em all arrested and whatnot. Sho' nuff, she pressed charges of sexual battery against the whole group. The cops showed up and put together a lineup of suspects, which included my brother. They were all taken to the station, and the girl was ready to start doing some identifying. "Well, which ones were involved?" the cops asked her. "Point them out."

Her finger made its way to each guy in the lineup, followed by words of condemnation for all. Except one. She finally pointed at Walter and said, "Yeah, he was there." Walter just knew what was coming next. He was sure she'd lie or remember incorrectly or something, and he was thinking he was going to need himself a good lawyer. Well, she did remember correctly and the lie never came. The girl lowered her finger and finished, "But he didn't do nothing." And that was absolutely right. My brother didn't do nothing. Well, nothing except find himself in a bad situation that he didn't know how to get out of. He knew what was right and wrong, and he didn't do a thing to that girl. I know he wouldn't have done that, even if he wasn't seeing Connie at the time, but the fact that he was committed to her made the temptation even easier to resist. He was in love with Connie, and nothing was going to get in the way of that.

So, what about the other guys? Did they go to trial? Did they have to go to jail? Well, the answers are no and no. And it was all thanks to Coach Hill. God bless that man for going through more crap with his players than a human being should have to endure. They did something wrong that night by taking that girl up on her offer, but they didn't do nothing illegal. Still, they should've at the very least been smarter than to do what they did. Coach Hill talked with them and then with the girl. I have no idea what was said by Coach Hill, but I do know the girl dropped all of the charges. There was just no way any of those boys were going to go to jail for a crime that never happened. Coach made sure of that.

Amazingly, that wasn't the only time Walter could've gone to jail while he was at Jackson State. During his senior year, right before the NFL draft, Walter, Rickey Young, Robert Brazile, and Vernon Perry (the young one just hanging around with the old guys) came up with a sort of "last hurrah" type of prank. They all knew they were about to be drafted, so Walter arranged to buy this Nissan 240Z sports car on credit. Everyone knew he was about to make a bunch of money, so he was good for it. And that car was good for picking up girls. It was a sexy little performance car, that's for sure. Thing is, Walter and the guys didn't want to pick up girls with that car. They wanted to scare 'em.

Walter and his boys of mischief went out and got this lifelike monster mask that resembled the Hunchback of Notre Dame, with bumps on it and bulging eyes and all kinds of just straight nastiness. They put the mask on Robert Brazile and put him in the trunk of the car (still not sure how they fit him in there), leaving it cracked open. Then they drove down to Lynch Street, just off campus, and found a group of girls just waiting to be scared, even if they didn't know it. The car pulled up to the girls and stopped in front of them. "Excuse me, ma'am," Walter said in his most polite Southern voice, "could you close my trunk that popped open?" One of the girls went to the back of the car to grant his request, and Brazile popped out wearing that mask. He didn't have to utter a word. In my opinion, he didn't even have to wear the mask, but that's neither here nor there. Those girls were scared out of their wits. They took off running, and the boys had the deep, end-of-an-era belly laugh that they were looking for. But that wasn't enough for them. They wanted more. They wanted to do some serious scaring and decided to take the show to downtown Jackson.

The boys cruised around downtown with Brazile stuffed down in the half-opened trunk, and then finally came across a couple of white girls walking down Capitol Street. Walter pulled up beside them, rolled down his window, and started up the conversation. "Excuse me, girls, could one of you slam that trunk down for me?" Well, both of them walked back there, probably unsure if they could say no, and Brazile popped out with the mask. Those girls were freaked out. And I mean, really freaked out. They went running down the street screaming, but that's not all. It didn't take them long to trip and fall, skinnin' themselves up but good. They were crying as hard as they fell, and the guys couldn't stop laughing until they were crying, too. Walter hit the gas, and they all headed back to campus, tired from all the scaring they'd done that night. Well, it turned out those two white girls weren't too scared to tell someone what happened.

The girls reported it to the police, and the police thought the description the girls gave sure sounded like some Jackson State football players. Word about the incident got back to you-know-who....yep, Coach Hill. The Jackson Police Department called Coach and let him know what was going on. "Coach," they said, "we're looking for a few football players who scared some girls so bad tonight that they fell down and got hurt. The girls say they were driving a 240Z sports car. Do you know anything about that?"

Coach didn't know anything about it when they called, but he knew who had a 240Z sports car. Everybody knew that. He said, "I know the car, Officer, and I think I know who did this. If I get the men responsible and handle it, they won't have to go to jail, right?"

Coach had a way with all sorts of people, and the Jackson Police Department was no different. "I promise they won't go to jail, Coach," they answered, "but only if you'll take care of it." Sho' nuff he would.

Coach Hill was now the one on a mission of causing fear and pain. But he wasn't looking for unsuspecting girls just walking down the street, minding their own business. Oh no. He was looking for some grown men who got a kick out of scaring unsuspecting girls just walking down the street, minding their own business. He walked right over to the football dorm, went up to Room 210, knocked on the door, and walked right on into the room without saying a word. Then he let it rip. "I need to see Rickey, Walter, and Brazile downstairs. NOW!" He turned and walked out of the room. The three amigos gathered themselves and marched downstairs right after him.

Coach was waiting at the bottom of the stairs, and the face he had on was scarier than any monster mask Walter and his friends could've dreamed of. "Give me the damn mask!" Coach shouted as soon as they got to the bottom of the stairs. "I don't want to hear nothing from none of y'all. Just give me the mask right now!" Brazile went back up the stairs as fast as he could to get the mask while Walter and Rickey stood in a mess of shame with their eyes looking straight down. Brazile came back down with the mask; Coach snatched it from him and walked away. As he went through the door of the dorm building, Coach turned to glare at the boys and said five words that were like daggers. "I'll talk to y'all later."

Well, it wasn't much later because Coach returned that night with his whistle. He walked back up to Room 210, knocked on the door again, and blew his whistle in the first face he saw when the door opened. "Y'all come with me!" he barked at the boys before turning around and heading back down the stairs. The boys followed again, of course.

Coach Hill led Walter, Rickey, and Brazile onto the football field and proceeded to run 'em all night long. They were seniors about to graduate and enter the NFL draft, but they were practicing like they'd just arrived on campus. The two-a-days from their first year were nothing compared to the punishment they endured that night. It didn't matter that they were about to go off into the world and make their mark. Those men were still boys in the eyes of Coach Hill. They were boys still living in Coach's house. They were still living under Coach's roof, and dammit, they were going to follow Coach's rules. For one night, right before they were about to go pro, it was like freshman year all over again. I've said it before, but I can't say it enough. You don't mess with Coach Hill.

All jokes aside, plenty of teams knew by then that you don't mess with Walter Payton, either. Not on a football field. He was a beast. He'd become a fine-tuned machine by the time his college days came to a close. Walter was a true phenom. He earned first-team All-American in 1974 and MVP in all of Division II football. Before Walter's senior season, Dick Young, a columnist for *The Sporting News*, boldly predicted Walter would be the first player from a traditionally black school to win the Heisman. Now, even though he finished fourth in the Heisman Trophy balloting, even being in the hunt for it meant he'd done the impossible for a player from a historically all-black college. Integration was one small step for education, but Walter took one giant leap for black athletes everywhere. In his career at Jackson State, Walter rushed for 3,563 yards on 584 carries for 6.1 yards per carry. He set the NCAA Division II scoring record at 464 points, which included 66 touchdowns, 5 field goals, and 53 extra points. He also managed to get his bachelor's degree in three and a half years. And you know, I think he was more proud of that than of all those awards and records he got playing football. In fact, during Walter's last semester, with a college degree already in hand, he began his quest for a master's. As it turned out, he wouldn't finish that up, because something else was waiting for him. The NFL was calling his name. He wasn't going to get that master's degree, but the temperature was about to drop a degree of two for him, I can tell you that. There was a draft in the air, and things were about to get windy.

CHAPTER 8

Bringin' In the New

The Bible tells you that if you ask for forgiveness with a pure heart, then forgiveness will be yours. There's no other price that needs payin' because Jesus Christ done already paid it. Walter and I had plenty of "come to Jesus" moments over the years, that's for sure. I mean, there are some things I've done throughout my college and professional football careers that I'm not proud of, and I've had to look to the Lord to wipe it all away. It's only through Him that I've been able to the throw out the old and bring in the new. I'm no different than anyone else. Same goes for Walter. And as for anyone else, well, nobody's perfect. We all need forgiveness. We all need to come to Jesus. We all need our sins washed away. Perhaps none of us more so than the men calling the shots for the Falcons, the Cowboys, and the Colts in the 1975 NFL draft. Those teams had the first three picks. Walter Payton went fourth. Sinners.

Steve Bartkowski, quarterback from the University of California, was taken by the Atlanta Falcons as the No. 1 pick, and there was no doubt who they were going with. Things were a little different after that. The Dallas Cowboys had the second pick, and they couldn't decide. They wanted to go one way and then another. Legendary

Bears coach Mike Ditka was an assistant coach with Dallas in 1975. He said, "In the war room, when we were trying to decide who to take, Dan Reeves and all the offensive coaches wanted to take Walter. Coach Landry was a little more defensive-minded, though he agreed Walter was the best player in the draft." Everybody wanted my little brother, and a lot of teams were trying to trade up to get him. But Coach Ditka said that in the end Dallas wound up taking defensive tackle Randy White out of Maryland. "Not a bad pick," said Ditka of White. "He was a great, great player and ended up in the Hall of Fame, too." Okay, so the Cowboys passed on one of the greatest players of all time to get another Hall of Famer at a position where they had a need. Maybe we can let that slide, but surely the next team would take Walter. Or maybe not.

The Baltimore Colts had the third pick and selected Ken Huff, an offensive guard out of the University of North Carolina. Should've been Walter. Ray Perkins was a scout for the New England Patriots at the time, and he was amazed to see Walter fall past the third pick. Perkins was from Petal, Mississippi, so maybe he was partial to someone from his home state, but I think it was more about what he saw as a scout. "I watched Walter practice, and he was simply unbelievable," Perkins said about scouting my brother. "That was the good news. The bad news was we had the 16th pick that year, and there was no way he would still be available by then." He was right.

As you know, the Chicago Bears chose Walter in the first round, making him the fourth player picked overall. Two picks later, Walter's close friend from Jackson State, Robert Brazile, became the sixth pick. Despite some rumors to the contrary, Brazile was not wearing that hideous monster mask at the draft. Coach Hill locked that thing away for good. All Brazile had on his face was a big ol' smile. Two boys from Jackson State were among the top six picks and going to the NFL.

If Walter didn't need a good lawyer back at Jackson State, well, he needed a good lawyer now.

A few weeks before the draft, Walter hired a guy named Bud Holmes to represent him. Bud was from Petal, Mississippi, just like Ray Perkins, only he didn't know anything about Walter like Perkins did. A friend of Bud's named Vernon Bowen called him one day and wanted to know if he'd represent a black athlete from Jackson State. Bud said, "Sure, there are a lot of good people at Jackson State. Tell me about him." And Vernon did just that. He told Bud about this kid named Walter Payton who was just such a good football player and was probably going to go in the first round of the NFL draft that year. Despite all Walter had done at Jackson State, he wasn't a household name in the area just yet since he didn't play at Southern Miss or Mississippi State. Most people didn't follow Jackson State, despite how good we were. Bud said, "Hell, I hadn't ever heard of Walter Payton, truthfully." Coach Hill called Bud after he talked to Vernon and said he was bringing down two boys for Bud to consider representing. Coach brought Walter and Robert Brazile down. Bud met with them and really liked Walter and Brazile right off the bat. They all hit it off, shook hands, and Bud agreed he'd represent them when the draft came around. That first meeting gave him a snapshot of my little brother, but it wasn't until about a month or so later that Bud got a closer look at the type of guy Walter was.

The graduating seniors from the high school in Petal were planning a weenie roast at Bud's farm to celebrate making it through. They knew Bud was connected to football down there and wanted him to get Bobby Collins, who was the head coach at Southern Mississippi, to come speak to 'em. Or, if he couldn't get Coach Collins, they wanted Ray Guy, who was Bud's first client, to show up to the party. Well, Bud tried his best, but those guys each had a conflict or something and couldn't make it. In an effort to give them something, he told the high school boys, "Well, I'm representing a kid from over here at Columbia that is supposed to be real good. He broke all kinds of records up at Jackson State, and I'll see if he'll come over and speak to y'all."

So, Bud called Walter and asked if he'd do him a favor and come speak to these boys graduating from high school in Petal. Walter jumped right at it and said, "I'll be glad to come."

Bud said, "Great. We'll have hot dogs and hamburgers, so yeah, just come on over and have a good time with us." The thing is, it was the first year of integration at Petal High School, so there was still some racial divide down there. Bud said, "So, here it is, I had all these white high school kids with all these pickup trucks and shotguns and rebel flags in the back of the trucks, and I was bringing in this black kid to speak to them. I guess I didn't really think anything about it at the time."

The white kids had a big ol' bonfire going, and everybody was having a good time roasting hot dogs and all that. Then Bud introduced Walter. With him being black and all those kids being white, and since Bud had never really been around Walter more than just to say hello and shake hands, he started to get a little nervous about the whole situation. He wasn't sure what those boys were going to say to Walter, and he wasn't sure what Walter was going to say to those boys. It finally dawned on him that perhaps he should've thought it all through a little better. But none of that so much as fazed my little brother. Walter just started talking, roasting hot dogs, and acting like he fit right in. He told a joke or two, but those kids didn't so much as crack a smile. Bud watched the whole thing unfold and saw Walter trying to break through the wall those white kids were putting up. Bud started getting mad about how they were treating Walter and thought, *Hell, these kids are being rude. I'm paying for everything out here, and they're going to act like this toward my guest? Boy, I ought to get in there and run every damn one of them off my land and just enjoy these hot dogs with Walter.* The whole time, Walter just never quit talking. He kept on and on and on, talking about this and joking about that. He was just one of the boys even if they didn't see him that way.

Finally, Walter got around to talking about the upcoming Super Bowl. Bud remembers what happened next like it was yesterday. "He asked the group, 'Who's going to win the Super Bowl?'" Then they all started talking about both teams and who'd win and all that. Well, every time one of them boys would say something, Bud said Walter would do the opposite of what they did to him. He'd just light up and, if appropriate, he'd fall over dying laughing. "I mean, if they told a joke, Walter acted like it was just the funniest thing he'd ever heard," Bud remembered. Soon those white kids were smiling and just talking back and forth, and the next thing you know, all of them wanted their picture taken with my little brother. Of course, Walter obliged. "They were all getting their picture taken with this black kid," Bud said, "and I'm not sure who was more excited, Walter or those high school kids."

Walter didn't get in a hurry that night, and he didn't let the rudeness from those kids get to him, and it really impressed Bud. After watching how Walter's attitude transformed those kids as the night went on, Bud just looked at Walter and thought, *Now, this kid's got something special. He's got a certain flair to him that you don't see every day. He can read people. He knows how to handle them.*

The only problem was, it wouldn't be all fun with Walter. When Walter was finally drafted in the first round by the Bears, he acted a fool and didn't get in touch with Bud until he was asked to give a press conference in Chicago. He was a bit panicked about it and called Bud for advice.

Bud didn't hear from Walter for about a week after the draft. There was a picture of him and Brazile on a motorcycle floating around, but that was all Bud saw of them. Both of them were drafted in the first round, and Bud was supposed to be representing them, but all he ever had with either of 'em up to that point was a handshake and a meeting or two. And Walter was out there saying some mess about how he's going to law school and would be representing himself. It was a joke that Bud didn't find too humorous. Well, all of a sudden, Bud gets a phone call from Walter, and he's in a panic saying, "Look, I'm supposed to be going to Chicago for a press conference."

"Good," Bud said.

"What should I do when I get there?" Walter asked.

"Okay, you got something to write with?" Bud responded.

"Yeah."

"Go to a phone booth, and as soon as you get there, get the yellow pages out. Look under attorney. That's spelled A-T-T-O-R-N-E-Y. Look that up 'cause you're going to need somebody to represent your sorry ass."

Walter was surprised by that. "Huh?" he asked, not sure what to do. "You not representing me?"

Bud wasn't about to put up with my little brother's antics. "Nah," he said. "Hell, I already told you. I thought you and I had an agreement that I represented you, but look how you've been acting. I only represent *proud* black men. I won't put up with this bullshit. You get drafted and don't so much as call me. How many times I got to tell you?"

"Come on, man," Walter said.

"Are you not hearing me? Listen, I haven't heard a word from you since the draft. So, I just want you to get somebody else, okay? Someone who will put up with that bullshit, 'cause I won't. Hell, I ain't got time to fool with somebody like you."

"Man, don't do me that way," Walter pleaded. "I need you, man. Come on and give me another chance."

Bud had an idea. "Okay, I'll tell you what, here's what we're going to do. Be in my office in the morning at 10:00 AM. I don't mean 10:01 or 9:59, okay? I mean 10:00. Then I'll see you."

So, Bud got down to his office at something like 7:30 the next morning, and Walter was already there outside, standing on the corner just waiting for him. There's no telling how long he'd been there, but Bud wasn't about to see him just yet. Bud walked right on by, only saying good morning to him or something like that. He just kept on going and went inside his office, leaving Walter outside. Well, a few minutes later, Bud's secretary came back to his office and said, "Walter Payton is out here to see you." Bud said, "I know it, but I told him 10:00. He can wait." So, Bud didn't do a damn thing but sit there and make Walter wait until 10:00. At exactly 10:00 AM, Bud called up to his secretary and said, "Okay, bring him on back."

Walter came in and said, "I want to apologize," but Bud cut him off right away.

"Now, Walter," he said, "we can either start over—and we're going to start over on the right foot, or there ain't going to be no foot at all for us. Do you understand that?" Walter nodded and then apologized, apologized, and apologized. After too much of that, Bud said, "Okay, that's good." They shook hands and had a new deal and a new understanding. That's when Bud Holmes really became my brother's agent.

When Walter first told me about Bud, it was like he was Walter's new favorite person in the world. I didn't know anything about Bud, but Walter sure seemed to love him. He was singing Bud's praises over and over and over. When I finally got a chance to meet him, I wanted to punch the guy.

Walter kept telling me, "Man, you got to meet my lawyer!" He'd talk about how Bud was just super cool and the best lawyer around. He even said Bud would be able to help me get back into football. Well, you know that sounded good to me, so one day we jumped in Walter's infamous 240Z and headed down Highway 49 toward Hattiesburg to meet up with Bud. Before I knew it, we were deep into the woods, out from Petal. We drove down a narrow driveway and followed a long winding road to this big cabin overlooking a lake. Walter was excited to be there and ran on in ahead of me while I was getting my stuff out of the car. I walked in through the door, and Walter said, "Bud, I want you to meet my brother. He can really play." There was some nervous awkwardness walking in, mostly from me, and I think Bud could tell. He decided to try to lighten things up and break all that down by throwing caution to the wind and slinging some fightin' words. After Walter introduced me, this whiter-than-white white guy got up out of the chair and said to Walter, "Yeah, yeah, come on in here. Sit your black ass down and tell me what you can do." I stopped in my tracks, and the grin I had walking in fell right off my face. I must admit, all the nervous awkwardness did, too. Now, it was just plain awkward. I thought, *Whoa, I know he didn't just say that.*

I was seriously shocked. I mean, I didn't know what to do. I thought maybe I was going crazy…or at least a little deaf…or both. I remember thinking, *Wow, I'm about to put a whoopin' on this guy right here.* I had yet to move a muscle, though, and that included my tongue. Not saying a word, I just looked at Walter in disbelief. What shocked me even more than Bud's words was that Walter didn't seem bothered at all by any of it. He was over there just saying, "Now, Eddie, don't worry about that, okay? That's just Bud, that's just Bud. He don't mean a thing by it." But at that time and in that cabin I saw things a little differently than that. I was asking myself, *Am I about to walk into a scene from* Deliverance *up in here?* I wasn't sure what sort of unsavory characters might be hiding in the other room, just waiting to jump out and do who knows what to Walter and me. Still, Walter insisted it was nothing and that everything was cool. Bud nodded, and I darted my eyes back and forth between them for a minute. They both smiled, and I started to follow my brother's lead. Maybe he was right. Perhaps Bud really didn't mean nothing by it.

It turned out that Walter was right. It took me a while to understand, but I eventually came to understand that Bud just liked to break the ice with a sledge hammer. He thought friends should be able to say anything to each other, even if that anything was shocking to the rest of world. Chances are, if you were ever shocked by Bud (or by Bud and Walter together), he (or they) was (or were) just messing with you. If you were on the inside, you got it. If you were on the outside, well, you might've suffered the same fate as Brent Musburger.

Musburger was a reporter at the CBS affiliate in Chicago at the time. He wasn't national yet, and he was trying to set up a press conference so he could interview Walter and introduce him to Chicago. When Musburger called Bud and presented the idea, Bud agreed it was a good one. The Bears hadn't yet signed Walter, and Bud knew if Walter could come out of the press conference looking good, it could only help his client. The plan was for Walter to talk about how he wanted to do nothing but play in Chicago, and that would serve to make the Bears look like they didn't know what they were doing having not yet signed him. In the end, Bud knew the whole thing would give Walter leverage in his contract negotiations. So, Musburger wanted to know if Bud could get Walter to come up there for the press conference, and of course Bud agreed. But he didn't just want Walter to talk about how much he wanted to be in Chicago. Bud also wanted to have some fun with it, because he'd heard Walter was a prankster extraordinaire. Walter and Bud would prove to be a match made in heaven in that way, but at the time Musburger called for the press conference, Bud was still trying to see what kind of sense of humor my little brother had. He found out pretty fast and in a big way.

Before heading to Chicago for the press conference, Bud said that he pulled Walter off to the side and said, "Let's go up there and let's have some fun with this, okay? Here's what I want to do. We'll fly to Chicago and get out and meet the local press and others out there. Now, you'll do the press conference just fine, but before you go on air, I want you to act like a dumb, ignorant, subservient, backwoods black guy, and I'll play the part of a dumb, ignorant, redneck lawyer that must be a member of the KKK. We'll just make 'em all a little nervous about what you'll say on air." Hmmm…sounds familiar. Guess they weren't much for coming up with new material.

Well, hearing Bud's little plan was music to Walter's ears. Bud was his kind of agent, that's for sure. Walter just loved the idea. And I mean, he dearly loved it. He told Bud, "Yeah, yeah, yeah, that'll be fun. Yeah, we'll do that." According to Bud, Walter really got a big kick out of thinking about pulling that prank, and all the nervousness he had about going to Chicago and doing that press conference just melted away.

The way Bud told the story, they flew into Meig's Field Airport in Chicago, and there was a limo waiting for them and everything. It was a big deal to the media folks of Chicago, and Bud and Walter smiled at each other as they sat there on the plane, looking at all the cameras pointed toward them. So, Bud and Walter let everyone else get off the plane first. They wanted to be the last ones off, and Walter was the very last one off the plane, walking behind Bud. Walter walked off that plane, and the press just looked at him. Walter was looking at all the snow, though, and he got an idea. He started right up with the gag by pointing at the snow and saying, "What's that mess?"

Bud followed right along. "Well, now, that's snow," he responded so everyone could hear. Then Walter took it to a whole new level.

"Nah, that's cotton," Walter said in the dumbest sounding voice he could muster.

Bud almost laughed and gave away the whole thing, but he somehow kept it together. "Nah, Walter, it ain't no cotton. Hell, come on over here. I'm telling you, it's snow."

"What, I got to play in that mess?" Walter continued. "I ain't getting off this plane."

"Now, now, you come on here," Bud said, sounding just as redneck as redneck could be. Bud and Walter then started to act like they were about to punch each other, with Walter not wanting to get off the plane. Finally, Walter got off the plane, got in the limo, and they went downtown. But the fun was just beginning. They walked into the studio to see Musburger, and that's when the joke got very interesting. Every other word Walter said was "nigger." You know; nigger this, nigger that. "How 'bout them niggers?" he'd say, or, "How many niggers y'all got? I don't see any." Stuff like that. And the whole time, Musburger was just sitting there getting all freaked out. He was convinced that what was going to be an exciting day for him was about to turn into the worst day of his life.

Everything Walter said made Musburger flinch. It scared the hell out of him. All of a sudden and far too soon for Musburger, it was 10 minutes before they were scheduled to hit the air. Walter went out there, and they set him all up with a mic and everything. They got Walter all situated, and he had a little camera he brought, and he was sitting there playing with everything like he was dumb as a box of rocks. All the CBS people were real frantic, because it was almost time to go on the air, and they didn't know what Walter was going to do. Walter and Bud could see them all huddled up not knowing what to do, with no idea what was about to go out on the air. They were actually trying to decide whether to cancel the show or not, from what I understand. They had all the press out there, too. I mean, everybody, so it would've been a big deal to cancel. Walter and Bud knew they wouldn't. So, anyway, they get ready to go, and Musburger finally came over to Walter and Bud just moments before show time and said, "Look, we're getting ready to go on air. I don't want to…I'm asking you guys…don't use the ethnic slur."

Walter looked Musburger square in the eye, acting as dumb as could be, and said, "What you talking about? What you mean by 'ethnic'?"

"You know, that word you all keep using. That ethnic slur," Musburger said, not amused.

Bud decided to cut in. "I don't know what you're talking about," he said, continuing the ruse. "Do you know what he's talking about, Walter?"

"No, sir, Mr. Bud. I don't." Then Bud looked at Walter and shrugged his shoulders.

Musburger was getting frustrated. "You know what I'm talking about, that word you use," he said again. He didn't want to say it, but Walter and Bud were determined to get Musburger to say the word.

"What word you talkin' 'bout, Mr. Musburger?" Walter said again.

"That word. You guys keep saying…." Then he whispered, "*Nigger.*" He had to choke it out of himself. Bud actually started feeling sorry for Musburger, but Walter smelled blood and wanted to make it worse for the poor guy.

"Mr. Musburger," Walter said in response, "I promise, I told you I's a good nigger. I ain't no bad nigger."

Musburger was completely freaked at that point. "No, come on, now, you can't use that word out there," he said, seeing his career flash before his eyes. "You understand me? You can't use it."

Walter didn't skip a beat. He just answered, "I's a good nigger, Mr. Musburger. I promise, I's a good little nigger."

Then the lights turned on, and it was show time. Musburger took to the air and started in for about five minutes. Bud says he must've been nervous as hell, but all he did was brag about Walter's career at Jackson State and all the records he set. He showed a bunch of video clips of his days at Jackson State and just went on and on about him like he was the best thing to come to Chicago since sliced pizza. Walter hadn't said a word or given any indication as to whether or not he'd be using "that word" on the air. Finally, Musburger was out of great things to say about Walter, and it was time to turn Walter's mic on. Musburger gave Walter the cue, "And I'm going to now introduce you to the Bears' No. 1 draft choice." The press, and especially Brent Musburger, held their collective breath. "This is Walter Payton," continued Musburger. "Now, I'm going to ask him if he has anything to say."

What they didn't know (and what you don't know yet, come to think of it) was that Walter had worked part-time at Channel 16 in Jackson while a student and did a lot of "on the scene reporting." He had a minor in radio and TV. As a matter of fact, when Bud's client Ray Guy, as a rookie, hit the Astrodome ceiling with a punt, Walter was down there that night with a camera, interviewing Ray for Channel 16 in Jackson. So, if they'd have done their homework, the Chicago press would've known that Walter was no rookie when it came to being in front of a live camera.

Walter switched back to his normal voice, smiled, and said, "I am so honored to be here today to just have the thought of being able to play for the same team that legends like Red Grange, Bronko Nagurski, Sid Luckman, Gale Sayers, and Dick Butkus played for. And the great George Halas. It is the wildest dream of my life to be able to have this honor, to be able to be out there where Gale Sayers has run up and down the field. I just hope that I don't embarrass." Walter did so much more than just not say "that word." He was downright eloquent.

There was clearly nothing dumb about Walter during that press conference. Nothing dumb in the least. It didn't matter what they asked him, my little brother answered it with style and class. Bud once noted that even Musburger appreciated the charade at that point. "As soon as the thing was over," Bud said, "Brent Musburger came up to us, made sure nobody was around, cut his eyes at Walter, shook his head, then turned to me and said, 'Damnit, you're right, he sure is a smart-aleck nigger, isn't he?' I never saw Walter laugh so hard before or since. He just laughed and laughed and laughed at what Musburger said."

Walter and Bud sure had some good times together and really clicked in an odd sort of way. And I think Bud fully appreciated what I was going through at the time, too. What's more, I think he cared. My situation reminded him a lot of his good friend, Hank Williams Jr. I'll never forget Bud's story of the two of them fishing on Barnett Reservoir the day after a Hank Jr. concert in Jackson. They got to drinking, and Hank Jr. got to spillin' his guts. He turned to Bud and said, "You didn't come to see *me* last night, you came to see my daddy." Bud didn't quite know what to tell him, so he didn't say much. Then Hank filled up the silence saying, "Well, I'm a musician, too," before he took another drink.

It was true, you know. Everywhere Hank would go there for a while, all anyone would want to hear him sing were his daddy's songs. Not long after that conversation with Bud, though, a song of his own bubbled up: "Standing in the Shadows". And these lyrics made their way to my ears:

I know that I'm not great
And some say I imitate
Anymore, I don't know
I'm just doing the best I can
After all, I'm standing in the shadows
Of a very famous man

Oftentimes, I felt like him, standing in the shadows of a legend who happened to be my little brother, the one I'd taught the tricks of the trade. But what good is a big brother if he's only there to give you something to follow or to keep you tagging along? No, there's more to it than that. Sometimes I think the greater test of a bond for an older sibling comes not in patting the younger ones on the head when they're coming up, but in patting them on the back when they've passed you by. When my little brother became a star, he found me standing in the shadows cheering him on. And when that era was over, I couldn't think of a better way to spend my time than to pour myself into some other young athletes as the head golf coach at Jackson State. I think of Mr. Bradley sometimes with all he did for us young athletes when he opened that sports complex in Columbia when Walter and I were kids. And now here was one of those kids all grown up and getting ready to make his mark on NFL history.

Eventually, with the help of Bud Holmes, Walter and the Bears came to terms. He signed a three-year contract that gave him the richest deal in franchise history at that time. Bud got Walter the highest signing bonus for any player ever from Mississippi, in the amount of $126,000 ($1,000 higher than the bonus Archie Manning got). Might not seem like much now when talking about a player like Walter, but back in 1975, it was a fortune. Walter was thrilled, and that's when things really started to fly in his life. He was a Chicago Bear. He was in the NFL. He had achieved his dream, and now he was getting ready to live it. And for a good little while there, I even got to live it with him. That's right— Payton & Payton was coming to the NFL.

CHAPTER 9

Becomin' Sweet P

Do you know how long a mile is? Well, it's exactly 5,280 feet. A football field, on the other hand, is only 300 feet long (360 feet if you include the end zones). There are almost 18 football fields in a mile. Now, it's 825 miles or so from Columbia, Mississippi, to Chicago, Illinois. That's around 14,138 football fields. Quite a long way no matter how you slice it. It'll take you about 14 hours by car to get from my hometown to the Windy City, and that's if you take the straightest of shots. Well, Walter certainly didn't take anything even close to a straight shot. There were many twists and turns on his path to the Bears. Hell, there were many *paths* on his path to the Bears. It took Walter 21 years to get to Chicago. And he went much, much farther than 825 miles. I can't even begin to count how many football fields he had to run along the way. Funny thing was, once he arrived, my brother's journey was just beginning. And so was mine.

Walter was living the dream when he became a Bear. All of his hard work had paid off, and he had reached the highest level of football. While he was settling into his new life in Chicago and training for his rookie season, I was starting a whole new phase of my life about 9,417 football fields away in Memphis, Tennessee. The CFL didn't work out, so I was out of football and had started teaching at Vance Junior High School before moving over to Booker T. Washington High School. That's where I became the athletic director, the math teacher, the PE teacher, and the football coach. Time rolled on by for Walter and me, and as the summer turned into fall, Chicago Bears fans got a glimpse of their new all-purpose athlete. Walter proved to be a beast returning kickoffs, and he slowly showed he could be a force running the ball through the line of scrimmage, too. But it wasn't easy for him at first.

When he first took the field in high school, Walter hit the ground running, but it wasn't like that for him as a rookie in the NFL. Of course, it wasn't really his fault, if you ask me. It was largely because the Bears didn't have much going on offense when Walter showed up. In fact, it wouldn't be much of a stretch to say that when Walter got there the Bears' best offensive play was the punt. After that, it was all pretty much downhill, and not in the good football sense of the term. Chicago just wasn't a very good team, and Walter wasn't going to be able to turn things around on his own. It doesn't work like that in the NFL. Every player in the league was a star on his high school and college teams. It's just that some stars were bigger than others, and when Walter came to the Bears, they seemed to have more of the "others."

Quarterbacks Gary Huff, Bob Avellini, and Bobby Douglass just couldn't provide the kind of potent passing attack that could keep opposing defenses honest. Noah Jackson, Revie Sorey, and some other young and inexperienced players made up the offensive line, so there wasn't a whole lot at the time to run behind. Dan Jiggetts came in the next year, and that would be the start of what would later become a great offensive line for Walter, but it was hard for him to find much room to run that first season. Any defense facing the Bears simply zeroed in on the rookie running back, and I mean that literally when talking about Walter's infamous debut. It's widely known that Walter totaled zero yards rushing on eight attempts in his very first game as a Bear. That was a tough beginning to a tough rookie year for my little brother, and in all honesty, it was probably even tougher for me, because I was pulling so hard for him. I wanted him to get out there and be bad-ass on the grass right away. That's just not how it was going to be, though. Unless, of course, we're talking about what he did as a kick returner.

Despite Walter's ability to play almost any position at Jackson State, one thing he never did in college was return kicks. I never did that in college, either, so I was surprised to see they had Walter back there catching the ball and running it back as a rookie. He was supposed to be their star running back, pounding through the line of scrimmage, leaving a trail of sweetness behind him, so I wanted to know why they had him returning kicks. I called him up and asked, "Why you doing that? Why you returning kicks?" He had a very simple and wise answer for me. "Because they pay me," he said. Okay, little brother, I can dig it. The Bears got their money's worth, too, because Walter led the league in kickoff returns as a rookie. That was something he made sure I knew and would never, ever forget. Never, ever.

Now, of course, if you don't know anything about Walter's stats during his rookie year, you might read what I just wrote and think he only returned kicks and did nothing as a runner. You'd be wrong. He didn't do what the world would come to expect from him, but he wasn't exactly a slouch either. He didn't get zero yards rushing in every game. He got better and better as the season went on. Even with a young Bears O-Line and no passing attack to speak of, Walter's talent eventually just had to shine through. There was nothing anyone could do about it. Uncommon, God-given talent like his has a way of doing that. As I mentioned, he led the league in kickoff returns, but he also finished the season with 679 yards rushing. Might not sound like a lot, but considering he was a rookie on a bad team, it was pretty good. Oh, and for some perspective, his 679 yards were actually the most for any Bears running back since 1969. If it was a poor first year in the NFL for Walter, it said more about the state of the Bears at the time than my baby brother's level of sweetness on the field. Still, it didn't hurt to get a little boost in the sweetness department over that following summer.

Remember how at Jackson State, Walter was in a funk from being rejected by that girl and her mother, and how he came out of that funk after meeting Connie? Well, the summer following his rookie season in the NFL, Connie (who was Walter's fiancée at the time) left Jackson State and came to Chicago to be with him. They wed a few weeks later on July 7, 1976. That was a wonderful day for my little brother, and I must say, it really topped off his sweetness tank. He started to explode during his second year. That season Walter really stepped it up and basically became the Bears' offense, carrying the ball 311 times, which was the most in the league. He led the league in kickoff returns as a rookie, like I said, and now here he was in his second year as a pro leading the league in rushing attempts. He gained 1,390 yards on the ground, which didn't lead the league, but it sho' nuff led the National Football Conference (NFC). The Bears finished the year 7–7, which was their best season in eight years. Maybe Walter should've married Connie sooner.

Whether Connie was the reason or not, Walter Payton was back in a big way. It was exciting for me to watch him doing what he was doing out there. He was in the best league in the world with the best players in the world, and he was playing like the best of the best.

Doesn't get much better than that. Well, except for being in the NFL with him. That would've been better for sure. I enjoyed watching Walter so much during that breakout second year that I started to think about our year together back at Jackson State. I was reliving all the fun we had together as Tigers, and I started to get the itch again. I mean, don't get me wrong—I was enjoying my job as a high school football coach and teacher in Memphis. It's just that watching Walter out there during his second season made me want to play again. And if I'm being perfectly honest, growing up I never dreamed that I'd have stopped playing and moved to coaching so soon. I was still a football player, really. It's just that I wasn't playing football. So, while I was coaching and teaching and watching Walter introduce himself to football fans everywhere, I just kept trying to stay in shape, wishing, hoping, and praying that somebody in the NFL would give me a shot. I thought maybe someone would remember the things I did in college or the type of athlete I was when I played. Eventually, I got a call that changed everything.

Al Tabor was the special teams coach with the Cleveland Browns during that time. When I was at Jackson State, Al was coaching at Southern University. I'd played against his team while a Tiger, so Al had firsthand knowledge of what I could do. He'd seen me run up and down the field in an up-close and personal kind of way. Well, he eventually left Southern University and became part of the Browns, and he remembered me from when he saw me play back in college. In the summer of 1977, he called me up and said the six most beautiful words I've ever heard anyone say to me. "You think you can still play?"

"Yes, sir," I said.

"Okay, you think you can return kicks?"

Now, again, returning kicks wasn't something I'd done in college, and I never really saw myself as that kind of player. I always imagined

I'd be a running back at the next level, carrying the ball, making guys miss, breaking ankles and records all at the same time. Then I remembered what my brother told me during his rookie year about why he was returning kicks, and I thought, *Okay, now, swallow your pride and get paid.* My response started out a little weak, perhaps, but I finished strong. "Well, I guess I...yep, I can. Sure can."

Al was happy to hear it. "Well, we want to bring you in and give you a look," he told me, "and then if everything works out, we'll sign you." I hung up the phone and un-hung up my cleats. I felt like a teenager again, just as thrilled as I could be and filled with the love I had for the game when I first started playing with the neighborhood kids. That call from Al was what I'd been waiting for, and I went out jogging right away to be sure I was in tip-top shape for the upcoming workout, thinking the whole time about all the kicks I was about to get a chance to return on the highest level in football. I was humbled and excited about the opportunity and couldn't believe it was really happening.

Well, the rest of the Browns coaching staff saw what Al saw in me when I was at Jackson State. I made Cleveland's team as a free agent, and I was finally in the NFL. I was getting my shot. The problem was, it wasn't much different than the shot I got in the CFL. I was only with the Browns for two games, a victim of the numbers. You see, our All-Pro defensive tackle, Jerry Sherk, was injured at the time, so they were allowed to have another player on the roster while he recovered. I was that player. We were trying to play games with one less defensive lineman until Jerry got well or we put him on injured reserve. Well, we ended up putting him on injured reserve a little quicker than I thought we would, so he couldn't play any more that year. They were just going to try to wait him out, so they signed me instead of another defensive lineman. But we just weren't doing well on defense, and with Jerry on injured reserve, they had to bring in another defensive lineman to replace him. Room had to be made for the new defensive lineman, so I got cut. As they say, the good Lord giveth, and the good Lord taketh away. Fortunately for me, sometimes when the good Lord does that, he giveth again right away.

I'd done enough in those two games with Cleveland that the Detroit Lions took notice. They picked me up off waivers, and I finished the last eight games of the season with the Lions. So, between the Browns and the Lions, I got to play 10 games, and I just have to mention what happened on December 17, 1977. It's my book, so you're just going to have to deal with me braggin' on myself a little here, okay? It was the last game of the year for the Lions, against the Minnesota Vikings. I was really feeling my oats that day and returned two kicks for touchdowns. I ran a kickoff back for a 98-yard score and returned a punt for an 87-yard touchdown. That's 185 yards and 12 points on two plays. And you know, I actually could've had a better game on November 6, 1977, which was about the third week I was with the Lions. We were playing against San Diego at home, and I was ripping up and down the field all day. It was the best I'd ever feel in the NFL, but holding flags erased some good runs and a lot of yardage. Still, I was showing flash out there, and a lot of people saw it. It was a great time for me, and I think more than anything, I was feeling like me again. On the day I scored two touchdowns, I established in the eyes of many that I could play. Some people realized that I was Eddie Payton and not just Walter's brother. Of course, it was inevitable that some would always compare me to him.

When I first got in the league, somebody said, "Man, you run just like Walter." I always responded with a wisecrack by saying, "Nah, Walter runs just like me." Still, some compared us, and I actually took that as a compliment. I even earned the nickname "Sweet P." Not

"Pea" like Sweet Pea from Popeye, but the letter P, for Payton. Walter was Sweetness, and I was Sweet P. I absolutely loved it. I mean, in the NFL, when you're known by a nickname, that means you've arrived. People don't really know what you're about until they know you by your nickname. When other players in the NFL hang a moniker on you, that sets you apart from everybody else; it's really something to wear with pride. Walter and I did just that as Sweetness and Sweet P out there on the fields of the NFL.

You know, when Cleveland first signed me and I made it into the league, people weren't yet calling me Sweet P. I was just a rookie like all the other newcomers. It's funny; I was older than Walter, but I was the rookie, and he was the third-year player. I was at a press conference for the Browns, and all us rookies had to step up to the podium and tell the media who we were. Of course, they all knew who I was already. And I don't mean they knew I was Eddie Payton. No, I mean they knew me as Walter Payton's brother. Well, I didn't exactly see it that way, and I let one particular reporter know all about it. He asked, "Well, how does it feel to be the brother of a superstar?" I came right back at him almost without even thinking about it and said, "I don't know. You'll have to go to Chicago and ask him how it feels." That line became my crowning statement and has been talked about by many. I thought it was a pretty good line, but I know it's been presented by some that I said it out of jealousy, resentment, or spite. Those folks need to get a sense of humor already. You know, if I couldn't be a football player or a teacher or a coach, I might've tried stand-up comedy. I just love cracking jokes, and that's exactly how my response to that reporter's question was intended—as humor. Of course, I'd be lying if I said it wasn't also a dig at the smart-ass reporter who asked such a dumbass question. I mean, "How does it feel to be the brother of a superstar?" Maybe I should have just asked, "How does it feel to be a dumbass?"

Now, I do understand what was behind that question. My brother was becoming a big star in the NFL. While I was waiting to get my shot in the league, Walter was busy casting his shadow on me. I finally made it to the next level of play, only to be standing in the shadow of Sweetness. The worm had turned, as they say, and I was now trying to emerge from his shadow to prove who I was. And you know, that's when I finally understood what it was like for Walter growing up as the little brother. That's when I connected with him in a way I hadn't before. I found myself reflecting on growing up with him, seeing things in a way I wish I could've seen them when we were kids. Everything we'd done growing up had a whole new meaning. Everything he'd talked about when he was a freshman at Jackson State, all his fears and what he wanted to do and what people expected from him... well, I don't think I fully understood all of that until I experienced it myself. I had to make it into the NFL to really get it. I had to put on cleats as a pro before I could know what it was like to be in his shoes. And despite how some have spun my response to that reporter in Cleveland, I embraced being the brother of a superstar. Hell, I even took advantage of it.

When Walter came to Jackson State, he was the freshman and I was the established player telling him how things worked, how you just don't mess with Coach Hill, what he needed to do in practice, and all of that stuff. I'd been there and done that, and I knew how it all worked. I was the big man on campus answering all the questions he had about why we were doing this or that, and what the coaches were looking for. Walter would come to me as a freshman in college and we'd sit up late at night just talking about things like how our other teammates were doing and how Walter could stand out from them. Well, when I came into the NFL, Walter was already there, and our roles had reversed. It was his turn to teach me what I needed to do as a rookie and how to make it in the league. I was now the one calling him up while I was at training camp, asking him what I should be looking for or doing to stand out from the crowd. The little brother was now teaching the big brother the tricks of the trade. And you know, I think the best advice he ever gave me was when he said, "The only thing you need to remember, Eddie, is that you are responsible for your job. It's up to you to do it right, and you can't get away with not doing it right. It's all on film."

He was the one on TV, but he was right that we were both on film. That's how he saw it. I was an NFL player who needed his advice. Sometimes we'd be on the phone, and he'd take time to talk about the other guys who were there at camp with me. We'd talk about who was doing well at the beginning of camp and who wasn't, and how I couldn't be one of the latter. I'd tell him the details of what was going on with all of that and which guys were getting cut, and he'd tell me why they got cut and how I could avoid it. Walter would also point out that at Bears camp, some guys would bring attention to themselves by messin' up, and they'd get released. He'd say you want to build yourself up in camp, start off doing well and each week just get better and better, because they're looking for improvement. The key, he said, was to just keep making progress, no matter how hard you need to work to do that. Oh, and he also mentioned that if you get injured or nicked up, you need to learn how to treat yourself without alerting the training staff. He presented it as inside NFL knowledge, but I think he actually learned that one from Coach Hill and John Ely back at Jackson State. As it turned out, "Too hurt to practice, too hurt to play" applied in the NFL, too.

Some might think it would've been a hard thing for me to take when the roles reversed for Walter and me. But let me remind you that when I was teaching him growing up and on into college, those were just some of the best days of my life. And it's not because he was under me or anything like that. It's because we were bonding through it all. When the roles reversed in the NFL, we were bonding just the same. You see, it's true that he was standing in my shadow growing up and heading into college, and yes, I was standing in his shadow in the NFL. What's important, though, whether I was casting the shadow or Walter was, was that we were standing together. You can't be in another man's shadow without standing right next to him. When we were both in the NFL, the roles were reversed, but we just got closer and closer to each other through it all.

Bud Holmes, Walter's longtime agent, knows more about it than anyone. He has said some very nice things about how I handled being the big brother of a superstar NFL player. He saw firsthand that it wasn't long before my limelight moved toward my little brother. Bud said it was kind of like the new guy coming into town and taking your girlfriend away from you. Perhaps he was right, but he also pointed out that, instead of resenting Walter, all I did was brag and brag on him and promote my little brother, even after I made it to the league myself. Bud tells everybody, "Eddie's attitude was, 'You think I'm good, you ought to see my brother.'" And I don't mind the things he had to say about how I carried the ball as a kick returner, either.

"Eddie Payton, pound for pound, was the better athlete," Bud once said of my skills. "If you could put Walter's frame on Eddie, add those extra pounds to him, he'd have been great, too. Eddie was quicker and faster. It's just that Eddie happened to come along at a time when the rosters in the NFL were short. If teams would've carried the same numbers on the rosters back then as they've got right now, Eddie would've had an even longer career than Walter, because no one has ever been any better in the NFL in the return game."

It's nice to hear those things from a guy who really knows his stuff like Bud does, but it's even nicer to know that Bud saw how Walter's success didn't get me down. In fact, instead of letting it get me down, I was always cheering on my brother. His doing good was like I was doing good, and vice versa. We were one and the same on the field back at Jackson State, but we were also that way generally in life. I loved him. I lauded him. I lifted him up. I wanted him to succeed, and I cheered him on when he did.

"Eddie never indicated to me one iota of resentment or jealously," Bud went on to say. "I never detected it. It would've been so normal to have had it, too. I mean, the Bible is full of it. Cain and Abel, they got to whipping up on each other. But you didn't have any of that with Walter and Eddie; they were always very, very supportive of each other."

My brother was a superstar, yes, but he was so much more than that to me. The reporter in Cleveland asked how it felt to have a superstar as a brother, but he should've just asked, "How do you feel about your brother?" It would've been out of place, but that's a question I would've gladly answered. I mean, Walter Payton was Sweetness to you, but he was my brother above all else to me. And I was his. We saw ourselves as the same, even if the sports reporters didn't.

While we were in the NFL together, Walter and I'd talk every week about what happened during the games, what we could do better, what was going on behind the scenes, and yes, we'd also usually laugh about who did something stupid (and trust me, in the NFL, someone is always doing something stupid). We'd just talk about some of the things that pro football players talk about, and we'd talk about some of the things that pro football players do after a game. You know, what different people did to relax, and the kind of things they'd enjoy off the field. Good or bad. But you know, Walter was a bit of a workaholic and was just obsessed with football at the time. He was different than a lot of other players in that way. He'd go lock himself up in a room after a game and watch other football games. Some other players, like yours truly, would be looking to enjoy what being a professional athlete can get you off the field. While Walter was locked up in that room with the TV, I (for example) would be looking to go lock myself up in a room with a woman…and try to get locked up with her, if you know what I mean. Walter wasn't into all of that. He wasn't a typical pro football player in that way. He was always doing something. He lived a hectic life, but he wasn't into wild living, and he was a one-woman man. I mean, the guy had more temptation in a week than most men have to deal with their whole lives, but he was pretty damn monogamous through it all. No, we weren't together every night (we were on two different football teams), so I can't tell you I saw his every move. I can tell you that we talked all the time, and we knew each other like we were a set of twins. Trust me, he was the good twin.

A lot of people actually never realized just how shy Walter was when he was coming up, from back when he was a kid all the way to when he was a star running back. It sometimes seemed like he had social anxiety disorder and couldn't really deal too well with the type of attention women threw at him. He had no trouble in front of faceless crowds, of course, but he wasn't so good with actual faces. He'd get in front of a big crowd and light up the room. His warm personality would just come out and make its way to everyone in a general sort of way, but one-on-one, he was a mess.

As far as being a womanizer, well, let me tell you that he couldn't have been one. I know some people say he was, and they get a lot of attention for themselves or sell a lot of books and magazines that way, but I'm telling you, as his brother, that Walter was not a womanizer. He just wasn't. You know, a lot of people ask me about Jeff Pearlman's book and all the accusations in there about Walter's womanizing ways, and I tell them that the guy made a mistake. He had Walter and me mixed up. I mean, listen, if somebody said "Payton" was out with three women or whatever, they weren't talking about Walter. They were talking about me. I was flying under the radar, of course, because I wasn't leading the league in rushing like my little brother, but when it came to rushing up to women, I had him beat big time. Whenever I was with Walter out at a party of whatever, probably 100 women would throw themselves at him. But at the end of the night, he'd just go home to Connie. Now, I know that's not headline news because people like to focus on the "dead fish," as I said before, but truth is truth. Walter resisted women far better than any other man I know could've done in his situation. And that, my friends, is the truth.

Of course, when Walter went home to Connie, I often picked up the pieces with the disappointed ladies he left behind. You see, I wasn't monogamous at that time. I didn't have to be because I was single, but still, I was basically a dog. I'll admit it, okay? Walter and I would be at some NFL function together or party of some sort, and women would just throw themselves at him looking for their 15 minutes of Sweetness (if not fame), but I'd be the one who ended up with 'em. To those women rejected by my little brother, I suppose I was the next-best thing. That was just fine by me. Walter would always figure out how to blow 'em off, and I'd always try to figure out how to get a…well, you can figure it out. Let me just say, there were definitely some benefits to standing in the shadow of Sweetness.

Of course, it got to where it didn't matter if I was in Walter's shadow or not. When I went to Kansas City, where I played one year, it was kind of like one continuous orgy. I won't say I'm proud of that, but I will say that's how it was. In Kansas City, just being on the team meant women would just flock to you. It was the damndest thing I've ever seen anywhere in my life. And they'd follow us everywhere. It didn't matter if we were playing at home or away, they'd be there trying to get with us. And let me tell you, they didn't need to try hard. If we were on the road, we'd get in the morning before the game and we'd go out on the field and warm up. Then we'd have our meetings and stuff like that. When we went back to the hotel, those women would already be there in the lobby just hanging around. As a player, you didn't pick them—they picked you. They'd already know our stats, our pictures, our shoe sizes, and some things that even we didn't know about ourselves. They'd all done their homework and knew exactly who they wanted.

There was this one girl I got with who was either Korean or Vietnamese. She had picked out one of our defensive linemen as her target, and she was pursuing him hot and heavy. He kept resisting her advances, though, and kept telling me, "Man, I wish she'd leave me alone. I wish she'd just go away. I don't want nothing to do with her. I've got a girlfriend." I was thinking, *Well…um…do you mind if I uh…?* He and I had become good friends that whole season, until he came over to the house one day to get a game tape and that Korean/Vietnamese girl answered the door. He never spoke to me again. I guess if he couldn't have her, he didn't want anybody to.

It's hard to be monogamous and in the NFL at the same time. I mean, my brother and that defensive lineman are two of the exceptions. But even though Walter shied away from the ladies, one

161

thing he never shied away from was good, clean fun. You already know how much he liked prankin' people, and that carried over to the NFL. How could Walter have so much social anxiety and at the same time be such a prankster? I'm not sure, but I know he never stopped punking people. He'd even go back to Jackson State as a pro and start looking for his next victim. One time that victim was his college coach. I guess once you leave college and become a big star in the NFL and lead the league in rushing and all of that, you've earned the right to mess with Coach Hill.

Coach Hill and Walter kept in touch and would often talk about Jackson State's current players, how they were doing and all of that. One time, Coach unintentionally gave Walter some ammunition for a prank. He told Walter about this one player who had a crazy girlfriend that he needed to get out of his life. Well, Walter was back in Jackson between seasons one year, and he and Brazile got bored (which was always a dangerous thing), so they decided to call up Coach Hill and have a little fun. They waited until about midnight so Coach would be asleep (or at least very tired), and they dialed his number. Coach picked up and Walter told him in a bit of concerned panic, "Coach, look here, this kid got in a fight with his girlfriend that he's been living with. You know, that girl you've been telling me he needs to get rid of? Well, they got into it big time, and they got them down there in the jail."

"Oh Lord," Coach said, seriously calling out to God for help. "Let me get up and go down there."

"Nah, nah, it's all right coach," Walter said, not pushing the prank too far. "We had a little money with us, so it's cool. We got our money together and put up bond, so we got him out."

"Oh man, I appreciate that," Coach said, ready to go back to sleep and to deal with the situation in the morning. "I appreciate y'all doing that for him." Then they hung up the phone and Walter and Brazile laughed and laughed about what was going to happen.

Well, Coach didn't sleep very well after that call and decided to deal with the situation at about 6:00 AM. Coach had this little guy appropriately named Shortman who worked for him, so Coach sent Shortman over to go get this player to come meet him at his house so they could talk about what happened. Well, the kid didn't know anything about anything, of course, because nothing had happened. He was just laid up there in the bed, sound asleep. Shortman knocked on the door until the kid got up and opened it. Shortman went in the room and said, "Look, Coach wants to see you."

"For what?" the kid said, his eyes still squinting out the sleep.

"I don't know. Coach just told me to come get you, so you better get up and go." The kid was still under Coach's control, unlike Walter, and he must have already learned that you don't mess with Coach Hill, because he got right up and went with Shortman.

When they got to Coach Hill's house, Coach started right in on him. Coach asked him to explain what happened, and the kid had no clue what to say. "Now, don't you lie to me," Coach said like a daddy about to give a whoopin'. "I already know what happened last night. Just tell me what's going on." This went on for a while, with Coach asking the kid to explain and the kid saying the whole time he had no idea what Coach was talking about. Finally, Coach believed him and realized that Walter had set the whole thing up. He thought about how he should've seen it coming given Walter's history, and he dreamed about seeing him running laps as punishment. But he knew he couldn't do anything about it. Coach just had to deal with it. Walter got 'em both—killed two birds with one prank. He tricked Coach the worst, but he also got the kid. Coach still won't admit it to this day, but he was punked. And if Walter would punk Coach Hill, well, then no one was immune. Not even his agent.

Bud was out on a pheasant hunting trip one day in North Dakota during Walter's rookie year, right after Bud had gotten him the highest signing bonus for any player ever from Mississippi. Someone from Bud's office drove out to find him in what was basically the middle of nowhere. When they finally got out to where he was and tracked him down, they said to Bud, "We have an emergency—Walter Payton's got to talk to you."

Bud was enjoying his trip and didn't want to deal with anything, but he knew he had to. With a hint of annoyance, he said, "Oh, what is it?"

They said, "Don't know, he wouldn't say. He just said he's got to talk to you and that it's an emergency." Well, there were no cell phones back then, so Bud had to leave what he was doing and drive all the way back to where he could find a phone. When he finally did, he called Walter, thinking, *Yeah, this better be an emergency.* Bud said, "Walter, what's up?"

"Well, I quit," Walter stated, almost in a pouty sort of way.

"What?" Bud couldn't believe what he was hearing and had no idea how to respond.

"Yeah, that's right. I quit. They got me out there at that practice, and they're trying to tell me to do things and stuff. They want me to do this and that and whatever. I just can't put up with it. I don't need this shit. So…I quit. I'm done with it. I've already gone home."

"Walter, come on, man," Bud said, trying to reason with him.

"Nah, I quit."

"I tell you what, Walter…" Bud said, not sure what he'd say next. It didn't matter anyway because Walter cut him off.

"Nah, I quit. That's it. I'll just do something else. I'm just not going to put up with it."

"Come on, Walter. Look, here's what I'll do. I'll change clothes, and I'll catch a flight out of here." Bud was up around Bismarck, pretty far away from the problem at hand. "So, I'll get a flight, and I can meet you over there. Just meet me in Chicago, okay? I'll just meet you over there."

"No, I ain't going to do it," Walter said emphatically.

Bud was shocked and confused. "Why not?"

"Because, I just ain't going to do it."

"You're telling me you're not going to do what I tell you?"

"Uh-huh."

Bud was getting frustrated. "You ain't going to mind me? Your agent? Haven't you learned your lesson on that? When the hell did you get so damn big that now you don't do what I say?"

Walter continued on, "Nah, I ain't going to go to Chicago."

Bud begged and pleaded, trying everything to get Walter to meet him in Chicago. "Come on, Walter," he tried one last time. "What the hell is wrong? How come you won't just meet me in Chicago so we can handle this?"

Walter then decided to let Bud off the hook. "Because I'm already here. I ain't going to meet you here 'cause I'm already here."

Bud was confused. "Huh?"

Walter laughed as he followed it up and said, in his signature playful way, "Yeah, I knew I could get you. I knew I'd get you out of the woods. They told me I couldn't get you out of the woods, but I told 'em I bet I could. Well, I won my bet." It didn't even matter who "they" were; Bud had been had. And Walter just laughed his pants off about it.

Bud was a good sport about it, and that wasn't the only time Walter pranked Bud. I wouldn't say Walter was a drinking man, but he sure did love him some Bud. When he wasn't pulling tricks on him, Walter would even go down to Bud's farm to train for training camp. Bud's farm really became Walter's home away from home, and Bud became his second father. Of course, Bud knew that if they ever got into it as "father" and "son," Walter would be the one whoopin' ass. He was as strong as an ox and a workout fiend in those days. His body was just unbelievable, like a sculpted piece of art—chiseled muscles everywhere. I'd go with Walter to Bud's farm sometimes to work out, too, but Walter would stay longer and train harder than I did. The man was more obsessed with hard work and being in better shape than anyone in the league; I couldn't keep up with that. I was just Sweet P, so how could I? Walter always said to me, "I want to be in the best shape of anybody on the team. If I'm the key person, then I got to set the pace and be the example." He was the key person for the Bears, that's for sure, and he definitely set the pace in terms of physical conditioning. No doubt about that, even if there was some doubt as to his sanity. I mean, his workouts were just plain insane.

He'd sometimes wait until the hottest part of the day, probably about 11:30 AM or so, and he'd go over to Southern Mississippi's stadium in Hattiesburg—about 20 minutes from Bud's farm. There was never any media out watching him, and very few people knew he was there. If they did, they probably would've all come out and seen the craziest workout of their lives. For three hours, from about 11:30 until about 2:30, he'd just run that stadium like it really meant something. He'd never slow down. Not a bit for the whole three hours. He'd just run, run, run…and run some more. When he finished, he'd go take a shower and get in the whirlpool and go back to Bud's farm to take a nap. Then after just a bit of shut-eye, another crazy (he'd call it "fun") workout would begin. Walter would dress up in camo pants and army boots and he'd take Bud's gun from Vietnam out into the woods with him. For the rest of the day, Sweetness would play Rambo. That crazy brother of mine would go all over the farm by himself, running up and down old ditches, and jump across the creek with that gun. He'd get down and hide for a few seconds, then belly crawl out like he was trying to elude the enemy. I was happy to know that some of what I taught my kid brother back in our plum-poaching days stuck with him all that time. Anyway, if you saw him out there, you'd think he was trying to take Hamburger Hill. To Walter, it was great fun. To me, it was a crazy-ass workout. To you, it might sound just plain crazy. But in all seriousness, there wasn't a six-year-old boy who enjoyed that shit more than he did. It was a dream come true for Walter to be in the NFL, but I think his favorite moments during his football career were those Rambo workouts on Bud's farm.

My brother worked so hard for his dream that a lot of people would say it was a nightmare. Those people just don't understand the level of dedication and commitment it takes to make it in pro football. The thing I try to tell young people now (well, the ones who will listen, anyway) is that if you have a dream and believe in yourself, just don't ever give up on your dream and don't ever stop believing. Most importantly, don't ever stop working crazy hard. Do whatever it takes. Because what you may view as a mountain to climb or an impossible fence to get over is just preparing you for what you're going to have to do when your dream presents itself as reality. Believe the impossible and work impossibly hard. That's what it takes.

I know most people probably think I couldn't hold a candle to my brother, and that's okay. As for me, I never once doubted that I was as good a running back as No. 34. You have to think about yourself like that or you won't make it. I just had to wait for somebody to give me a chance, and when that chance came, I proved that my running can give cavities, too. Sweetness wasn't the only Payton sending people to the dentist. Sweet P was also out there bringing the sugary funk. It's just that I was too small to be remembered.

Walter was listed as 5'11", and the 5'10"/5'11" players got a lot more attention than us little guys. Shoot, there weren't even a lot of 5'7" guys like me in the league at all at that time. We were few and far between. And those of us who were in the league didn't get a fair shot at running back because of our size. We were all fully capable runners—people like Noland Smith, "White Shoes" Johnson, Mike Garrett, guys like that—but we were labeled as specialists. Howard Stevens played for the Saints at the time, and he was like 5'5", so there was no chance he was going to carry the ball. All of us little guys returned kicks. I guess 5'8" and under kind of became the ideal size for kick returners, at least in the minds of the coaches. That's what they asked us to do, and that's what we did. They were the ones signing our paychecks, and we were determined to get paid. Even today, though, I think most kick returners are either frustrated running backs or frustrated receivers. They're not getting their shot at their natural or desired positions for whatever reason (maybe even reasons they have no control over, like size), but they are good enough athletes to help a team.

I helped the Detroit Lions for two great seasons. I was so good returning kicks that they didn't just pay me...they paid me more. Things were looking good for Sweet P. Then they went and changed coaches. They brought in Monte Clark as the head coach, and the next thing I knew, I was on a plane for Kansas City. The new guy up and traded me to the Chiefs for the 1978 season. It was good for the Chiefs and for all those women waiting for me in Kansas City, but I wasn't sure about the place at first. Still, I gave it my all, both in the bed and on the field. I finished fourth in the AFC in punt returns and fourth in the AFC in kickoff returns. I was on my third team, yes, but I couldn't complain. I was still in the NFL, playing with my brother. Things were going well for us Payton boys. Then, the week before our last game of the season, I got a phone call that turned our family's world upside down.

CHAPTER 10

Thinkin' What-Ifs

On Monday, December 11, 1978, I was just sitting in my place in Kansas City, trying to relax after a hard practice with the Chiefs. We had just gotten our butts kicked by the Denver Broncos the day before, and the coaches made us pay for it on Monday. Though the Chiefs and the Bears found themselves in the same position (with one game left in the season, neither team would be going to postseason play), Walter probably had an easier Monday than I did because the Bears had played at home against Green Bay and won that game 14–0. They had no trouble running all over the Packers. Walter had 97 yards on the ground, another 13 through the air, and he scored one rushing touchdown. Just another day at the office for Sweetness. But that Monday wouldn't be just another day of any sort for Walter and me. While I was recovering from practice, the phone rang. I ignored my tired legs and got up to answer it. My brother-in-law was on the other end and he wasn't calling to see if I was doing all right after the Broncos beatdown. "Hey, Eddie," he said, "I have some bad news for you."

That's not something you ever want to hear when you pick up the phone, but I was curious. "Oh yeah?" I asked. "What's up?"

"It's your father. He...uh...he died."

I don't think I even believed it at first, but I knew my brother-in-law wouldn't be telling me this if it wasn't true. Shoot, even Walter—prankster extraordinaire himself—wouldn't joke about something as serious as this. "Whoa, whoa," I responded before steadying myself. "What!?!" Then I was silent. I didn't know what to say after that. I felt like I'd been punched in the gut. I was devastated. It felt as though *I* had died. After all, I was Daddy's look-alike. Bud even said recently that Daddy looked a lot like I do today. "[You] were even the same size," Bud added, "and really mirrored each other." I found myself just holding the phone, wondering what had happened and how I was going to deal with losing Daddy. Then I stopped thinking about myself and started talking again. "How's Momma?" I asked my brother-in-law.

"She's all right, man," he said, not telling me the truth. Momma was right there with him and snatched the phone. Of course, I expected her to be upset since it had just happened and all, but she was more than upset. Momma was nothing short of hysterical. Even angry. "Eddie," she yelled into the phone, "they killed your daddy!"

I didn't know what to do with what I was hearing. I had no idea how to respond to Momma's words. *What did she mean by that? They killed him? Who killed him?* The room was spinning, and then my brother-in-law got the phone back.

"Hey, man," he said.

I pulled myself together and got the room standing still again. "Look, I'll be there tomorrow," I said. "Just take care of Momma."

I hung up the phone and immediately called my brother. Walter had already gotten the same call from my brother-in-law, so he'd heard the bad news. He was as shocked and unprepared for it as I was. We spent a few moments in stunned silence together on the phone, both standing in the shadow of our fallen father. Walter broke the silence by saying Bud was already making plans to pick us both up. You could always count on Bud, especially in times like that.

The next 24 hours were sort of crazy for me. They all ran together in a big blur. I got up in the morning and went to the Chiefs' headquarters to tell coach Marv Levy that my father had died and that I needed to go take care of family business. He said that was fine, of course, and that if I got back before our last game of the season to just let him know, or I could just join the team in Seattle for that final game. He also said if I needed to miss the game altogether, he would understand. It was great to have a coach who understood what was most important in this life. Football is football, and family is family. The two don't even compare. And we weren't just talking about family here. We were talking about Daddy.

I'd had uncles and aunts who'd died before, but Daddy was the first immediate family member I ever lost. My daddy, Peter Payton, was gone. *How could it be? He wasn't more than 52 or 53. That's just way too young!*

Now, I'm not a drinker and wasn't back then, either, but I needed a drink to cope with all that was happening. I called a friend of mine because I just needed to be around another human being while I waited for Walter and Bud to pick me up the next day. My friend came right over, and I broke down. She fixed me a drink, and it definitely helped ease the pain a little. I got woozy and fell asleep (that drink was probably the only way I would've been able to sleep at all that night), and got up the next morning haunted by Momma's words once again. I kept hearing her voice over and over in my head. "They killed your daddy." I was desperate for answers, and soon Bud would give them to me.

I really can't say enough nice things about Bud Holmes and how much he cared for all of us Paytons like we were his family. As soon as he found out Daddy had died, he dropped what he was doing and flew his personal plane, at his expense, out on that Tuesday to pick up Walter in Chicago. Then they came to Kansas City to pick me up. During the flight, Walter and I didn't say much. We just let Bud explain as much as he could about what happened. Bud had already started his investigation and talked to a number of people the night before, finding out as much as he could about what went down. Though he didn't yet know how Daddy died, he told us what he did know.

Daddy and Momma had a beautiful little garden about three miles up the street from their house on a small piece of property they'd bought. They called it their "plantation" and simply adored the place. Daddy worked at it real hard and spent as much time as he could tending to that garden. Bud explained to us that on his way to check on the garden on Monday, Daddy stopped by a small service station and got himself some beer. He was planning on going to the garden and drinking a beer or two while he worked. Just like a lot of other normal guys, Daddy's four favorite things (outside of Momma and us kids) were hunting, gardening, fishing, and, yes, drinking a few beers every now and again. He mainly liked to drink on the weekends with his friends, just sitting in a rocking chair and shootin' the breeze. But he wasn't a drunk by any stretch of the imagination. He just had a beer or two every now and then, and that's what he had that day while he worked that beloved garden of his. Just a beer or two.

On his way back home from the garden, Daddy must've noticed he was low on gas, because he pulled up to that same station to fill up. He'd gone inside to pay and talked to the girl at the counter, who later said he was slurring his words. Everybody knew my daddy, and this girl could tell something was off about him that day. She figured he'd been drinking too much and later said she told him, "Now, Pete, you need to go on home." From what Bud was telling us, Daddy staggered around a little bit after that, got in his truck, and promptly backed into another vehicle. The people hanging around the station were obviously surprised by that and started asking Daddy things like, "Pete, what's the matter with you?" Then someone called the police.

Daddy didn't know what was going on, and when the police arrived, they immediately thought he was drunk. Some of the folks there that day told Bud that the police said to Daddy, "Pete, you better let us take you down to the station. You don't need to be hurting anybody or hurting yourself, and you know you're not capable of driving." Daddy stumbled around some more before collapsing to the pavement. The cops were convinced at that point that Daddy was stone-cold drunk, so they picked him up, put him in the police car, and took him down to jail. They didn't give him a sobriety or breathalyzer test or anything like that. They thought they'd seen enough and didn't think they needed to mess with all that, so they just took Daddy to jail. Well, Bud said once they got him to jail, Daddy had a seizure. Eventually, the police took him to the hospital, and then he died. That was all he knew at that point.

What he didn't know was that earlier in the day, Momma was driving home from Chicago where she'd been to watch the Bears play against Green Bay. Daddy had yet to stop by the service station where he'd begin his fatal downward spiral. Pam had previously begged Daddy to go to the game with Momma, because we didn't like Momma traveling on her own, but he didn't want to go. Like I said, he simply loved his garden and really just wanted to spend his Sunday out there working it. So, Pam made sure that our close family friends, Bertha Brewer and Johnny Hale, went with Momma to the game.

On their way home from Chicago, Momma's main concern was making it back to Jackson by 9:00 PM Monday night. As you know, Walter had a good game, and Momma was hoping to catch the news on WGN (a nationally broadcast Chicago station) so she could watch the highlights from the Bears game. She was getting frustrated because, according to her, Johnny was driving too slowly. He was just kind of taking it easy, not fast enough for Momma's liking, so she made him pull over so she could take the wheel and get a move on it. Hey, what can I say? That's our momma! Where do you think Walter and I got all that get-up-and-go? Anyway, thanks to Momma's NASCAR-worthy driving, they made it to a friend's house in Jackson in time to watch the news. After she saw her baby boy on TV running all over the Packers again, Momma, Bertha, and Johnny got back in the car and went on to Columbia. As soon as they got home, Daddy's sister came running out of the house to meet them. It was late, so they knew something was wrong. Daddy's sister was frantically repeating, "They put Peter in jail!"

Momma was quite surprised to hear that, to say the least. "Put him in jail?" Momma asked.

"Yes, Ma'am," my daddy's sister said.

"For what?"

"They say he was drunk."

Momma immediately knew there had to have been a mistake. "Oh no, he couldn't have been drunk. I know him better than that," Momma said. "I've never seen him drunk. No, no, he wasn't drunk."

Daddy's sister already knew that about Daddy, but she wasn't sure what to think about what the police had told her. "Well, they say that he was staggering and couldn't talk," she continued. "When they were taking him to the police station...when he went to get out of his truck, they say he fell out onto the ground, and they think he was drunk, so they carried him out and put him in jail. They put him in jail, Alyne!"

Well, Momma wasn't convinced. She knew her husband better than anyone, and he wasn't a drunk. Johnny got out of the car and stayed with Daddy's sister while Momma and Bertha jumped back in to go downtown to the police station to sort it all out. When Momma

Payton showed up, she wanted some answers…and right quick. The police told Momma that Daddy had indeed been staggering and that they just locked him up for his own protection. Momma started right in with them and said, "No, no, no, he wasn't drunk, he couldn't have been drunk. He doesn't drink that much. He might've had a beer or two maybe, but that's all!"

Just like everyone else in the area, the police all knew and respected Momma and Daddy, so they listened to Momma and went to the cell where Daddy was lying on the bed to see if maybe he was coherent enough at that point to talk. Well, he wasn't. The police arrived at his cell to discover he'd had a seizure. They came scrambling back out to get a patrol car and see Momma and said they were taking Daddy to the hospital. Momma was floored. *The hospital? What was going on?* Momma knew at that point that something very wrong was afoot. She said they then loaded Daddy into a patrol car and took him to the hospital. Momma and Bertha got back into their car and actually beat the police to the hospital. I guess Momma was driving. Well, that trip to the hospital would be the last trip Daddy would take alive, and Momma didn't even get to see him.

"We got out there," Momma remembered, "and they wouldn't even let us sit in the waiting room. They said, 'He ain't made it here yet. We're looking for a sick patient and y'all can't stay in here.' So, they moved us to another room. I think it's because they knew he was already going to be dead when they brought him through there, and didn't want me seeing him. They never did let me see him."

So, after a little while of waiting in the other room, one of the black policemen came in and told Momma that Daddy had passed on. I think that officer knew even back at the station that Daddy was already well on his way to being dead. Momma stayed at the hospital until 2:00 AM, waiting and hoping and praying that somehow they'd be able to revive him. The doctor working on Daddy later said he did everything he could but that, in the end, there really was nothing he could do. He told Momma that night that Daddy probably had a heart attack. He was gone.

The next day, Bud took Walter and me to the hospital, along with a board-certified pathologist he knew. Bud went in to observe the autopsy on Daddy while Walter and I waited outside. Everybody was assuming he'd had a heart attack, because of what that doctor told Momma. There was no indication of any outside trauma or anything, so that's what they thought it was. Turned out to be a guess, though, and not a very good one. Bud said they opened Daddy's chest, pulled out all the vital organs, and got into the heart. They started dissecting it and looked closely at all the tissue. "They couldn't believe how clean his arteries were, like an 18-year-old or something," Bud said of the doctors' response to seeing Daddy's heart. They were just amazed by it. There was no problem with the aorta or the pulmonary arteries going out to the lungs or anything at all. Everything was perfectly clear. Once they realized it couldn't have been a heart attack, Bud said they were going back and forth with each other, finally agreeing the only things they thought it could be was some kind of a stroke or some issue in his brain. What Bud said happened next is a little on the gross side, so you might want to skip ahead a little if you don't have a strong stomach for this sort of thing.

"So, [the coroner] cut the top of the skull," Bud described, "and lifted off the skull plate and looked at the brain. He started slicing, and sure enough there was a big ol' thing in there about fist-sized, bigger than a goose egg. It was an aneurysm, which I was told is a weakening of the walls of the artery that enlarge until they basically explode or start leaking. When they got into the aneurysm, there were a bunch of white, wormlike things. They said it was protein. It takes so many hours or days for it to build up like that, and then it just bursts or leaks."

The doctor told Bud that Daddy had developed a small leakage deep in his brain. It slowly grew and grew over time and reached its peak on that Monday. I later learned that the symptoms of a brain aneurysm often make it seem like a person is dealing with other problems, such as intoxication or diabetes. For Daddy, it started putting pressure on the sensory nerves that go to the tongue, the mouth, and control a person's equilibrium. That made it so he couldn't really talk, and it caused him to lose his balance and stagger around like he did in front of the cops. It gave him the appearance of being drunk. So, Momma was right and the cops were wrong. Daddy wasn't drunk. It was a brain aneurysm.

Walter and I were just outside the autopsy room while Bud was in there getting all the info. We didn't want to see them cutting open our daddy. Once the autopsy was over, though, Bud asked us to come on inside and look at Daddy's brain so we could see the evidence for ourselves. He didn't want there to be any question in our minds as to what had happened, about how and why Daddy died. We'd all been hearing rumors, and Bud wanted to put those to rest, at least for us. Neither of us wanted to go inside, so we refused the offer. No way did I want to remember my father that way. We accepted what the professionals had found. It took Momma a little longer to acknowledge it. She was hurting and confused, and people were telling her all sorts of things.

Some of the people in town were saying things like, "Well, ya know, they let him die in there. They abused him and killed him." But given what happens with a brain aneurysm, I really don't think anyone could've done anything for him. Daddy could've died in the booking cell, in the holding cell, or on the way to the jail. It was entirely up to the progression of the aneurysm and had nothing to do with the cops. Still, as seems to happen a lot, people who didn't really know anything and who weren't privy to the facts just speculated about what had happened to Daddy. People were telling Momma they killed him in jail, and she was just clinging to whatever she could. Hell, people to this day still think he died in jail. He was *dying* in jail, yes, but I'm convinced he actually died on the way to the hospital.

We had all sorts of people saying we should've sued the city. But when Walter and I found out the nuts and bolts of the issue after that autopsy, we knew we weren't going to be suing anyone. We accepted the facts and moved on to grieving. Of course, that's not to say little things didn't creep into our minds here and there. I mean, even when you know something for sure and you can understand what happened, when you're talking about losing your daddy or someone close like that, you always have a few what-ifs that come along. You know, what if they'd gotten him to the doctor faster? What if they hadn't just jumped to thinking he was drunk? What if they'd given him a breathalyzer or something to be sure? I mean, there are a lot of what-ifs that will just drive you crazy if you let them, but I've had to just look past them. Listen, Columbia is my hometown, and I grew up with the people there, and I knew most of them, black and white. They're all good people down there. Walter and I were a source of pride for the folks of Columbia, too, so the feeling was mutual. They all knew our parents. Even the cops did. No one would have killed our daddy.

Momma wasn't able to accept the facts as easily as I did, and she still harbors a few what-ifs about the whole thing to this very day. That's why when she goes back to see some friends, to her, it's sort of like Columbia's not her hometown anymore. I moved her out to Jackson in the later part of 1980 so she could be closer to my sister Pam and me, and she eases on down to Columbia every once in a while to visit for a wedding or a funeral. But she doesn't really *like* going back. I guess there's still an edge from what happened with Daddy, and she just can't kick those what-ifs. But hey, that's okay. If anyone in this world is allowed to have questions about what happened to my daddy, it's my momma. I mean, Peter Payton was our father, but he was the love of Momma's life.

Momma has certainly been able to deal with it better and better over time. She recently shared: "I had five doctors say that if the police had carried Pete straight to the hospital, he wouldn't have lived anyway. When that aneurysm hit him, it covered his brain, and that's what killed him. He had a brain aneurysm, and he had it for a while. It just all of a sudden came on when he was trying to get home. It was just his time. The Lord called him to his real home."

To me, there wasn't really ever a controversy surrounding Daddy's death. After a couple of days, things settled down a bit in town, and people stopped spreading the crazy conspiracy stuff. And you know, I can't really blame them for saying those things to begin with. In a town like Columbia, Daddy knew everybody, and sometimes rumors get started about people who know everybody. Also, having two sons who were playing football in the NFL kept all of us under the microscope, and that probably made it easier for people to about Daddy's death and to get rumors going. You know, "Hey, did you hear they killed Eddie and Walter Payton's daddy?" Stuff like that. So, I don't really blame the people of Columbia, especially since they all squashed it pretty quickly. Now, I can't say the same for the media.

Shortly after the autopsy, there were a bunch of media types from Chicago hanging around Columbia. There were all kinds of folks camping out at the Payton house, hoping to get the inside scoop about how "they killed Daddy in jail." It didn't help that some of the family were hanging around the house and adding fuel to the fire. Bud drove up to the house at one point, and some of the family pointed toward him and told the media, "Hey, look…there's Bud Holmes. He's our lawyer! He's here to represent us, and we're going to sue the city over Pete's death."

The media did what the media does, and they came right over to put microphones in Bud's face. Some of the family and some of the other folks in town had been talking about all this stuff that happened down there at the jail as if it were fact, and the media had overheard a thing or two. They wanted Bud to answer some questions. They said something to him about hearing the cops had beaten Daddy up because he was black and they were white. Some of the media were trying to make it a racial thing. Knowing the facts, though, and being from Mississippi unlike those media people, Bud took offense.

Bud responded by saying, "Okay, I need your name, because the grand jury is going to be convened, and they're going to want to call you before the grand jury so you can bring all of this evidence you're collecting to back up what you're saying." They didn't really like hearing that and didn't know how to come back at it. After some awkward silence, Bud said, "What? Don't y'all have some evidence to back up what you're saying? Hell, the grand jury will want to hear it, and I'll see to it that they do. I'll get us an attorney, and we'll have a federal grand jury convene and come down here, okay?" Talking to all those still trying to kick up dust with their words, Bud continued, "I want y'all to be sure to come before the grand jury since you're saying all these things. Of course, if they aren't true, well, there are things called contempt of court and obstruction of justice we'll have to deal with. Minor details like that. If you know something, we want to hear it. But if you don't know it, let's don't be spreading false rumors, okay?" There was a lot of "I heard this happened," or "I heard that happened" going around at the time. Bud would tell them to tell him who they heard it from, and they always gave him the same response. "Well, I can't remember."

Bud agrees with me that all these conspiracy theories came about because it was happening in Mississippi. Still, Bud told the Chicago media camping at our house that "We have better justice here than y'all have up in Chicago." If they had some evidence, Bud wanted to hear it and would've been the first to do something about it. Of all the lawyers in the world, Bud would've been the last one to let someone get away with doing something to our daddy. But all his inquiries for real evidence prompted nothing. Some of the other family members told him, "Hey, I got this lawyer in Jackson who wants to represent the family and help you sue everybody." Bud said, "That's great, have at it. Tell him I'll be glad to come testify. He ain't gonna like what I say, but he ain't got to subpoena me to testify, either, because I damn sure conducted an investigation down here. But if he's got some evidence that I'm not aware of, maybe I didn't do a good enough job of investigating." Nothing ever came of any of it, so I guess the evidence was never there.

And as for the media, Bud knew they were just going after a story like they always do. The facts weren't as juicy as the rumors, so it was hard to get the media to move away from all that. Bud would later say, "To Eddie, Walter, and Alyne's credit, they didn't foster any of it. They didn't spread any rumors. It'd have been easy for them to say, 'They killed my poor daddy because he was black and they were white.' That'd have been the easy thing to say. And you know, even now, Eddie is the epitome of what I think brings about the great, great relationships that we have in our racial community down here in Mississippi." Bud really appreciated the way Momma, Walter, and I didn't jump all over the race thing and try to make a fuss where there wasn't one. "I'll put our racial relationship in Mississippi above any other state in the United States," Bud said. "We get together down here. We share a genuine love and respect for each other."

Now, ain't that the truth.

Walter sure did preach truth at Daddy's funeral. People were crying and squalling and having a real hard time with it all, but Walter was more composed than ever before. I was so proud of him up there. He got up and talked to all those people, and he told them that if Daddy were still there, he'd have wanted them to celebrate his life and be happy living theirs. There weren't any tears from my baby brother, and not because he wasn't sad. There weren't any tears because he knew that's how Daddy would've wanted it. After the funeral, I was talking to Walter about what he said, and we agreed that something else Daddy would've wanted was for his two boys to go back to work. The funeral was on Thursday, so on Friday, Bud flew Walter back to Chicago and took me back to Kansas City for our final games of the 1978 season. Daddy would've wanted it that way, and we were going to honor his memory by giving him what he wanted. We also gave him a bunch of yards (Walter rushing the ball and me returning it) and another touchdown from my baby brother. And then, we both flew back home to look after Momma. We came home out of our love for her, of course, but that wasn't the only love bringing us back. You see, Daddy loved our momma more than anyone. It was largely his love for her that called us home. He would have wanted us to be happy and go on living. He would have wanted us to keep playing football, which we did. But, when the season was over, Walter and I went back to Columbia to look after our dear momma because, well, that's what Daddy would have wanted most of all.

CHAPTER 11

Runnin' Against Time

Momma missed Daddy in a big, big way. Without him around, Walter and I were the men in her life. She wanted to see us as much as possible, but to do that, she had to come to most of our games. It was a logistical nightmare at times with us being on different teams and all, but she was a real trouper and was determined to make it happen. Of course, we made it easier on her by paying for the travel. Walter and I had a good system in place for that. If she came to my game, I'd buy her plane ticket. If she went to Walter's game, he'd buy her ticket. If our teams played each other in the same game, the losing Payton would cover her ticket. Not that we needed it, but that gave us each a little extra incentive to win.

During my rookie year, when I was with the Lions, we played Walter and his Bears on Thanksgiving Day in Detroit. The Lions flew Momma in for the game. She was in the parade and even got the key to the city, so it was a real fun time for her. For the first half of the game, she sat on the Bears' side, and for the second half she sat on the Lions' side.

So, I like to think she started out rooting for Walter and the Bears, but in the end she really wanted me and the Lions to win. Really, though, she cheered for us equally. She treated us equally. And what's crazy is, on that day, she saw her boys run equally. Walter rushed for 137 yards, and I returned kicks for—yep, you guessed it—137 yards. Momma got to see us each run exactly the same distance in that Thanksgiving Day game. We didn't plan it that way, but maybe someone did.

Of course, Momma wasn't always around, so I spent the rest of my time in the NFL taking full advantage of all the fringe benefits it had to offer. For somebody with a libido like mine, the NFL isn't a good environment. Or maybe I should say, it's not a good environment in which to be good. After they retire, players are often asked what they miss most about the NFL, and the guys will say all sorts of things. They often say they miss the camaraderie with their teammates or the exhilaration of running out on the field in front of thousands of people (millions on TV) or the money they made or blah, blah, blah. If they'd tell the truth, though, I bet 95 percent of 'em would say they missed the smorgasbord of beautiful, sexy women crowding around them day and night. They're in every city you play in, everywhere you go. There're women who'll give their right arm just to be seen in the presence of an NFL player, and they'll give more than that to be in the presence of an NFL star. I ain't talking about no dogs, either; I'm talking about 9s and 10s. These are the kind of women you're proud to be seen with. And it was just too easy to get them.

You'd be out with one woman, and another would be sending you notes from the other side of the table. Or if you were out on a date and got into an argument or something, the girl you're with would always have girlfriends hanging out in the room. Though they weren't dogs, like I said, they did run in packs. Well, one of those girlfriends would come over to see what was going on, and if y'all were still fighting, that girlfriend would offer herself to you as a replacement. Things sure did get complicated for me a time or two thanks to the nonstop flow of irresistible women.

Now, I say "irresistible" as a figure of speech, not because no one could resist them. Walter could resist them much better than most. People talk about Walter as a womanizer, but the truth is he was kind of sanctified compared to other NFL players, including yours truly. We were equals in the eyes of our momma, like I said, but we certainly weren't equals when it came to womanizing. He knew how to say no. Me? Well, I'd open my mouth with the intent of saying no, and it just wouldn't come out. I often meant to say no, but I guess I just felt like I'd be letting somebody down if I didn't say yes. You know, like I was supposed to be living the life that every other guy out there dreamed of living. Walter just didn't think the way I did when it came to all of that. Walter's nightlife as an NFL player was boring compared to mine. He wanted to be a good football player, but he mostly wanted to be a good husband and a good father. And if I ever envied him for anything, it was for that. I never really felt like I wanted to be like Walter in the game of football, but it sure wouldn't have hurt to have been a little more like him in the game of life. People like Walter are unique in the NFL. Guys like him are out there trying to find that one person who will make them whole, while the rest of us are out there trying to find that one-night stand. Walter was a family man from the get-go, but it took me until I got out of the league to settle down, have kids, and watch them grow up.

I went into the league married, but got divorced after the first year. Then I ran wild, more off the field than on, for about eight years. I guess I was just young and enjoying the spoils of who I was… or who I thought I was. And you know, though I don't really regret the things I did (I mean, nobody got hurt), I do regret the fact that I missed watching my first two kids growing up. I was just never there; I was always away playing football, golf, baseball, or fishing. Later in life, I found someone who'd put up with my shit, so I got married again and have enjoyed watching our kids grow up. (I actually get to coach my daughter now as she's on the Jackson State girl's golf team.) But for a while there, it was all about the NFL life for me.

I was only able to enjoy all those women in Kansas City for one year. That's when the team cut me. Then I was out of the NFL for a year during the 1979 season, but I sure kept playing football. Right after my release from the Chiefs, Forrest Gregg, who was my head coach at Cleveland, called me up. He was out of the NFL, too, coaching the Toronto Argonauts in the CFL, and he needed a return specialist. So I was like, "Yeah, where do I sign?" I packed up all my things just like that and headed to Toronto. I got a big bonus for signing, too, so it was a good deal all the way around. I wasn't in the NFL enjoying all the women that come along with it, but those Canadian women were awfully sweet, and I was still getting paid to play football.

While I was playing in Canada, Walter was in "the States" (it took a while to get used to everyone up in Canada calling it that) having one of his best years to date, running up and down NFL fields week after week. He won the rushing crown that season by carrying the ball 369 times for 1,610 yards. That sort of yardage total is mind-boggling even for today's juiced-up league, but that wasn't even Walter's best year. He had 1,852 yards in 1977 and 1,684 yards in 1984. His highest touchdown total was 14, which he reached twice. One of those 14-touchdown seasons came while I was in Canada. Oh, and he added 31 catches for 313 yards that season to boot.

I was in Toronto for a year, and then I came home, because I got sick with a terrible case of the flu. Or maybe it was "Eh" fever. Who really knows? Regardless, I was happy to be back in "the States" and even happier when the Vikings became the fourth NFL team interested in my services. I was on the move yet again, and though I was headed north this time, at least I was going to be south of the CFL.

Minnesota was a great place to play. As a bonus, I was reunited with Rickey Young (a teammate at Jackson State, if you'll recall), who'd been with the Vikings since 1978 when he was traded from San Diego to Minnesota. So when we played the Bears, it felt like me and Rickey against Walter in a Jackson State scrimmage. And me and Rickey had the better team at that time.

Before 1982, when the Bears finally got a good quarterback (more on that in a bit), it was basically just Walter left, Walter right, Walter day, and Walter night. There was nothing but Sweetness every which way pretty much from 1976 to 1981. He gained over 1,000 yards and made the Pro Bowl each of those seasons but one. He was taking a beating, though, and he couldn't win games by himself. My first year with Minnesota, we played the Bears at Soldier Field in 1980, and we kicked their butts 34–14. Our defense held Walter to 39 yards on 16 carries (less than 2.5 yards per carry). And big brother actually had more total yards in the game than he did. Walter had 53 yards, including receiving yards, while I returned five punts and one kickoff for a total of 61 yards. But it wasn't Walter's fault. He was running behind a patchwork, inexperienced offensive line, and he was frustrated.

After that game, I was hanging out with my brother, and he complained all night about the bad mistakes the Bears were making. It was all truth, too. As talented as Walter was, he couldn't run through holes that just weren't there, and he couldn't keep the offense from sputtering when he didn't get the ball. "We're going to get rid of some of these guys who're making all these mistakes," he finally said, "and we're going to come up with a passing game." Most guys would think a player as good as Walter would actually want to be the whole offense, but that just wasn't the way he saw it. Just like at Jackson State, he wanted to win above all else, so he knew the Bears needed an attention-grabbing passing game.

I just smiled and gave my baby brother a little jab. "As long as y'all keep playing like that," I said, "we're gonna keep beating you." And sure enough, we beat them again later that year, though I do have to admit it was closer. We got them 13–7 in a defensive struggle, but Walter wasn't held in check this time. He got 102 yards of the Bears' 161 yards rushing. I didn't do as well in that one, gaining just 38 yards on one kick return and four punt returns. Oh well. I guess that's why they say "Scoreboard!"

Fortunately for me and the Vikings, we ended up with the high number on the scoreboard in two out of the remaining three head-to-head games we had against the Bears in my time there. Our defense keyed in on Walter every time, and we were able to hold him under 100 yards in three of the five games we played against each other. The very last time Walter and I stood on opposite sidelines was in 1982, and I'll never forget it. It was one of the best victories I was a part of in the NFL. The Bears and Vikings only played once that year because of a 57-day players' strike, and the Bears were simply dismal in that game. We crushed them 35–7. It felt good for me and my teammates, but things were about to change in Chicago. Walter wouldn't be frustrated for much longer. He was about to get his wish…even if he thought it was a curse at first.

When the Bears drafted Jim McMahon in the 1982 draft, I'm not sure any of them knew what they were getting. They found out, though, when McMahon showed up to his first press conference in a big ol' white limousine. He got out of that thing wearing a white fur coat and tokin' on a long cigarette holder. He looked like the front man for some glam rock band, not the quarterback of the Chicago

Bears. I remember everybody in the league thinking, *Is this guy for real?* Walter was no exception.

Walter called me up shortly after that press conference, and he was raising himself a little hell. He couldn't believe this was the guy they brought in to turn the passing game around. "Man, we wasted a draft choice!" he shouted through the phone. "We've needed a quarterback for so long, and they draft this idiot?!" Walter wasn't happy. I just let him vent until he calmed down and said good-bye. Then one night I was sleeping when the phone woke me up. It was Walter calling again after the Bears played in San Diego, only this time he was singing a different tune. It turned out to be sort of like a glam rock anthem. "Man, I've never seen anything like this boy in my life. Man, I ain't shittin' you."

I was still trying to wake up and hear what he was saying. "What? What's that?" I asked.

"Man, he got in that game and he went absolutely stone crazy. He was throwing that ball around, screaming and hollering. Them boys scored three or four touchdowns in no time. Man, that boy is crazy! He's gonna be a tremendous quarterback!"

I looked at the clock, realized what time it was, rubbed my eyes, and then said, "Bro, it's 3:00 in the morning! Who the hell are you talking about?"

"McMahon, man!" Walter said with the excitement of a 12-year-old kid. "Jim McMahon! He got in the game and was out there just having fun, hollering shit at the defense like he ain't scared at all. He told one guy, 'I was fucking yo' mama last night, and she ain't worth shit!'"

Well, that woke me up. "What? Really? He said that?" I asked, thinking I should've come up with that line. "That son of a bitch is going to get killed out there."

"Man, the guys love him. That stuff fired 'em up. Boy, the dude's crazy, but he can play! He's gonna be good."

Yeah, he was going to be good, but that didn't mean it was all going to come together for the Bears in 1982. It didn't matter much that year, I guess, with the season shorted by a strike and all. Walter had only gotten a glimpse of the wonder drug that Jim McMahon would prove to be for the Bears. But during that 1982 season, there were some other kinds of drugs going around.

Missing all those games was stressful for a lot of guys. An eight-week vacation might sound good on the surface, but when it's not planned, some guys don't know what to do with themselves. It's sort of like the lottery. There are some people who just have no business winning it, and they'll be broke again in a few short years. Well, give some players eight weeks off, and the same sort of thing happens. A lot of guys were doing everything right and working out hard for the first couple of weeks. Everyone wanted to stay in shape because we were told the strike wouldn't last long. After three weeks, though, a number of players kind of backed off their conditioning because it looked as if the strike could drag on for months. Some guys were doing a little less training and found other things to keep themselves occupied. They made more personal appearances, went home and hung out with family and friends, went to bars, and went to women. And yes, without any testing for weeks, some thought it was safe to do a little drugs. Then a little more. Then all of a sudden, we players had a drug test dropped on us, and a lot of guys were up shit creek without a paddle. Hell, for the Vikings, half the team was about to fail, and that's probably not an exaggeration. I was part of the clean half, so there were no worries for me.

Being an entrepreneur at heart, though, I saw an opportunity to enter the drug-testing biz and ran with it. It just seemed brilliant to me at the time. Not only would I make a little cash, but I could also help keep my team together. My teammates became my clients, and the men's restroom became my office. You see, as guys came in to pee in the cup for the drug test, the ones who were guilty of illegal drug use were my targets. And I didn't even have to know exactly who they were. "Fifty bucks for a cup of clean pee," I'd bark out to the guys as they came in. Thirty years ago, they didn't have a monitor to accompany the pee-er during a drug test, so it was easy to fool 'em. I would just take the $50, pee in a cup, and hand it back. It was as simple as that. And thank goodness they didn't require a completely full cup, either, because with such high demand at the time, the supply was a little hard to provide. "Pass the word to the next guy to bring me more water," I'd say as one customer would leave with a half-filled cup of my pee. My bladder was empty, but my pockets were full. And so was our roster.

I had some good times up there with the Vikings, but pee wasn't the only thing I was running out of in those days. My time in the NFL was running out, too. As Walter and the Bears looked to be on the brink of shining bright, my football career was in its twilight stage. I really did enjoy my time in Minnesota. If it weren't so damn cold up there, I could probably live there even now. I just love the place. I had three good years with the Vikings and am grateful to this day for the opportunity and the honor of playing for them. I didn't want it to end, but sometimes it doesn't matter what you want. When it comes to playing in the NFL, at some point, well, you just get old. And you're usually very young when it happens, if you know what I'm saying. It's just such a competitive league and such a hard place to play, and younger, faster guys are always coming in. For me, it was getting more and more difficult to avoid the new young headhunters looking to make a name for themselves, coming in there and trying to take my head off every time I'd catch the ball. At some point, it just ain't worth it, and when three years passed for me in Minnesota, it was time for me to hang it up. I thank God every day for the blessing of having played pro football for a living, and I thank Him even more that I made it out in one piece.

With my cleats hung up for good, it was time for Walter to carry on the Payton name in the NFL by himself. And boy, did he ever carry it. The Bears improved each year as McMahon gained experience and the passing game became a real weapon. It wasn't just on offense that they started peaking, either. Buddy Ryan's "46" defense was beginning to dominate opposing offenses, and it became clear to everyone that the ingredients for a championship team were coming together in Chicago. Walter was having his best year yet, just ripping through the league, but it still wasn't easy for him. Despite the improved play all around him, he was still taking a beating in the league. Walter and I talked after games, and he'd tell me how much he was hurting. Bud Holmes saw it firsthand, as he traveled to most of the Bears games. "No one on a football field gets beat up more than the running back," Bud said. "Walter got pounded so damn bad, I'd walk him into the training room and sit him down, and his old knees would look like basketballs. They were so swollen that the trainers would have to drain the fluid."

After a game Walter would sit in the whirlpool and he'd look like somebody had taken a sledge hammer and beaten on his knees. Really, it was that bad there for a while. The NFL is unforgiving, and the training staff would furnish some sort of pills as the only type of mercy he could get. Now, when I say pills, I ain't talking anything illegal. Walter had no addiction issues of any kind. Let's just put it this way: he wouldn't have been one of my pee customers in Minnesota. The only pills Walter ever took were provided by trainers and were available to all NFL players. I know other people have said that Walter had a problem with drugs, and like I said before, I wasn't with him all the time, but I just don't believe it. We talked about everything, and I never once heard a single word that made me think he might be into that shit.

Walter played in the league longer than the average NFL player, so he consumed more medication than the average NFL player, too. The long-term effects of painkillers weren't truly known 30 years ago. And I suspect all those pain pills had something to do with his death. Any time you take any type of medicine, it's got to go through your liver first. It's just my belief that all that stuff he was taking for pain while playing in the NFL was detrimental to his liver. He had frequent headaches from getting pounded so much and took lots of meds for that, and they're saying now that long-term use of anti-inflammatory drugs might be bad for the liver.

At the time, Walter wasn't thinking about how all of that could affect his health. He wasn't really thinking about his future. He was thinking about his present, and he wanted to win. Playing through the pain, he finally helped the Bears rule the NFL in 1985, only losing one regular season game, to Miami. They finished with a record of 15–1. Then they breezed through their two playoff games, pitching shutouts in both of them. Walter was still the team's clear-cut leader and producer during that historic season, finishing with 1,551 yards rushing and another 483 through the air on 49 receptions. My little brother realized his big dream by first realizing a bunch of small ones. Everything he'd done in high school, at Jackson State, and during his first 10 years in the NFL led him to that glorious 1985 season. And he led his team to Super Bowl XX on January 26, 1986, where the Bears hammered the New England Patriots and won by a score of 46–10.

The Patriots' defensive plan was a carbon copy of everyone else's. That is, their plan was to stop Walter. Though teams often failed, the Patriots succeeded, holding my brother to 61 yards on 22 carries and no touchdowns. Perhaps he should've gotten a chance to score from the 1-yard line, but that's all water under the bridge. I give Coach Ditka a pass on that because he gave Walter what he really wanted all along anyway. I mean, my brother wasn't a stranger to scoring touchdowns. He had more than his fair share of those. But what he didn't have at the time was a Super Bowl ring, so getting that was the important thing. Walter was all about team and all about winning, so he was all about being happy on that day. The Chicago Bears were world champions!

Despite his subpar individual stats, that Super Bowl was the highlight of Walter's career. And really, the 1985 season was the beginning of the end of it, too. Walter's last great season came in 1986, a year after leading one of the best teams in NFL history. In 1986, Walter rushed for 1,333 yards, which was the 10th time in his career he gained over 1,000 yards. The problem was, when you do anything for the 10th time in the NFL, things are probably winding down for you. Walter was really beginning to feel his age at that point. Even his rigid training regimen, which had become famous in its own right, was starting to slow up. The cruel fact was that he was now facing an opponent he couldn't beat. In his prime, Walter was hard to stop, but time is impossible to stop and never loses a step. It just keeps going. Keeps moving. No matter what you do or how hard you try, you move further away from your youth with each passing day. My brother was one of the best who ever played the game. He started out with so much promise, took the field by storm as a kid, changed things for black colleges everywhere as a young man, and led the Bears to a Super Bowl victory as a grown man. Yet still, after all that, he was slowing down. He was running against time, and time was catching up to him.

One thing that never slowed down through the years was Walter's obsession with practical jokes. I could write a whole book on his pranks (actually, I kind of feel like I have), and I think it's only fitting to talk a little more about that now. And speaking of talking, we all know Walter had a high-pitched voice. But what you might not know is that Walter could imitate a woman's voice so well that he could even fool a woman.

Thomas Sanders was a running back for the Bears behind Walter when they won the Super Bowl. Sanders also returned kicks for Chicago, so you know he's a good and talented guy. Anyway, on Thanksgiving Day during his rookie season, Walter got on his car phone and called up Sanders' wife, sounding just like a girl. "Hello," Walter said when she picked up the phone. "Look, when Thomas comes in, tell him if he's not going to have Thanksgiving dinner with me, at least he could buy the baby some shoes that are the right size. They just too little. Tell him I don't appreciate it. I come all the way up here from Texas, bring the baby, and he don't even buy the right size shoe for that baby."

About an hour later, Sanders drove up to Walter's house in a panic. "Man, I gotta see ya," he said, desperate to talk with someone. "I gotta see ya."

Walter knew why Sanders was there, of course, but he acted totally innocent. "What is it?" Walter asked, like he was just the most understanding friend in the world.

"Man, some bitch called my house, got the wrong number," Sanders said. "I know it was the wrong number 'cause she's talking about a baby, and my wife's throwing a fit. I mean, she's packing up to go home right now thinking I got some baby and some woman's up here to see me for Thanksgiving dinner. Man, I don't know what to do. What do I do?"

Walter couldn't contain himself and erupted with laughter. Sanders didn't think it was so funny. Walter finally had to talk to

Sanders' wife to get him off the hook. She didn't believe him until he re-created the voice for her to prove it was all a joke. If he hadn't finally done the woman's voice on the phone for Sanders' wife, I'm not sure she would've ever come back to Chicago. Walter might've been the only one who thought that gag was funny, but he sure did laugh his ass off about it.

Walter's famous for being a running back, but really, he could've made a career out of pulling tricks on people. Pranking was a way of life for my brother. Making fools of his friends was as much a part of him as making fools of opposing defenses was. I know I said this once before, but he just loved to get Bud with that high-pitched voice of his. He often dropped by Bud's office and assumed the secretary's desk and answered the phone in her place. Sounding like a girl, he'd sit and answer the phone for hours, sometimes saying things the secretary would never say. He just loved messing with people. The phone would ring and Walter's fun would begin. "Hello, Bud Holmes' office," he'd say, listening for a moment. When they asked to set up a meeting with Bud, Walter would said, "Nah, he's too busy to see you. And he even told me if you call back down here again, not to let you talk to him." Then he'd just hang up. He'd do that kind of stuff to Bud's friends all the time…and sometimes, like with Musburger, Bud was in on it.

One of my favorite Bud/Sweetness pranks was played on Bobby Collins, the head football coach at Southern Mississippi. Walter was fishing down at Bud's lake one day, and Bud hatched an idea. I guess the fish weren't biting, because Bud said, "Hell, let's have some fun with Bobby Collins. I'm going to tell Bobby some story about this unknown kid being down here and how he wants to play for Southern. You'll be the unknown kid." Walter quickly jumped all in.

"Yeah, yeah, okay, I like it," Walter responded.

So, Bud called Bobby Collins and said, "Bobby, look, I got this woman I represented once, some family—hell, I've known them forever. I think my daddy even used to represent them. Anyway, she's got a nephew, a grandson or something. I don't really know the relationship, but whatever it is, the family wants him to go to Southern. He's a nice kid. She asked me if I can help him, because they can't afford out-of-state tuition."

Coach Collins was listening, not yet sure what to think.

"Here's what I'll do, Bobby," Bud continued. "I'll bring him out there, and if y'all will just kinda be nice and take a look at the kid, I'll give y'all enough money to hire him on as equipment manager or something. You know, so he can at least get his education."

Coach Collins was willing to help out, so when Bud and Walter went, Walter disguised himself with a baseball cap and sunglasses. Coach Collins came out and met Bud and the "kid" at the practice field...and it was on.

"What's your name?" Coach Collins asked.

"My name is Robert Johnson," Walter blurted out. Robert Johnson was a blues legend, and Walter must've had one of his tunes stuck in his head. Maybe "Sweet Home Chicago"? Still, it was an odd name for him choose. I mean, Johnson was such a good musician that folks thought he must have sold his soul in exchange for that guitar-picking talent of his. What's really strange, though, is that Johnson died a mysterious death before his time. Most think he was poisoned. It's not the name I would've chosen, that's for sure. Of course, maybe Walter didn't really *choose* it. That name might've just popped into his head for a reason that even Walter wasn't aware of at the time.

"Well, we're glad to have you come here, Robert. Where do you go to school now?" Coach Collins asked.

"Well, I go out there to Monterey Junior College," Walter—uh, I mean—Robert said.

Coach was curious about the physique of this kid. "Did you play any sports?" he asked.

"Oh yeah," Walter/Robert said. "I played basketball over there, and I played football, too."

"Oh yeah? What kind of record in football?"

"Oh, we had a good record," Walter/Robert responded. "We should've won the championship. A lot of people want to blame the referee. But I say, if you don't win, you don't win. I don't say nothing about the way the referees call it. I keep my mouth shut about it. We should've won the game, though." Coach Collins was ready to hear more.

"You look pretty fit. How much do you weigh, Robert?"

"Right now I'm weighing 205," Walter/Robert said. "You know, I get a little bit off that sometimes, but I'm basically 205."

"Goodness. Well, have you ever been timed in the 40?"

"Oh, yes sir, yes sir."

"What'd you run?"

Those fish weren't biting earlier when Bud came up with his plan, but Coach Collins was sure taking the bait now. And Walter was *really* ready to have fun. "Well, most of the time when I ain't really running real hard, I run like a 4.4. But when I really, really feel like I need to get it, I run a 4.3 most anytime. Now, one time, I don't know if it's true or not, and there was a pretty strong wind, I think, but they gave me a 4.25. But really, I run 4.3, 4.4. Something in there."

Well, by this time, Whitey Jordan, another Southern Miss coach, had come out and was listening in on the conversation. After all the 4.3/4.4 talk, Jordan and Collins got to looking at each other and started drooling over what they were beginning to believe was a 20-carat (black) diamond in the rough that they'd just discovered.

"Well, what about your grades?"

Walter started laying it on thick. He wanted to make them think they'd done died and gone to heaven. "I majored in math and computer science," Walter/Robert said. "I got a 3.8 GPA. I should've gotten better, but I wasn't feeling good on that last exam. I should've had a 4.0." The two coaches were now worked up into a full recruiting lather.

"Coach, how about going out there and seeing what this kid can do," Jordan said. "You mind letting us time you, Robert?"

"Oh nah, I don't mind. I'll be glad to go run for you. I likes to run."

"He needs some shoes, Coach Jordan," Coach Collins said.

"Well, I can run barefooted," Walter/Robert offered. "It don't matter none, I run barefooted back home all the time."

"Nah, we got shoes back there," Coach Collins said. "We'll get you some. What size you wear?"

"Ten and a half."

This whole thing was unfolding beautifully. Walter figured he could give 'em at least a 4.45 with a good warm-up. Walter went inside the locker room to change into some shorts and lace up his shoes when a coach from Columbia strolled in to see Coach Collins. He spoke to Walter and Bud as he walked into the back where Coaches Collins and Jordan must've been developing a strategy for landing Mr. Robert Johnson. Coach Jordan already had his stopwatch around his neck and was ready to go when Coach Mason said, "What's Walter Payton doing here?"

And that's when the whole thing came crashing down. "What? Walter Payton?" a very surprised and embarrassed Coach Jordan asked.

Well, Walter and Bud didn't know Mason had let the cat out of the bag, so they walked outside and were waiting to be timed. Then Coach Jordan walked out to the field by himself (I suppose Coach Collins figured he'd wasted enough time at that point), but he just kept walking right on past the two pranksters. Bud was surprised and hollered, "Hey, Coach Jordan, aren't you going to come time Robert?"

"You smart-ass son of a bitch!" Coach Jordan yelled back. "You go out there and time him your own damn self!"

Walter and Bud looked at each other in stunned silence for a moment. Then smiles came to their faces right before they busted out laughing. Walter had no trouble at all pulling pranks like that on coaches. And he wouldn't just do that stuff to coaches he didn't play for. You already know he pulled some on Coach Hill, but even one of the most legendary coaches of all time wasn't off Walter's target list. Little did Mike Ditka know when he took the head coaching position for Chicago that he had moved into Walter Payton's crosshairs.

"Walter was the biggest practical joker on the team," Ditka recalled. "He kept everybody loose in the locker room, and it was mostly all in good fun. Well, with the possible exception of when he called me at night and disguised his voice—sounded just like a woman."

Coach Ditka tells the story well. He started getting these very enticing calls from an unknown woman. The woman would say, "How 'bout meeting me tonight?" and Ditka would just let it go, brushing it off. Coach would get these calls a couple of times a week there for a while and just ignored them.

"I was out on the practice field one day," Ditka said, "just standing around, watching practice, and then I heard this voice behind me say, 'Would you meet me at the hotel tonight?' It was her! It was that woman who had been calling me. Only I turned around to find out that woman was Walter. I tell people all the time that I'm glad I never went."

I know exactly what Coach means, too. Walter was one ugly woman.

My baby brother was constantly doing stuff like that. If he wasn't setting off firecrackers in some guy's locker, he was setting the clocks back in the locker room to try to make guys late for meetings. Or if he wasn't leaving notes on teammates' windshields from "crazy women," he'd be busy tying shoelaces together. He just had that type of personality, and anyone was fair game for a Walter prank. Well, almost anyone.

I suppose Walter wouldn't have been so quick to pull a prank on a fan. One thing he took very seriously was his relationship with his fans. Walter and I often talked about the people who'd come to see him play. He was very humbled by the fact that some of the guys who'd come to see him play had to work an entire month to save enough money to take their wives and kids to the game, then had to sit in the nosebleed section and could hardly pay for parking, much less buy a drink and popcorn for the kids. Walter always wanted to give those guys what they came to see. He wanted those guys he'd never met to be able to say, "I was there that day when Walter Payton did this" or "I was there when Sweetness did that." He wanted those guys and their families to leave and say, "I got to see Walter Payton play today." While other guys like me in the league were trying to live the life other guys could only dream of, Walter was busy trying to give those guys something to dream about. Besides winning, that was his primary motivation. He played pranks on his friends, but he truly, truly respected his fans.

Walter could even find joy when he was going to a hospital to see some kid who was sick and wanted to meet him. He loved meeting those kids and their families. Nothing made Walter feel better than when he could make those kids feel a little better, even for a moment. Bud helped Walter arrange those hospital visits, and he and Walter often talked about the effect it had on his life. "That's what Walter really liked to talk about," Bud explained. "His heart would just melt, and he'd say things like, 'Aw, Bud, you should've seen the look on that child's face. He was so glad to see me. That little fellow came up like he'd always known me and just talked and talked. I just sat there, and we talked, and I even got to pray with him.'" I'm sure those kids felt blessed to be spending some time with such a big star, but I can tell you, Walter was the one who felt blessed.

Bud went on, "Walter believed if he was a celebrity, then by God he was going to use it to bring joy to somebody even if it was for only one minute in his life. I asked Walter once, 'Walter, what'd make you happy?' He said, 'Just tell me about 10 kids who are sick and where they are so I can go cheer 'em up a little bit.' That was from his heart. That was who he was. There was no limelight of publicity during most of those times, no photo op. It was just being there with that kid to make a positive difference. That's what he really loved doing."

My brother even inspired me to extend a helping hand to our youth. Even today I try to speak to high school, junior high, and elementary students at least once a week. During Black History Month, I'll usually do two or three per week. I talk to the kids about what I've accomplished, and they look at me and don't see a big, huge athlete telling them these things. They see me, a little guy, not much bigger than them, actually, and they think, *If he can do it, I can do it.* I always tell them to seize the day, 'cause you won't be young forever.

By 1987, time had finally caught up with my little brother. Injuries, age, and the Bears front office took so much out of Walter that he announced his retirement at the end of that season. It became obvious to Walter and me (through our talks) that the Bears were trying to figure out a way to get him out of the game so they could go in a new direction. Seems to happen a lot in the NFL. In the 1986 draft, the bears picked Neal Anderson out of the University of Florida. They thought he was the next coming of Sweetness, and they were more interested at the time in having the next Sweetness than the real Sweetness. Anderson was even about the same size. A clone, maybe? The Bears management might have said "yes" at the time, but I say "no way." And I mean that then, now, and forever. Walter was more than just an outstanding running back. It should be clear he was an outstanding person. There will never, ever be another Sweetness. Period.

Still, management folks for NFL teams aren't usually interested in hearing all of that. Walter had been there long enough to understand what was happening. The writing was on the wall. There were less carries for him and more attention was being given to Anderson in practice. Walter knew he'd lost a step, but he also knew what he had given to the city. And there were the Bears, trying to figure out how to get Walter to retire. As he did his whole life, my baby brother would call me and pour his heart out. In truth, he was a little bitter about all of that. He didn't like the feeling of being pushed out, especially not after how hard he'd worked for the Bears and their fans. Walter realized he couldn't play forever, of course, but he wanted to go out in a way befitting somebody who did what he'd done for the organization.

Eventually, the organization realized that right was right and made it happen. The way they sent him off, with all the accolades and celebration, made it easier on him. They had this big retirement celebration for him at the last regular season home game. But as usual, Bud Holmes made the real difference. Bud worked it out so that Walter (or his family in case of Walter's death) would draw $240,000 a year for 44 years or for life, whichever was longer. Walter loved football, and he hated to leave. But at least he knew that he'd be able to continue providing for his family even if something should happen to him. Just like always, Walter was thinking of more than himself as he prepared to join me in life after football.

CHAPTER 12

Wreckin' the Car

Have you ever had one of those cars that you just love and never want to stop driving? I'm talking about the kind of car that looks great and just feels right and makes you think, *Why would I ever want a new car?* You drive it and drive it and drive it until the wheels are about to fall off. But no matter what you do, no matter how much you want it to keep going, the wheels eventually do fall off. Then you need a new car. Well, that's how it was with the Bears and Walter there near the end of his football career. The Bears drove him into the ground and loved every minute of it, of course, and they wanted to keep running him. But they also knew he was wearing down, and they just couldn't resist the shiny new things, like Neal Anderson, rolling up behind him. "The Bears office called me and said they didn't want to cut Walter," Bud said. "Instead, they wanted to just do the 'move in another direction' thing." Bud knew it couldn't last forever, so he met with Connie and Walter to discuss retirement, trying to sugarcoat it as best he could.

"Well," Bud started with Walter, "Alexander cried when there were no worlds left to conquer, but he still had to stop conquering." Walter had done his thing on the field and had left his mark on the

Bears and the NFL forever, so Bud was smartly appealing to that sentiment. Walter had broken this record and that record, and the road was coming to an end. I mean, he broke Jim Brown's record for crying out loud. What more was he going to do? Bud knew the time had come and suggested that Walter get out of football and head into the business world. It's just that Bud might have underestimated how important playing football was to keeping Walter balanced.

Now, I made light of Walter's ADHD earlier, but it really was a serious matter. Though he was never officially diagnosed (adults back in the day weren't even tested), there's no doubt in my mind that he was afflicted in a big way. You didn't have to be a brain scientist to figure that out, and it started to affect his behavior again as he transitioned to life after football. Playing for the Bears and everything that came along with it had consumed Walter's life for 13 years. He had a purpose out there on the field and always had something to do. There was always another game to win, and his life was extremely busy in preparation to win that next game. His ADHD was mostly held in check during that time. Life after football, though, was just so foreign to him. Walter was so good on the field for so long that when he wasn't playing anymore, it sort of blindsided him. You know, the hardest day for a pro athlete like Walter is the day it all ends. When players at his level step out and go into another phase of life, they've got to fill the inevitable emptiness that comes with no longer being able to run out of that tunnel and do battle on Sunday. And the harder a guy plays, the harder it hits him when he no longer can.

For average athletes like me, it's a little easier. I didn't really struggle with it like Walter did. I hung it up, and that was that. I was thankful for everything I got out of the game of football. I was just lucky to be out there playing for a living for a little while. But for somebody who was the all-time rushing leader, an MVP, a nine-time

Pro Bowl selection, and placed on a pedestal by the entire football-loving nation, well, when that was gone, he basically had to try to find something to fill an unfillable void. Walter almost instantly started to feel worthless when he stepped away from the game. And instead of going to his family to find his worth, he tried to deal with it by spending an enormous amount of time away from them. He tried to fill his life with activity. It started with something good.

As soon as Walter retired, the Bears appointed him to their board of directors, and then he had Bud set up a foundation for him with a guy named Mr. Halas. Halas took care of older NFL players from back in the '30s and '40s, guys who had no health insurance. The new union contract at the time only provided coverage for players back to like 1955 or so. All of the guys who played before that were stuck without coverage. Mr. Halas had been trying to take care of those guys, and Walter wanted to team up with him. It was the kind of thing he could really get into, because, as you know, he loved helping people. The foundation was going to be called the Halas-Payton Foundation. The money raised was simply going to help those older players get medical care. There was going to be a huge kickoff event at Soldier Field, and Hank Williams Jr. even looked set to come and put on a big concert and everything. Walter was excited and planned on staying there all night long, even until noon the next day if necessary, just as long as anybody wanted to come by and get an autograph and a picture with him.

Bud loved the idea and wanted Walter to end his career by leaving that legacy of helping former players. It was just what Walter needed, and it was all in the works. But then, before it could fully come about, the NFL amended their policy to include all former players. Now, that obviously wasn't a bad thing, and perhaps what Halas and Walter were planning on doing led to that positive change, but it made their foundation's mission completely unnecessary. This thing Walter had been putting his energy into was no longer needed. And though the goal of covering those older players had been achieved, Walter couldn't help but feel a little deflated about the whole thing. He really had been looking forward to helping those guys himself and sharing the foundation name with Mr. Halas. He had been excited about doing something worthwhile, and now the air had been squeezed out of the balloon. After that, the foundation shifted completely and was converted to a charity for inner city kids, renamed the Walter and Connie Payton Foundation. And though great things have been done through the foundation, of course, Walter had a hard time letting go of the original plan.

The real problem, though, was that other business-minded people had an insatiable hunger for Walter's time. All Walter really wanted to do was help people who needed his help, but he couldn't get away from the guys who just wanted him to help them out with appearances, endorsements, and other business dealings. Walter felt like an item up on eBay that everyone wanted to buy. Just a few months into retirement, he had so many people pulling at him that the football field seemed like child's play in comparison. All of these people were coming at him, telling him he needed to do this, asking him to do that. He didn't know which way to turn or look. Bud saw firsthand the tug-of-war that went on between those who loved Walter and those who loved his fame. "I'll say one thing," Bud said. "Eddie and the people in Mississippi—I call it the Mississippi Payton side—they stayed 100 percent true to Walter. Down deep Walter was very much committed to them, too. But it created conflict with the business people in Chicago wanting Walter's full-time presence."

I guess the business people in Chicago pulled harder than we did.

Once the foundation was rolling, Walter's time started to fill up quickly with business and even recreational opportunities. He went into race car driving for a bit to try to fill the football void and to get that same satisfaction he got from performing on the field. It just couldn't compare, though. He loved race cars, of course, but no matter how much he wanted it to be something more, that was more of a hobby for him than a purpose. So then he just sort of started trying any and every kind of business he could, hoping something would stick and keep him occupied and satisfied. He threw his hat into food service, construction, and even bought into several Studebaker's franchises. He set up an office for himself in an effort to make it feel good and real, but it just wasn't the same as being on the field. Then came along an idea with some serious promise. It was an idea that'd combine business *with* football.

Bud had talked with Jim Finks, who everyone thought would take Pete Rozelle's place when Rozelle stepped down as NFL commissioner, and the idea of getting Walter a franchise came up. "Why don't we see about working on Walter becoming an owner?" Finks said. "You know, the first black owner, and he has such a great image. We need to make that happen."

Bud liked the idea right away and presented it to Walter. "Let's go hard after a franchise," Bud advised. "You can be the first black owner." Desperately trying to find something that made sense in life after football, Walter was in full agreement, and the timing seemed to be perfect. Walter was available and willing, of course, and the professional sports world needed the kind of public relations boost that a guy like Walter could bring. You see, around that time, a firestorm of bad racial publicity had been created by a few high-profile sports personalities. In April of 1987, for example, Al Campanis, general manager of the Los Angeles Dodgers, was asked on live national TV why there weren't more black managers in Major League Baseball. His answer: "I don't believe it's prejudice. I truly believe that they may not have some of the necessities to be, let's say, a field manager, or perhaps a general manager."

"They" don't have the "necessities?" Ouch.

Then in January of 1988, Jimmy "The Greek" Snyder, a CBS football analyst, told a Washington, D.C., television reporter that "The black is a better athlete to begin with because he's been bred that way. This goes all the way back to the Civil War...the slave owner would breed his big black to his big woman so that he would have a big black kid."

Okay, uh, yeah. Let's just say the NFL was worried to death about its image, and for good reason. Enter Walter Payton to help bridge the racial divide, as he'd been doing his whole life. After several discussions between then-commissioner Pete Rozelle and Walter and Bud, Rozelle promised Walter an expansion franchise. They were told at the time that Oakland and Phoenix were possible spots. And location aside, Walter liked that a lot. He thought it was the challenge he'd been looking for, and he was up to it.

Soon after that promise from Rozelle, Phoenix was taken off the table. Billy Bidwill moved the Cardinals from St. Louis to Phoenix, so Arizona no longer needed a team. Of course, that meant that St. Louis became a possible spot for an expansion team. Well, Rozelle soon left his post as commissioner to focus on his fight with cancer, so the thought was that the whole "Walter will be an owner" baton was going to be handed off to Finks. Well, it wasn't exactly going to be that easy. As Bud explains it, "Jim Finks missed being the commissioner by one vote. Still, everybody knew that Walter was going to get a franchise. Jacksonville and Charlotte became likely cities. Things were still moving in a positive direction."

Walter and Bud kept upbeat and kept moving forward. Of all the possible cities, Walter zeroed in on St. Louis and decided to go for that one. There were to be three partners. Walter was going to be the minority owner (in more ways than one) of the franchise. One of the other partners, a member of the Busch family, was putting up the lion's share of the money, and the other partner was a real estate mogul who would be building the stadium. Those two and Walter had gotten together and were deciding how things were going to go. The problem was, things started to go not so well.

The other two partners got to bickering about who was going to have the controlling interest in the franchise. They were basically arguing over the 1 percent vote. You know, "One percent more than y'all." It got ugly, and I'm talking lawsuit kind of ugly. As the 11th hour approached for a deal that'd give them a St. Louis team, Walter called me to talk about his frustration with the process. "Man, you ain't going to believe this shit that's going on," he said. "These people up here are arguing about who's going to own what percentage and all that."

I was just listening and letting him vent. "That's crazy," I said.

"Yeah," Walter continued, "the NFL doesn't want to hear it either, and they got me in the middle 'cause one guy has the money and the other has the property. They got me all jacked up here trying to take sides and smooth it out. I just feel like taking a stick and whoopin' everybody's ass who's involved in this whole thing. I mean, it's just going along fine and looks like it's going to happen, and then they start with all this?"

I wasn't an expert on all the ins and outs of NFL business dealings, but it didn't sound like it was going to work out to me. "Well, I guess that means I ain't going to be the personnel guy in St. Louis," I said. Walter and I had talked about my becoming the personnel director once the team got going.

"I don't know," Walter responded. "We'll see how that all works out. We got to get over this hurdle first. If they don't quit this bickering, we're going to lose the franchise. They'll just award it to somebody else."

Well, they never quit the bickering, and I guess Walter had had enough because he went missing. They had built a new stadium for the team and people were getting nervous about the way things were going, so a private plane was waiting for Walter at Butler Aviation in Chicago to fly him to St. Louis for a big press conference to promise the new stadium wouldn't go empty. You know, just to set minds at ease by building up the idea that it'd all work out in the end. The problem was, the airplane waited and waited for Walter. Then it waited some more. Walter didn't show. The other partners kept calling Bud, wanting to know where Walter was and why he wasn't on that plane. Bud didn't know. Nobody knew. He just didn't show up, and that was all there was to it. He'd had enough, and instead of calling someone, Walter was just calling it quits.

With the threat of a lawsuit already hanging over the partnership, and now with Walter pulling his disappearing act, the NFL awarded the expansion franchise to Jacksonville instead. St. Louis was still going to get a team, but it was going to be an existing one. The Los Angeles Rams moved to St. Louis, but they already had an owner, so they didn't need Walter. He was out.

"Walter, what the hell?" Bud asked once he finally connected. "Why'd you do that? Man, we hunted you and hunted you and everything, and you never showed up. Where the hell were you?"

"I just was riding around," Walter said, as if he didn't know or care about the trouble he'd caused. "That's just business, man. Sometimes things don't work out, okay? Sometimes you just have to back up, regroup, and change your game plan, like in a football game."

"Walter…" Bud tried to interrupt.

"If I can't be an owner, I don't want any of it," Walter said.

"Well," Bud came back with some frustration, "you're gonna get your wish."

As it turned out, they wanted to give Walter 5 percent ownership, which would be worth about $30 million on today's market. That's what he was giving up. At that point, though, he was bitter about it all and just wanted to get away from it. He wasn't thinking about percentage points or money or nothing like that. He just felt burned by the NFL and the whole process. Walter had already gone down and done a ton of work over a period of three and a half years, helping to set the stage for the team, and getting the stadium built in St. Louis in anticipation of the expansion. They put a bond issue together for like $450 million to build the stadium, and now some other owner's team was going to be in there. Though he didn't help matters by skipping the press conference, Walter was bitter and pissed off and just felt used and abused. He put three years of his life into schmoozing and being paraded around like a prize pony to everyone, and it was all for nothing. He was slapping backs and shaking hands and smiling and taking pictures to make the whole thing work, but he didn't have anything to show for it. That was one of the low points in his life because he really wanted to be the first black owner of an NFL football team. That would've put him back where he wanted to be, back in football and part of a team.

Walter started to lose his identity through all of that. He no longer had the football field on which to escape, and all he could see was his fame and the hounds gathering around it. He was starting to lose himself a bit, and Bud could see what was happening. As Walter's manager, partner, shrink, father, and friend on all of his business (mis)adventures, Bud knew better than anyone how much it was all weighing on him and how much Walter was struggling to find his place in this new post-football world. "When Walter would spend time with Eddie and come down and go hunting and just be with the boys out in the woods…that's when Walter was really, really, really on top of the world," Bud said. "You take him out of that environment and it's kinda like a Hank Williams song written after Hank made a bunch of money and became famous and all that. The basic idea of the song is, *We now have the finest of everything, but in this world, there is no place for me."*

Walter felt out of place in that corporate dog-eat-dog world he was in, where everybody wanted to get a piece of Walter Payton for themselves and their pockets. The pressure was getting to my baby brother in a big way, and he wasn't blind to what was going on. He'd lost his team and his sport, and now all he had was his fame. He was starting to feel like that was all he was to the people around him. "All anybody wants out of me is to make a dollar for themselves," Walter said at the time. "They don't give a damn about me."

Like any normal person, he was feeling down about it, especially because he felt like with the whole franchise fiasco, he'd wasted three and a half years of his life that he couldn't get back. He now had to start from zero again, and I think the thought of starting from zero just made him long to start from the beginning. You know, before he had fame. Before people knew who he was. Before people stopped loving him for being Walter and started loving him for being Sweetness. He just felt down about how everybody saw him, and he wanted to find someone, anyone, who didn't know who he was.

Well, that someone came in the form of a young flight attendant— I'll call her Linda. Walter was on trip to Atlanta, and for the first time in a long time, he'd met someone who didn't know his name before he told it to her. Linda was a very pretty woman who didn't know anything at all about Walter Payton, and that proved to be a very dangerous combination for my brother. After all those years fighting off the aggressive advances of other women, along came someone who just didn't know to be aggressive. After all that time resisting the irresistible, Walter had finally found a woman he just couldn't resist.

Now, I'm not excusing it, of course, and neither would Walter, but it was sort of a perfect storm for him. Linda came along at just the right (or maybe I should say wrong) time and gave Walter just what he thought he was looking for. Walter and Linda hit it off immediately, and he came to the conclusion that this girl liked him for who he was and not because he was a celebrity football player. They started dating and getting more and more serious as time went on. Walter kept his two worlds separate for a while, but eventually they had to collide.

It started with Bud. At one point, Walter decided he wanted to introduce Linda to Bud. It didn't sit well with Bud at first because, though he said Linda was very pleasant, it was the first time he'd ever seen Walter with any woman other than Connie. He just wasn't sure how this could end up in a positive way. Perhaps Walter wasn't either, but he apparently got deep enough into it that he wanted someone close to him to know about Linda. "Walter always treated me like a daddy, I guess," Bud said. "Actually, when his daddy died, he asked if I'd be his daddy. Anyway, I guess he just wanted to introduce his girlfriend to me as if I were his daddy, you know?" Walter was struggling at the time with who he was, being pulled one way by his celebrity and another by his desire to be removed from it.

Introducing Linda to Bud was the start of what eventually led to Connie finding out. Obviously, the relationship between Walter and Connie had deteriorated over time, partly because of Linda, and they eventually filed for divorce. Bud wasn't having it, though. He explained, "I told Connie, 'You are a hell of a lot better off being a miserable Mrs. Walter Payton than the ex–Mrs. Walter Payton.'" Bud talked Connie out of divorcing Walter, but he couldn't keep her from meeting Linda. In fact, he facilitated it.

Walter brought Linda with him to his 1993 Hall of Fame induction, and they had a hotel room to themselves. Connie and the kids were at the induction, too, which proved to be a tougher balancing act for Walter than tiptoeing down the sidelines ever was. Walter was torn between two things: what he knew was right and what he wanted to do. He could only keep the shell game up for so long. Tension was understandably high there at the Hall of Fame induction, and Walter and Connie got in a scrap at some point.

"I wasn't with Walter when he and Connie got into it, thank God," Bud said. "But Connie called me up later and said she wanted to know if I'd introduce her to Linda. I said, 'Connie, if you want me to. I'll see what I can do. I think they are all down there in the lounge.' So, I went down there with Connie and introduced them. They were very pleasant to each other. Connie, Amanda [Connie's close friend], Ginny [Walter's personal assistant], and all of them were bunched up there with Linda. Connie and Linda got off to themselves for a few minutes at one point and had a very nice, pleasant talk, from what I could tell. And trust me, I was paying attention."

I think Linda wasn't as comfortable as she was "pleasant," because after that meeting, Walter started getting pressure from her to leave Connie. Walter told Linda he wanted to marry her but that Bud was the reason he and Connie weren't getting a divorce. "So, I became the goat, you know, to Linda," Bud said. "I was the problem for them. I was the reason they couldn't ride off into the sunset and live happily ever after. I was preventing it, in her mind. But I told Walter, 'Hell, I just think it'll be a damn mistake. The public has you sitting up on a pedestal. You're going to get your image so damn tarnished if you up and abandon your wife and kids.'"

Well, Walter and Connie weren't divorced but they did separate, and Walter was living with Linda. He just couldn't stay away from her. He could always talk with me, Connie, Bud, and a few other people about his problems before, but I guess Linda gave him something none of us could. She was someone he could talk to who wasn't a part of his famous football life. She didn't bring any of that baggage. He got into that relationship because he felt like he had nobody to talk to and that everyone else just liked him because he was a big star. The problem was that he still knew it was wrong, and so he became depressed even about having Linda in his life. He was torn between what he was supposed to do and what he wanted to do. And in that sense, he was no different than anyone else. Except, of course, he was different.

If you are in the public eye like my brother was, you just can't behave like Joe Blow, because nobody gives a damn what Joe Blow does. Walter was so open to public scrutiny, and it was hard for him to be happy living his life when he really couldn't do what he wanted to do. I mean, at that time, he really was torn between his relationship with the mother of his kids (who also happened to be his college sweetheart) and the relationship with Linda. He couldn't fully commit to either one of them because of who he was at the time. He was already down about losing three and half years of his life to the unfulfilled pursuit of the St. Louis franchise, but he was really depressed about the conflict between his two relationships. We all get depressed to one degree or another. We all go through periods of depression. We all deal with it at some point, even if it's just for an afternoon, and most of us come out of it on the other side. Still, knowing suicide rates among former NFL players are six times the national average, we all had to pay attention to what Walter was going through.

Bud really was like a father to Walter, and that was a role he took seriously. He stayed as close to Walter as Walter would allow and knows more about his alleged suicidal tendencies than anyone else. Bud said he got to feeling horribly sorry for my brother during that time. Walter would call him up and say things like, "I'm going to commit suicide. I'm going to end it." That worried Bud for sure. And then one night, Walter's longtime assistant, Ginny Quirk, called Bud and was hysterical. She said, "I promise he's going to kill himself! Bud, he swears he is. He's told us all good-bye and that he was never going to see us again. We'll never see him again!"

So, Bud started thinking things were getting out of control with Walter, and he wanted to do something about it. He knew Walter was flying to L.A. and was going to be interviewed by Roy Firestone before going down to drive in a celebrity car race with Jay Leno, Paul Newman, and some other celebrities. Ginny told Bud it'd be all right if he just showed up, so he hopped on a plane in Houston, where he was on a day trip at the time, and flew straight to L.A. He beat Walter there and was waiting for him when he got off the plane. Walter was surprised to see him. "What you doing here?" he asked, and then, according to Bud, he just laughed. Bud didn't quite know how to respond. He said something about having nothing better to do and stayed out there with him for three days. Everything was fine. "You know, looking back," Bud said, "I've often wondered if Walter just did that to prank me. I thought about it at the time, too, wondering if Walter wanted to see if he could trick me into leaving my day trip in Houston. I really wonder. I still wonder about that."

Listen, you can think what you want about my brother's depression and whether it ever got to a point where he wanted to kill himself. If he was suicidal, it wasn't because he was depressed (more on that in a minute). Walter was so squarely in the public eye that when he started to pull back from it, trying to deal with all the shit he was dealing with in retirement, some saw it as him being depressed to the point of wanting to end it all. Rumors got going as they always do when it comes to big stars like him. Really, though, pulling back just reflected who he was all along. He loved playing football in front of his fans and loved spending time with people he thought he could make a difference for, but he really wasn't a social being like I was. He'd have rather spent time shooting at his gun range or fishing on a lake or playing with his kids as opposed to going to some party or gathering and being introduced as "Walter Payton" to a bunch of people he didn't know. He much preferred to be by himself, generally speaking, and certainly when it came to dealing with struggles and private matters.

And I can also tell you that his depression was really more like anger. I mean, things would happen in his life that were not fun things to deal with, and he'd get more mad than depressed. Still, when he started to withdraw, some people would say, "Well, he's not coming out, so he's gotta be depressed." Most of the time, though, when he was dealing with something, he'd call me up and just get pissed off about whatever the situation was and want to talk about everything that was going on, who was to blame, etc. He never threatened to kill himself; he just threatened to kick someone's ass. Where Walter and I are from, we don't call that depression. We just call it getting mad.

When reporters and other people started pointing to the supposed evidence that Walter was suicidal, well, I didn't buy any of that for one minute. Not one bit. Listen, Walter liked to push buttons, we know that. Did he pull a prank on Bud? Well, I wouldn't put it past him, but the fact is we'll never know for sure. If he ever was suicidal, it was the concussions talking.

"Dr. Frank Jones explained a concussion one time to a jury," Bud detailed. "He referred to a concussion on cross examination like this: 'If I were to take a handful of mud and sling it up against that wall, and it splatters, well, that's what a concussion is.' When your brain is jarred so heavily that the brain is flattened out against the skull, that's a concussion."

I'd say logic tells you that anybody hammered as many times as Walter was over the course of his career is bound to have suffered numerous concussions. "He hit a lot of people a lot of times because that was his running style," Bears legend Gale Sayers said. "I think he got hit a couple of times more than I would have on the same running play." My little brother just refused to go down. Anyone who ever played with him will tell you that. If he was going to get hit, well, he was sure going to be doing some hitting of his own... but he was still going to get hit. Plenty of times. A bunch of times. Too many times.

How many times did one of those hits result in a concussion? Hard to say, but I'm certain he had a lot of them that no one ever knew about or kept track of. Officials at all levels of the game are pretty cautious about concussions these days, and for good reason. When Walter and I were playing high school and college football, those injuries weren't called concussions like they are now. Growing up, what was likely a concussion was just called a "dinger" or "getting your bell rung." It's extremely hard to figure the number of concussions players suffered back in the day. I mean, my first couple of years in the NFL, I don't even remember calling for a fair catch. Maybe that's just because my brain is mush. I don't know. What I do know is that smelling salts were my best friend. I played five years in the NFL and Walter played 13 (just like the chapters in this book). He was tackled something like 35 or 40 times a game, and was blocking on other plays. There's no telling how many concussions he suffered.

Nowadays we know repeated concussions can lead to chronic traumatic encephalopathy (CTE), also known as "punch-drunk syndrome," which is a degenerative brain condition that has long been associated with boxers. In the early stages of CTE, sufferers might display such symptoms as memory loss, confusion, suicidal behavior, lack of concentration, headaches, mood disorders (including depression), emotional instability, erratic behavior, problems with impulse control, and sleeplessness. However, CTE eventually progresses to full-blown dementia, similar to early-onset Alzheimer's. The problem with it is that you don't know you're in trouble until it's too late. A mark of CTE in football players is that years after a guy leaves the game, the condition starts affecting his personality and behavior.

Walter's former teammate, Dave Duerson, took his own life. He shot himself in the heart and left his brain to the Boston University School of Medicine. After a study of his brain, they found that the problems he had were directly related to the number of concussions he suffered. Like Walter, Duerson had a long NFL career, playing 11 seasons (which is a lot, but still two fewer than Walter). He was actually on the Bears' 1985 Super Bowl team with Walter and was one of the best defensive backs to ever play the game. I think it's pretty conclusive that he had CTE.

Another player who was the best at his position was Junior Seau, a future NFL Hall of Fame linebacker who committed suicide, also by shooting himself in the chest, at the age of 43. Seau's death brought immediate attention to the concussion crisis we have in sports. The harmful effects of repetitive head trauma on the long-term health of guys who played at all levels of football is now rightfully in the spotlight.

Yet another suicide victim was a tough defensive back, Ray Easterling, who played with the Atlanta Falcons in the mid-'70s. Easterling killed himself on April 19, 2012. He was actually the lead plaintiff in a lawsuit against the NFL before he took his own life. The suit, which also included another teammate of Walter's, Chicago Bears quarterback Jim McMahon, claimed that both suffered from CTE.

Those three victims all had something in common besides their terrible fates—they were personal friends of mine. I knew them well, along with their symptoms.

And the list doesn't stop with the guys I knew. Andre Waters took his own life in November of 2006. It was determined that he had sustained brain damage as a result of playing football. Prior to Waters' death, Terry Long, a former Pittsburgh Steelers offensive lineman from 1984 to 1991 who had attempted suicide before, succeeded on June 7, 2005, by drinking antifreeze. It was determined that Long committed suicide because of CTE, which was caused by the multiple concussions he suffered as a football player.

Tom McHale, who spent nine seasons with the Tampa Bay Buccaneers, Philadelphia Eagles, and Miami Dolphins, died on May 25, 2008, due to a drug overdose, but the autopsy showed that McHale also suffered from CTE. Did the CTE cause him to drug himself to death? Who knows? One thing is clear, though: McHale makes at least six former NFL players who have been diagnosed with CTE since 2002 and died by suicide or overdose.

Ted Johnson, a former New England Patriots linebacker who retired in 2005, said he suffered between 100 and 150 concussions in his 10-year career. Doctors have told Johnson he is afflicted with post-concussion symptoms. Dozens of retired NFL players have been found to have CTE, so we're just seeing the beginning of what I think is a crisis about to explode.

Me? Well, I have my share of memory loss and mood swings. I go from euphoria to depression more and more the older I get, and I sometimes wonder what's going on. It's scary, really. There is no telling how many concussions I've had in my life. When I played, you just went out there, got hit on the head and saw stars, and then somebody helped you to the sideline, gave you smelling salts, and you shook your head. After that, it was right back in the game. Well, chances are, each time that happened to me, that was a concussion. If I had to guess, I'd say I averaged a concussion every other game.

So, what about my brother? I watched Walter from the sideline for about six years, as you know. I've also watched a bunch of film of him playing. More often than I can count, when he got knocked down, he'd just come right back again. That was him never dying easy, but I'm sincerely convinced, based on the number of concussions and the blatant symptoms Walter had, that he had at minimum severe brain trauma—and at worst, CTE. If I was a betting man, I'd bet on the latter. I don't believe anyone would debate that Walter exhibited all of the symptoms I mentioned earlier. Memory loss, confusion, perhaps some suicidal behavior, lack of concentration, headaches, depression, emotional instability, insomnia, erratic behavior, problems with impulse control…those were all there at some point late in Walter's life, and each one is a symptom of CTE.

Looking back on it all, and knowing what I know now about concussions and CTE, I just can't say for sure whether or not my brother was suicidal. But I can say that if he was, it wasn't because he was depressed. If he ever did suffer from suicidal thoughts, it was because of all his concussions. Of course, I want to emphasize that I'm not saying he was suicidal, and I have to point out one very important fact that we just can't ignore: he didn't kill himself. Actually, as far as I know, he never attempted to take his own life. No matter what people say or think about whether he was suicidal and why, the fact that he didn't ever try to kill himself is one key piece of evidence that most have not been talking about.

Of course, some people will always say Walter was depressed and was therefore suicidal. They'll also say he didn't just take painkillers, but that he was addicted to them. Talk about jumping to conclusions.

Listen, 13 years of getting beat up every Sunday like Walter did, well, aside from symptoms of repeated concussions, he was going to have aches and pains that the normal 40-year-old person wouldn't have. A lot of people think it'd be great to be a pro football player, but those people don't have to deal with the pain that comes along with it. Walter did, and sometimes he had to take something to deal with the residual pain, even in retirement.

Walter was deathly afraid of needles. The only needle he'd reluctantly allow was when they had to drain fluid from his knees during his playing days. Really, whenever he took something, he was basically just taking the equivalent of Aleve. It was just aspirin or whatever a doctor would give him to relieve the pain he was dealing with. To say he didn't take pain medication would be a lie, but to say he was addicted to painkillers, that'd be a lie, too. Listen, when you hurt, you take something, right? When I hurt, I take something. It doesn't mean we're addicted. It doesn't mean we get up every day and take 'em even when we don't hurt, just out of habit. To me that's where the line is between somebody who's addicted and somebody who has to take pain meds for relief. Walter was the latter.

Keep in mind, too, that Walter was a guy who refused to run out of bounds. NFL players take far more abuse than most people in life, and Walter took far more abuse than most NFL players. That was just his do-or-die attitude coming out. And that do-or-die attitude of his would keep on coming out, even after he left the game. "Once I saw him driving a race car," Bud said, "and Walter fell back a lap or so. I said, 'Well, get ready to watch it blow up.' Sure enough, about that time, you could see him push the car so hard he'd done jammed the gears or something. He'd rather wreck the car than lose the race. It was always going to be the car's fault, not his. That's just how it was going to be."

And I'd say that's just about right. That's who my little brother was. He'd never die easy. He dealt with physical pain, sure, and he took some pills to get rid of it every now and then, but he was not addicted to anything. Pills would help him cope, but they didn't consume him. He'd never die easy. Walter dealt with emotional highs and lows, of course, just like the rest of us, but he was not going to let depression take him down. He'd never die easy. If he was suicidal, it was a consequence of the hits he took due to his unwillingness to give up on the field. He'd never die easy. Addiction? Depression? That's just not who Walter was. No matter what he did in life, he wouldn't be haunted by the regret that comes from not giving it your all. He wouldn't let anything beat him. Not football. Not pain. Not pressure. He'd never die easy. No, not my baby brother. This was true even as he suffered with what I'm convinced was CTE. True even when he got sick with primary sclerosing cholangitis. True even through his fight with cancer. True even to his death, which was not at his own hands. And that brings us back to Illinois, to his house, to his bedroom, where I last saw him alive, on Halloween Night, 1999.

CHAPTER 13

Livin' Ain't Easy

'll never forget my last night with Walter for as long as I live. It was Sunday, October 31, 1999. Halloween. Momma, Pam, and I'd been in and out of Walter's bedroom all day. My momma and sister left the room to give me some alone time with Walter. The colored light of the TV flickered all over the walls of Walter's room like some sort of rainbow promise from God that Walter would soon be with Him. Walter was extremely weak and fighting to get comfortable in his bed. He'd had too many visitors that day, and I could see it had worn him out. We talked that night about faith and how God was in control. Walter looked right at me and had a face of calm confidence that I'd never before seen on any man. "It's in God's hands, bro," he said, as if he knew something I didn't. "If it's His will to take me, I'm ready to go."

"His will be done," I answered in quiet and sincere agreement.

"Tomorrow is promised to no one," Walter said with a level of understanding that only someone can have when they are ready to pass on from this life. Dyin' ain't easy, but Walter knew it was something we all have to face. "I want you to do me a favor," he said.

"I got your back, dawg. What is it?"

Walter looked straight at me, and it was well beyond the surface. His look let me know that he was very serious about what he was getting ready to ask. He wanted me to promise to look after Momma. And that's when it hit me. That's when I fully realized what was about to happen. Walter was getting ready to leave me behind here with Momma. My brother was going on ahead of me to the other side. And that meant he'd soon see Daddy. I leaned over and hugged my baby brother around the neck, told him I loved him, and promised that I sure would take care of Momma. Then I asked him to do me a favor, too. I whispered in his ear, "Look, man, if you end up leaving, would you tell Daddy I love him?" I winced, trying to hold back tears before I continued. "I didn't get a chance to tell Daddy before he died."

Walter didn't say a word. He just looked at me once again with a wink and a grin that said it all. He did that a lot.

When I left Chicago that night, I was at peace knowing that my brother would soon be gone. But I still headed home not knowing exactly when that would be. I didn't know that night would be the last time I'd see him alive. I talked to him on the phone early Monday morning, November 1, 1999, and he sounded pretty good, but I didn't know how long he had. Then I talked with Momma for a few minutes, and she said he looked good, but we couldn't be sure how much time was left. My brother's life was slipping away, and even though I could see the end coming, I still wasn't prepared when it finally arrived. Walter died later that morning, and I flew back to Chicago the next day.

You may remember that the highest point total Walter ever got in a game was 46. You might recall that, in their Super Bowl victory with Walter, the Bears lit up the Patriots for 46 points and shut them down with Buddy Ryan's "46" defense. Well, on November 1, 1999, my beloved brother was gone...at the age of 46. That's one thing that has been rightly reported before. Walter's age wasn't what everyone thought. What some haven't gotten right, though, was why Walter had pushed his age back in the first place. It didn't have anything to do with his pursuit of the Heisman Trophy. Walter changed his age when he was entering the NFL, because he wanted to play as long as he could. Back then, you just filled out a form and entered your date of birth; no one checked it like they do now. When I got to the league, I followed his lead and did the same thing for the same reason. Walter pushed his age back one year, because he didn't want to be pushed by others to retire any earlier than necessary. At the end of his life, I was wishing he could've added that year back. Or two. Or 50.

Losing a younger brother, especially one only in his forties like my brother was, stirs a unique set of emotions. I never had to deal with anything like it before and haven't since. Even when I knew it was about to happen, being comforted by our last face-to-face conversation, I still didn't want to accept it. I didn't want to believe it. Somewhere deep inside, I thought if anybody could make it through what he was dealing with, it was Walter. I thought if God had a miracle out there waiting for somebody, it was going to be for Walter. But Walter didn't make it through. That miracle just never came. For reasons only God knows, Walter was taken home. Heaven is lucky to have him, of course, but the world is definitely worse off without him. That's what happens here when we lose a person who strives to make the world a better place.

Matt Suhey, a former teammate and dear friend to Walter, shared a story once that really shows what we lost. About two months before Walter passed, Suhey and Mike Lanigan (one of Walter's business partners) were sitting with Walter, watching TV. The mood in the room was somber, according to Suhey. Walter was sick, and they were walking on eggshells, understandably not knowing what to say.

Then out of the blue, Walter decided to break the tension. "You know what?" he asked. "This is going to be another *Brian's Song*, only in this one, the brother dies." Well, that did it. Walter's humor put everyone at ease. "Mike and I were supposed to be there to cheer Walter up," Matt remembers, "but there he was making a joke, trying to be sure we were comfortable." That's who Walter was. And I don't just mean he was funny. He had a great sense of humor, yes, but what Suhey's story shows is that he had an even greater sensitivity for those around him.

Gale Sayers also knows just how special my brother was, and how big a loss his death was to the world. "He was a great, great person," Sayers said. "If you were around Walter, you would know how great a person he was. I knew him on the football field, and I was around him off the football field when he was doing charity work for people. *That's* what I remember. And that's what I *want* to remember. If I knew something bad about Walter Payton, I couldn't say it. Ain't no way. Ain't no way I could say anything bad about him, because of all the times I saw him out there trying to help people."

To put it simply, Walter cared about people. My little brother was what every mother and father should want their son to grow up to be. And I ain't talking so much as a football player. I mean, he was obviously a great football player, and every football player should want to play like he did, but he was an even better person. If every little boy out there grew up to be like Walter, the world would be a much better place to live. He became a big star, but his heart was always with the "common people."

It's funny because, yes, I'm the older brother, but in remembering Walter, I don't really see it that way. I'm the one who learned a lot from him about being a professional athlete and, more importantly, a man. It took me nearly a decade after he passed to even begin to recognize how much his life *and* death impacted me. Even when I didn't know it growing up, my little brother influenced me. Even gone, Walter is shaping me. In fact, part of what led me to write this book is my quest to know exactly how big a part of my life Walter was…and is.

If only those he left behind acted more like him, perhaps then we could've avoided the ugliness, the bickering, the fighting over his estate, the jealousy, the power struggles, and on and on. But we didn't avoid all that. The Payton family was not immune to those evils. And it all started the night Walter died.

Bud was in Chicago with Momma the night Walter passed, and Momma wanted to go in to take some pictures of Walter's body. Well, a guy named Mark Alberts, who was married to Walter's assistant Ginny Quirk, took issue with that. "Mark…started hollering, 'You can't go in there, I'm representing the estate!'" Bud said. "'You can *not* take pictures.' Connie also said Alyne couldn't take pictures." Though they didn't want her to, Momma did get some pictures of Walter, but Mark wasn't happy about it. And Momma wasn't happy about how she'd been treated.

We went to the funeral home on Wednesday night to see Walter's body one last time before he was cremated. I thought he looked better than he'd looked in months, and we all had a nice time remembering our fallen family member. But on Thursday night, the night before the funeral, I was upstairs getting ready at the church and heard all kinds of commotion downstairs. I rushed down to see what was going on, and an employee of the church said that I needed to go check on Momma. I figured she was just getting emotional, breaking down and causing a ruckus on account of Walter's death starting to really sink in. But it wasn't that at all. Momma was with Mark Alberts, and she was fighting mad. I said, "What's going on, Momma?"

"Eddie, that's my boy who died," Momma said. "*My* boy! No one's gonna tell me what I can and can't do. No one's gonna take away my pictures of my baby!" Mark Alberts was at it again.

"What do you mean?" I asked, trying to get to the bottom of what was going on.

Momma pointed at Mark. "He wants my camera and my pictures of Walter!" I guess Mark had been down there trying to take the camera from Momma, and with pictures of Walter in there, he might as well have been trying to take a cub from a momma grizzly bear. I was on one side with Momma (somebody was actually holding her back), and Mark was on the other side. I looked at Mark in a way that said, *You better start explainin'.*

"Well, your mother took some pictures of Walter right after he passed," Mark said in my direction, "and we wouldn't want those pictures to end up in the *National Enquirer* or something like that. So, I wanted to get the camera and destroy the pictures." I couldn't believe my ears. Did he just say he thought my momma might want to sell pictures of her son to a tabloid? Was he for real? Unfortunately, yes, he was. And I was thinking, *Yeah, right, if anybody's going to sell those pictures, it's you, dude!*

"Don't you say another word to her," I said as diplomatically as I could. "That's her camera, and that's her baby. She wanted to take them pictures of Walter, and she ain't gonna do nothing with them. But even if she does—even if she wants to put them on every billboard from here to Jackson—well, she has the right to do so."

Mark tried to start in with something, but I wasn't done. "And who do you think I'm going to trust with the damn pictures of her baby, you or her?" I continued, my voice getting a little louder as Mark started to walk a little closer. "And furthermore, you need to get out of my face, because I'm about to get really pissed off." Everybody in the room started to realize that the one who was sent down to break up a fight was about to start another one. They all started scrambling, trying to get between me and Mark before anything could get going. Let's just say Momma got to keep her camera. In fact, Momma still has the camera and has never had the pictures developed.

For whatever reason, Walter trusted Ginny, and I guess Mark, too, but looking back, I can't think of one good reason he should've. Momma and I surely didn't trust either one of them. Ginny had way too much control over what Walter did, in my opinion, and I think she even tried to keep him from us at times. She's quoted in Pearlman's book as saying that when I'd call Walter, he'd tell her to tell me he wasn't there. Well, that's bullshit. All I know is Walter and I talked all the time before she got involved. Also, I'd call sometimes, and I know she never even told him it was me on the phone.

And don't get me started about the memorabilia. Ginny had Walter sign a bunch of stuff to send to kids, but I believe she'd just sign the rest herself. I, for one, didn't think that was right, sending something to someone signed in Walter's name but not by his hand. Momma even said Ginny had a warehouse full of Walter's footballs, jerseys, and other stuff out in California, and believed she was making a living off of selling those things. I think it was all about the dollar for Ginny, and I don't think it was any different for Mark. I felt like they were always trying to keep Walter and all things associated with Walter to themselves. "All the memorabilia you see for sale on the Internet is being sold by Ginny," Momma said. "Where did she get it? It wasn't hers to start with, and it's certainly a lot more valuable now that Walter is dead. I mean, she had a Super Bowl shirt she was asking $5,000 for on the Internet." Now, didn't I tell you not to get me started on the memorabilia?

No matter how you slice it, I don't think Ginny had Walter's best interests at heart. Anyone who reads Pearlman's book about my brother knows she still doesn't. Why would someone who cared about my brother say the kinds of things she said to Pearlman? Even if those things were true, why would she want to drag my brother's memory through the mud? To me, that just doesn't sound a whole lot like a person who cared much about Walter, so I have to wonder what's really behind anything she says or does. At any rate, my momma has found peace with it all. "The Lord says, 'Vengeance is mine,'" Momma said. "It's in His hands to bring justice if there's justice to bring. I can accept Walter's death, because I've turned it over to the Lord."

It's unfortunate that some have used Walter's death to divide our family and to do well for themselves. No matter what happens, though, one thing they can never take away are the memories I have of my brother. Those are all mine, and they're engraved here in this book forever. My brother will never be forgotten, even if some seem to have forgotten what he was all about.

Walter was an amazing football player. There's no doubt about it. I was so proud of all his out-of-this-world accomplishments as an athlete. But they were only a part of who Walter was, and I was never more proud of him than when I left his house on the night I last saw him alive. It was a very special moment for me that I'll treasure for the rest of my days, along with the priceless gift we'd given each other when we were just kids—the gift of brotherly love and unconditional acceptance. That's a bond that even death can't break.

Though I didn't want to think about it at the time, I knew that Walter would soon leave this place. The overwhelming pain of a broken world hit me like it never had before. Here was a super athlete so recently in his prime, now gone. This was a man who refused to fall, now fallen. He was unstoppable, and now he was still. It was all pretty hard to swallow. I couldn't help but think about where we'd come from, all of our birthdays and Christmases growing up, all of our times together stealing plums, hunting squirrels, playing baseball, chasing girls, exploring the woods, pulling pranks, dominating college football, achieving our NFL dreams, dealing with pain, and trying to figure things out all over again once we were out of the league. It hit me that now it was all over. Our journey together had ended. I was only comforted in knowing that by now, Walter had seen Daddy and told him I love him. I also knew that one day I'd be with them, too, and would get a chance to tell Daddy face-to-face, right before giving Walter a good pat on the back. Father and sons together again, just like the good old days back in Columbia, Mississippi.

We all return to where we came from at some point or another. Dust to dust. No one knows when that time will come, but I believe when it does, it's not by accident. It's just your time to go. Our days on this earth are numbered from the time we take our first breath. "So teach us to number our days, that we may apply our hearts to wisdom," as the Good Lord says in the Psalms. From the moment we're born, we're on a path toward dying. From the time we hit the ground, we're on a road back home. Perhaps Walter hit the ground running so hard that he got there a little faster than the rest of us. Only God knows for sure. What I know is I'm no longer waiting on Walter to join me like he did in high school and college. Now, I'm just looking forward to the day I get to join him, and I'm sure he'll have a thing or two to tell me about how things work up there when I arrive. Until then, I'll continue remembering Walter and me as children, as young men, and as adults. And I'll keep looking forward to when we're together again, walking side by side as two imperfect people made perfect in heaven. Walter and me, standing in the presence of our Lord. No more pain. No more strife. No more shadows.

Now, *that's* Sweetness.

Acknowledgments

This book was written in part to dispel many inaccuracies that have been written about my brother, Walter. It's not out of anger or offense, but simply to set the record straight. I also wrote this book because I have a story to tell, as well. Once I decided to write this book, I was all in. I have many to thank for their help along the way, enabling me to write a story with which I'm intimately familiar: *Walter & Me*.

I'm so blessed to have a loving and supporting mother who taught me the basics of how to be a good person.

Thanks to coach Charles Boston for teaching me the fundamentals of the game of football that I love so much.

A special thanks to coach Bob Hill for believing in me, for giving me a stage to perform on, and for surrounding me with great teammates.

Thanks so much to my wife, Rica, and to my children—Edward, Erica, Terry, and Bridgett—for their love and support. And to my sister, Pam, for her love and support.

I'd like to also thank the Jackson State University fans and family for their support and enthusiasm, which encouraged me to graduate and pushed me to another level.

I'm especially grateful to my coauthor, Paul Brown, for his friendship, steely resolve, and commitment to this book. Without his perseverance, this book wouldn't have happened. And I give a special thanks to literary agent Craig Wiley of the Craig Wiley Agency, for his professionalism in pulling us all together and for his role in the writing.

My gratitude to Bud Holmes can't be overstated. His unwavering support of my family and me over the years has been priceless.

And I'd like to give special credit to the Triumph Books team for giving this book top priority.

—Eddie Payton

It's been a true pleasure working with Eddie Payton on this book. Thanks to Eddie for his candor in answering countless questions, often awfully sensitive and sometimes just plain dumb.

Thanks to my editor, Adam Motin, and the amazing team at Triumph Books. Adam was a pleasure to work with from the opening kickoff.

A special thanks to Alyne Payton, Bud Holmes, Charles Boston, Gale Sayers, Matt Suhey, and Mike Ditka for their patience and insight during their interviews. And many thanks to Coach Ditka for writing the foreword.

I'm grateful to Angie Chitty, Janet Watkins, Jessica Brown, Ken Anderson, and Terry Brown for their assistance, feedback, and help in transcribing tapes.

I'd like to give special credit to my agent and friend, Craig Wiley, of the Craig Wiley Agency. We found a home for *Walter & Me* at a great publisher because of him. Craig's contribution to the writing was invaluable. We continue to work as a team, and I look forward to working with him for years to come.

—Paul Brown

Acknowledgments

First and foremost, I'd like to thank my Lord and Savior, Jesus Christ, from whom all book opportunities and other blessings flow. I'd also like to thank my talented wife, Darcy, for her editorial help and creative advice. My kids should also be thanked for putting up with a little less daddy time while Eddie, Paul, and I were dealing with crunch time.

I'd like to thank Tom Bast for seeing promise in the idea when I first pitched it as an agent, and also Mitch Rogatz for ultimately buying into it. Adam Motin deserves a special thank-you for balancing schedules, listening to ideas, and dealing with everything else that is a part of managing a book project.

Thanks goes to Eddie Payton for allowing me the honor of playing a part in the telling of his and Walter's story, and also Paul Brown, my longtime client and friend, for being so good at connecting with people like Eddie who have such interesting stories to tell. Paul should also be thanked for doing all the hard work of interviewing, researching, and piecing this project together. He is a very talented man.

Finally, I'd like to thank you, the reader, for picking up the finished product and taking time to read it, whether on paper or on screen. Without you, books, and all they bring to the world through their pages, would not be possible. And if you have a project of your own, I'd love to know about it. Feel free to get in touch with me through the Craig Wiley Agency.

—Craig Wiley